The Teacher Career Cycle

The Teacher Career Cycle

Understanding and Guiding the Professional Development of Teachers

RALPH FESSLER
The Johns Hopkins University

JUDITH C. CHRISTENSEN
National-Louis University

Lead Authors
and
Editors

ALLYN AND BACON
Boston   London   Toronto   Sydney   Tokyo   Singapore

Copyright © 1992 by Allyn and Bacon
A Division of Simon & Schuster, Inc.
160 Gould Street
Needham Heights, Massachusetts 02194

Library of Congress Cataloging-in-Publication Data

Fessler, Ralph.
  The Teacher Career Cycle: Understanding and Guiding the Professional
  Development of Teachers / Ralph Fessler, Judith C. Christensen.
      p.   cm.
  Includes bibliographical references and indexes.
  ISBN 0-205-13340-1
  1. Teachers.   2. Teaching—Vocational guidance.   3. Teachers—
  Psychology.   4. Teachers—Training of.   5. Teachers—In-service
  training.   I. Christensen, Judith.   II. Title.
  LB1775.F44   1992
  371.1'0023—dc20   91-26445
                                                                        CIP

Printed in the United States of America

10 9 8 7 6 5 4 3 2 1   95 94 93 92 91

Brief Contents

Contents

Preface

This book is the product of a unique collaborative effort. In 1980 a group of faculty from different universities began to meet to discuss common research interests in teacher growth and development. The group soon became a mutual support system and catalyst for a variety of research projects. In 1982 the informal network evolved into the Collegial Research Consortium. The major project since that time has been the development and refinement of the Teacher Career Cycle Model, which is the focus of this book.

The model is based on a process of theory building that is described in Chapter 2. The model constructs have evolved over the past eight years based on data collected from extensive literature reviews, interviews of more than 160 teachers, and a research project that supported the components of the model and provided data on environmental influences, incentives, and appropriate professional development support systems. Although the model is data-driven, the authors decided that this book would not be a detailed report of the research underlying the constructs. Readers interested in those data are directed to appropriate sources. The major purpose of this book is to use the model constructs as a foundation to understand the stages that teachers experience in their careers and to assess and guide their professional growth and development.

In order to emphasize the practical applications of the Career Cycle Model, we have used scenarios and case studies throughout the book. These "vignettes" have been carefully selected to illustrate various model components. While based on interviews with real teachers, the names and other identifying characteristics have been changed, and in some cases, individuals cited are actually composites of several teachers.

We envision this book as appropriate for several populations. First, we believe the book would be appropriate for graduate courses in staff development and in supervision courses that emphasize individualized, developmental approaches. It might also be considered for other courses in administrative leadership programs and programs that prepare staff developers.

Second, we would recommend the book for school personnel who are concerned with understanding and supporting the professional development of their teachers. We hope that staff developers, supervisors, and principals will find this book valuable in assessing the differentiated needs of teachers and in planning for their continuing professional development.

Third, we believe the book is valuable to teachers themselves. By understanding the dynamics of the career cycle, they will be better prepared to assess what they are experiencing and to plan their personal and career goals. We believe it is important for teachers to understand that they are not the first to experience the insecurities of the induction phase, the acceleration of the enthusiastic and growing period, or the depths of despair often associated with career frustration. We hope that the model constructs and the accompanying vignettes will assist teachers through a process of introspection and reflection that will contribute to their personal and professional growth.

Finally, the book will be of interest to researchers concerned with teacher careers and personalized approaches to professional growth and development. This book provides an example of how a research-derived model can lead to very practical applications for teacher growth and development. In addition, the model provides numerous possibilities for additional research.

The structure and development of this book are unique. Ralph Fessler and Judith Christensen, listed as the editors and lead authors, and other members of the Collegial Research Consortium have taken responsibility for authoring individual chapters. This is not, however, a typical "edited" book. The chapters tie together closely as components of the Career Cycle Model, and all of the authors have contributed to the research that led to this book and in determining the structure and organization of this project. This book is truly the product of a team effort.

Many people have contributed to the completion of this project. Thanks to the Department of Education for funding the grant on "The Role of Teacher Career Stages and Professional Development Practices in Determining Rewards and Incentives in Teaching" (Contract No. G0084100031, 1985). Special thanks to the teachers who were interviewed and to all those who participated in the research related to this project. Shirley Belz was responsible for the final typing and editing of the manuscript. Her attention to detail and her nurturing, warm personality were appreciated by all who worked with her. Special thanks as well to Betsy Savage, who contributed to the typing of various chapters, and to Mike Fessler, whose assistance with the graphics helped the pictures match the words. The Allyn and Bacon professional staff were most supportive and wonderful to work with, especially Ray Short, Sean Wakely, and Carol Chernaik. In addition, the editorial assistance of Ellen Silge and Michael Bass & Associates was of great value in fine-tuning the manuscript. Finally, thanks to Marge, Lynn, Carol, and Marv (and John and Judy) for their support and their understanding of the long hours we devoted to this project.

As indicated at the beginning of this preface, this book is the product of a unique partnership of members of the Collegial Research Consortium. It must be noted that our own careers and personal and professional development have been enriched through this effort. Throughout all our discussions, debates, and occasional conflicts, we have grown professionally, and our friendships and mutual respect have been maintained and enriched.

Ralph Fessler
Judith Christensen

Contributing Authors

Ralph Fessler
Professor and Director
Division of Education
The Johns Hopkins University
Baltimore, Maryland

Judith C. Christensen
Graduate Faculty, Interdisciplinary Studies Division
National-Louis University
Evanston, Illinois

Peter J. Burke
Director, Bureau for Teacher Education, Licensing, and Placement
Department of Public Instruction
Madison, Wisconsin

Esther Letven
Director, Regional Staff Development Center
University of Wisconsin—Parkside
Kenosha, Wisconsin

John H. McDonnell
Professor of Education and
Director, Master of Arts in Teaching Program
Beloit College
Beloit, Wisconsin

Jay R. Price
Professor of Education
University of Wisconsin—Stevens Point
Stevens Point, Wisconsin

CHAPTER ONE

Teacher Development As a Career-Long Process

JUDITH C. CHRISTENSEN   RALPH FESSLER

Becoming a teacher is a process that spans many years of preparation and experience. It typically begins with a period of concentrated study in a teacher certification program and continues through an often meandering path of successes and failures, enthusiasm and despair, growth and stagnation, and confidence and doubt. Since the needs of teachers change dramatically through this career-long journey, the support systems available must adjust to these changing needs.

The recognition of teacher education as a complex process has evolved in recent years. The traditional view held that teacher education was a simple two-step process: (1) preservice teacher education received at a college or university and (2) inservice teacher education that occurred from the time the teacher began employment in a school system and lasted throughout the career. Frequently there has been a well-defined line drawn between these two components of teacher education, with colleges and universities claiming control over the initial certification component, and inservice education being under the domain of school systems.

Recently there has been a growing realization that this two-step view is overly simplistic. Many changes occur within individuals and systems that require a more differentiated view of teacher education. A major breakthrough in creating a flexible view of this process has been the emergence of a growing concern over the special needs of beginning teachers. This awareness reflects an important recognition that teacher education does not end with the receipt of a degree and a teaching license, nor is teacher education the same for teachers of all levels of experience and expertise. The novice teacher has many continuing educational needs that must be addressed in the new work environment: needs related to teaching skills, classroom management, and personal adjustment to the

1

demanding responsibilities associated with full-time teaching. Teacher induction programs are an important bridge between preservice and inservice teacher education.

As a result of this interest in the special needs of beginning teachers, the simplistic two-step process is being replaced by a slightly more sophisticated three-step model consisting of (1) preservice, (2) induction, and (3) everything else for the rest of the teacher's career. While the emerging prominence of teacher induction programs is an important development in differentiating the components of a career-long approach to teacher education, this development should not be viewed as a final response of the profession to the individual needs of teachers. As a teacher progresses through the career cycle, special needs emerge, some related to changes in job expectations and demands and some related to changes in the teacher's personal life. These special needs, too, must be addressed as they emerge. Indeed, the "everything else" must be further differentiated. This book provides a framework for such differentiation as a model for career development is examined. The literature related to teachers' personal and professional lives is a starting point for an analysis of specific cases in later chapters.

The following sections of this chapter provide an overview of the theoretical works in the areas of psychological aspects of adult development and theories of organizational development. The interaction of the two dimensions will be used extensively in the Career Stage Model presented in Chapter 2.

Considering Adult Development

The body of literature on adult development is essential but not sufficient for making decisions about teachers' professional development programs. It is essential because it stresses the fact that 26-year-olds are not the same as 56-year-olds and therefore cannot be treated the same nor be expected to respond in similar ways. It is not sufficient, however, because so much of the research is based on male subjects who were primarily in career situations dissimilar to teaching.

In teaching, about 68 percent of the total population is female, and at the elementary level the percentage rises as high as 83 percent (Grant & Eiden 1982; Snyder 1989). These statistics point to a need to look at the adult development literature in a serious but critical manner. Although the body of literature on women's development is growing (Belenky, Clinchy, Goldberger, & Tarule 1986; Gilligan 1982; Levine 1989; Lightfoot 1983; Lortie 1975; Spencer 1986), the major works to date reflect studies of adult male development. The importance of the work cannot be ignored because it creates the theoretical bases for empirical study that eventually will lead to the knowledge that will help us better understand human behavior. It has been said that the research on adult development is at the point where child development research was fifty years ago. The next twenty to thirty years will undoubtedly yield research results that will be beneficial to everyone involved with adult workers.

For the present, the literature is divided between theorists who stress a developmental approach and those who stress stages of development. They have contributed different ways of viewing adult development, and further research probably will show an interactive relationship between the two.

For the purposes of this discussion, a brief review of several major theorists will be presented. The work of Erik Erikson (1959) is viewed as one of the earliest of the stage theorists. His descriptions of crises or turning points in a person's life have been seen as occurring in a specific sequence at predictable times of life. Erikson divides the life span into eight developmental phases with corresponding conflicts or crises. The phases and their conflicts include:

Infancy	Trust vs. Mistrust
Early Childhood	Autonomy vs. Shame, Doubt
Play Age	Initiative vs. Guilt
School Age	Industry vs. Inferiority
Adolescence	Identity vs. Diffusion
Young Adult	Intimacy vs. Isolation
Adulthood	Generativity vs. Self-Absorption
Mature Age	Integrity vs. Disgust, Despair

Continuing research using Erikson's model presents some interesting ways of viewing the conflicts. Gilligan (1982), for example, points out that Erikson found that the female child develops differently from the male child. Gilligan states:

> She holds her identity in abeyance as she prepares to attract the man by whose name she will be known, by whose status she will be defined . . . while for men identity precedes intimacy and generativity in the optimal cycle of human separation and attachment, for women these tasks seem instead to be fused. (p. 12)

The importance of this observation is that, although the differences exist, the model remains the original male-dominated interpretation. The need for studies with women as subjects is recognized, and future studies will strengthen the existing literature base.

Bernice Neugarten (1968) claims that the social framework must be examined along with the biological phases of life. As social norms change, so will the life-cycle expectations. Neugarten contends that:

> The major punctuation marks in the adult life line tend (those, that is, which are orderly and sequential) to be more often social than biological—

or if biologically based, they are often biological events that occur to significant others rather than to oneself, like grandparenthood or widowhood. If psychologists are to discover order in the personality changes that occur in all individuals as they age, we should look to the social as well as the biological clock and certainly to social definitions of age and age-appropriate behavior. (p. 146)

Lowenthal, Thurner, and Chiriboga (1975) also tie adult life stages to socially significant events. Their stages include: (1) early adulthood, (2) parenthood, (3) postparenthood, and (4) retirement. The importance of events in one's personal life cannot be ignored in their effect on one's interaction in and out of a professional role.

Life-stage theories became popular in our society through the works of researchers such as Gould (1978), Levinson and colleagues (1978), and Sheehy (1976). They all stress the importance of transitional periods of change or turning points in adult lives. The chronological age boundaries the researchers suggest are only rough indices of development but have captured the public's attention and caused considerable self-diagnosis among readers. Cross (1981) synthesized the ideas of many of the age-related life-cycle theorists and the significant characteristics of each phase as shown in Figure 1-1. The table combines the effects of each phase on an individual's personal and work life. The inseparability of these two dimensions is crucial when considering any phase of adult development.

Paralleling the life-cycle research is the work of the stage/developmental researchers. Jane Loevinger's (1976) work in ego development, Kohlberg's (1981) research in moral development and Hunt's (1975) work involving conceptual levels are examples of how cognitive development influences the adult and his/her growth throughout life.

In his work regarding moral development, Kohlberg (1984) asserts that moral thinking evolves over the life cycle and that the stages are hierarchically structured. The levels and stages are identified in Figure 1-2.

Gilligan (1982) has questioned the results of studies on moral reasoning and identity development and has conducted research to determine differences in perceptions of men and women. Her concern for more attention to women in research about the human life cycle is clear when she states: "Only when life-cycle theorists divide their attention and begin to live with women as they lived with men will their vision encompass the experience of both sexes and their theories become correspondingly more fertile" (p. 23).

Gilligan's work has widened the path of interest in research on women's developmental stages. The women's movement has encouraged publication of their points of view on personal and professional development. The literature base, which began in the early 1960s with Friedan's *The Feminine Mystique,* has grown significantly in thirty years.

Unlike Kohlberg's model, where the hierarchical nature of the stages imply

FIGURE 1-1 • *Cross's Descriptions of Life-Cycle Phases*

Phase and Age	Marker Events	Psychic Tasks	Characteristic Stance
Leaving Home 18-22	Leave home Establish new living arrangements Enter college Start first full-time job Select mate	Establish autonomy and independence from family Define identity Define sex role Establish new peer alliances	A balance between "being in" and "moving out" of the family
Moving Into Adult World 23-28	Marry Establish home Become parent Get hired/fired/quit job Enter into community activities	Regard self as adult Develop capacity for intimacy Fashion initial life structure Build the dream Find a mentor	"Doing what one should" Living and building for the future Launched as an adult
Search for Stability 29-34	Establish children in school Progress in career or consider change Possible separation, divorce, remarriage Possible return to school	Reappraise relationships Reexamine life structure and present committments Strive for success Search for stability, security, control Search for personal values Set long-range goals Accept growing children	"What is this life all about now that I am doing what I am supposed to?" Concern for order and stability and with "making it" Desire to set long-range goals and meet them
Becoming One's Own Person 37-42	Crucial promotion Break with mentor Responsibility for three-generation family; i.e., growing children and aging parents For women: empty nest; enter career education	Face reality Confront mortality; sense of aging Prune dependent ties to boss, spouse, mentor Reassess marriage Reassess personal priorities and values	Suspended animation More nurturing stance for men; more assertive stance for women "Have I done the right thing? Is there time to change?"
Settling Down 45-55	Cap career Become mentor Launch children; become grandparents New interest and hobbies Physical limitations; menopause Active participation in community events	Increase feelings of self-awareness and competence Reestablish family relationships Enjoy one's choices and life style Reexamine the fit between life structure and self	"It is perhaps late, but there are things I would like to do in the last half of my life" Best time of life
The Mellowing 57-64	Possible loss of mate Health problems Preparation for retirement	Accomplish goals in the time left to live Accept and adjust to aging process	Mellowing of feelings and relationships Spouse increasingly important Greater comfort with self
Life Review 65+	Retirement Physical decline Change in finances New living arrangements Death of friends/spouse Major shift in daily routine	Search for integrity versus despair Acceptance of self Disengagement Rehearsal for death of spouse	Review of accomplishments Eagerness to share everyday human joys and sorrows Family is important Death is a new presence

Source: From Patricia Cross, *Adults as Learners* (San Francisco: Jossey-Bass, 1981), pp. 174–175. Taken from original source material: Chickering and Havighurst, 1981; Gould, 1972; Lehman and Lester, 1978; Levinson and others, 1974; McCoy, Ryan, and Lictenberg, 1978; Neugarten, 1968; Sheehy, 1976; Weathersby, 1978. Reproduced with permission.

FIGURE 1-2 • *Lawrence Kohlberg: The Six Moral Stages*

LEVEL AND STAGE	Content of Stage		SOCIAL PERSPECTIVE OF STAGE
	WHAT IS RIGHT	REASONS FOR DOING RIGHT	
Level 1: Preconventional Stage 1: Heteronomous Morality	To avoid breaking rules backed by punishment, obedience for its own sake, and avoiding physical damage to persons and property.	Avoidance of punishment and the superior power of authorities.	*Egocentric point of view.* Doesn't consider the interests of others or recognize that they differ from the actor's; doesn't relate two points of view. Actions are considered physically rather than in terms of psychological interests of others. Confusion of authority's perspective with one's own.
Stage 2: Individualism. Purpose, and Exchange	Following rules only when it is to someone's immediate interest, acting to meet one's own interests and needs and letting others do the same. Right is also what's fair, what's an equal exchange, a deal, an agreement.	To serve one's own needs or interests in a world where you have to recognize that other people have their interests too.	*Concrete individualistic perspective.* Aware that everybody has his own interest to pursue and these conflict, so that right is relative (in the concrete, individualistic sense).
Level II: Conventional Stage 3: Mutual Interpersonal Expectations, Relationships, and Interpersonal Conformity	Living up to what is expected by people close to you or what people generally expect of people in your role as son, brother, friend, etc. "Being good" is important and means having good motives, showing concern about others. It also means keeping mutual relationships, such as trust, loyalty, respect, and gratitude.	The need to be a good person in your own and others' eyes. Belief in the Golden Rule. Desire to maintain rules and authority that support stereotypical good behavior.	*Perspective of the individual in relationships with other individuals.* Aware of shared feelings, agreements, and expectations that take primacy over individual interests. Relates points of view through the concrete Golden Rule, putting him- or herself in the other guy's shoes. Does not yet consider generalized system perspective.

6

Stages	What is Right	Reasons for Doing Right	Social Perspective of Stage
Stage 4: Social System and Conscience	Fulfilling the actual duties to which you have agreed. Laws are to be upheld except in extreme cases where they conflict with other fixed social duties. Right is also contributing to society, the group, or institution.	To keep the institution going as a whole, to avoid the breakdown in the system "if everyone did it," or the imperative of conscience to meet one's defined obligations (Easily confused with Stage 3 belief in rules and authority; see text.)	*Differentiates societal point of view from interpersonal agreement or motives.* Takes the point of view of the system that defines roles and rules. Considers individual relations in terms of place in the system.
Level III: Postconventional or Principled **Stage 5: Social Contract or Utility and Individual Rights**	Being aware that people hold a variety of values and opinions, that most values and rules are relative to your group. These relative rules should usually be upheld, however, in the interest of impartiality and because they are the social contract. Some nonrelative values and rights like *life and liberty,* however, must be upheld in any society and regardless of majority opinion.	A sense of obligation to law because of one's social contract to make and abide by laws for the welfare of all and for the protection of all people's rights. A feeling of contractual commitment, freely entered upon, to family, friendship, trust, and work obligations. Concern that laws and duties be based on rational calculation of overall utility, "the greatest good for the greatest number."	*Prior-to-society perspective.* Perspective of a rational individual aware of values and rights prior to social attachments and contracts. Integrates perspectives by formal mechanisms of agreement contract, objective impartiality, and due process. Considers moral and legal points of view; recognizes that they sometimes conflict and finds it difficult to integrate them.
Stage 6: Universal Ethical Principles	Following self-chosen ethical principles. Particular laws or social agreements are usually valid because they rest on such principles. When laws violate these principles, one acts in accordance with the principle. Principles are universal principles of justice; the equality of human rights and respect for the dignity of human' beings as individual persons.	The belief as a rational person in the validity of universal moral principles and a sense of personal commitment to them.	*Perspective of a moral point of view* from which social arrangements derive. Perspective is that of any rational individual recognizing the nature of morality or the fact that persons are ends in themselves and must be treated as such.

Source: From Thomas Lickona (Ed.) *Moral Developmental Behavior.* (New York: Holt, Rinehart and Winston, 1976) pp. 34–35.

7

higher is better, Loevinger's (1976) model of ego development does not define one stage as necessarily better or more adequate. Her stages are outlined in Figure 1-3.

The importance of the ego development studies for school personnel is emphasized by Levine (1989) when she states that

> school people will need different kinds of incentives and supports at various ego levels. At the Conformist level, a teacher's need for acceptance and acceptability makes frequent, positive feedback a key form of support. At the Conscientious stage, when standards of performance are more deeply internalized, evaluation from others alone will likely be insufficient. Instead, both personal and shared or mutual evaluation will provide a more appropriate kind of support. (p. 100)

The need to consider the conceptual levels of adult thinking was proposed by Harvey, Hunt, and Schroder (1961). They identified four conceptual levels:

Stage 1—Unilateral Dependence
Stage 2—Negative Independence
Stage 3—Conditional Dependence and Mutuality
Stage 4—Interdependence

The conceptual systems theory integrates both levels of information processing and personal maturity. For example, Hunt and Sullivan (1974) indicate that individuals at more concrete levels of conceptual development can function better in a more structured environment while those at higher, more abstract levels can function in either a high or less structured environment. Teachers at higher stages of development were more adaptive in their teaching style and more flexible and tolerant toward individual differences. They also tended to provide a more varied learning environment for students.

The age and stage theories of adult development take on particular importance as we look at the demographics in our society and see how society at large and the teaching force in particular have changed in the past two decades. The average age of teachers has increased, and the general ability levels of entering teachers has decreased. These trends make career-long education more important than ever.

Considering Teacher Development

Turnover in teaching has decreased as opportunities for movement within the profession have diminished and as more women have remained on the job rather than exiting to raise children. The need for two incomes in families as well as an

FIGURE 1-3 • Jane Loevinger: Milestones of Ego Development

STAGE	CODE	CHARACTER DEVELOPMENT	INTERPERSONAL STYLE	PREOCCUPATIONS	COGNITIVE STYLE
Presocial			Autistic		
Symbiotic			Symbiotic	Self vs. nonself	
Impulsive	I-1	Impulsive, fear of retaliation	Receiving, dependent, exploitative	Bodily feelings, especially sexual and aggressive	Stereotyping, conceptual confusion
Self-Protective	I-2	Fear of being caught, externalizing blame, opportunistic	Wary, manipulative, exploitative	Self-protection, trouble, wishes, things, advantage, control	
Conformist	I-3	Conformity to external rules, shame, guilt for breaking rules	Belonging, superficial niceness	Appearance, social acceptability, banal feelings, behavior	Conceptual simplicity, stereotypes, cliches
Conscientious-Conformist	I-3/4	Differentiation of norms, goals	Aware of self in relation to group, helping	Adjustment problems, reasons, opportunities (vague)	Multiplicity
Conscientious	I-4	Self-evaluated standards, self-criticism, guilt for consequences, long-term goals and ideals *Add: Respect for individuality	Intensive, responsible, mutual, concern for communication	Differentiated feelings, motives for behavior, self-respect, achievements, traits, expression	Conceptual complexity, idea of patterning
Individualistic	I-4/5		Add: Dependence as an emotional problem	Add: Development, social problems, differentiation of inner life from outer	Add: Distinction of process and outcome
Autonomous	I-5	Add: Coping with conflicting inner needs, toleration	Add:Respect for autonomy, interdependence	Vividly conveyed feelings, integration of physiological and psychological, psychological causation of behavior, role conception, self-fulfillment, self in social context	Increased conceptual complexity, complex patterns, toleration for ambiguity, broad scope, objectivity
Integrated	I-6	Add: Reconciling inner conflicts, renunciation of the unattainable	Add: Cherishing of individuality	Add: Identity	

Source: From Jane Loevinger, *Ego Development: Conceptions and Theories.* (San Francisco: Jossey-Bass, 1976), pp. 23–24. Reproduced with permission.
**"*Add*" means in addition to the description applying to the previous level.

9

increase in one-income families has necessitated this change. In addition, the tightness of the teaching market drastically cut down on easy exit and reentry into a teaching position. A study of the American teacher by Feistritzer (Feistritzer & O'Rourke 1983) reveals the following portrait.

> A profile of the "typical" American teacher suggests a woman approaching her 40th birthday. She has taught for 12 years, mostly in her present district. Over those dozen years, she returned to her local college or university often enough to acquire enough credits for a master's degree. She is married and the mother of two children. She is white and not politically active. Her formal political affiliation, if she has one, is with the Democratic Party. She teaches in a suburban elementary school staffed largely by women. In all likelihood the school principal is male. She has about 23 pupils in her class. When counting her after-hours responsibilities, she puts in a work week slightly longer than the typical laborer, and brings home a pay check that is slightly lower. (p. 1)

The study goes on to report that today's teachers are entering middle age. In 1970, about 17 percent of the teachers were under 25 years old. In 1980, that age group was 8 percent of the teaching force. The number of teachers over 55 is also shrinking. Early retirement plans to help accommodate reductions in force have encouraged teachers to leave the profession earlier than the usual retirement ages. The experience and stability of the teaching force today should be viewed as a positive situation considering classrooms are staffed by people who know their jobs well and are at the peak of their careers. However, Feistritzer reports that many teachers feel they "reached a plateau and are stranded there. They see no real opportunities for further growth or real reward on the horizon" (p. 3).

Levine (1989) notes the problems that occur when trying to motivate a veteran staff.

> When mobility in the profession was more common, teachers and administrators came and went, changing the configuration of adults in the school. As they came, they often brought fresh ideas and energy. As they went, they may have disrupted on-going projects and disbanded both good and poor working relationships. When teachers and administrators grow old together there is more time for either planned change or stagnation. (p. 52)

Retirements in a school create a situation where there are veteran teachers at one end of the spectrum and novices at the other. The need for individual staff development plans and incentives to keep a staff vital is imperative. Consider the following scenario of a staff development offering:

> The children are released from school 30 minutes early so all teachers can attend a presentation scheduled to last 90 minutes after school. The topic is on organizing lesson plans for more effective teaching. The meeting is

supposed to start 10 minutes after the children have been dismissed. However, some parents have forgotten about early dismissal and must be called to remind them to pick up their children, and one bus is late; thus many teachers don't have time for a break before the session begins. The speakers have been brought in from a university seventy-five miles away. They are planning to talk about the topic for 45 minutes, then get teachers involved in a simulation for 30 minutes and have 15 minutes for questions and answers. The teachers enter the all-purpose room and sit at lunch tables equipped with built-in benches. The room is chilly because it is also used for a gym. The speakers are introduced by the principal and they begin the session 10 minutes late. The principal leaves immediately after introducing the speakers to check on the late bus and to handle the students whose parents forgot about early dismissal.

Some of the teachers are interested in the topic, some are making lists of tasks they must do before going home, some are grading papers, one is reading a newspaper, and a few others are just there.

The speakers conclude the lecture portion of the presentation and ask the teachers to divide into groups to complete a task that involves applying the information they have just heard. The principal returns to the room and joins a small group. There is considerable grumbling about doing the task, and many people are not sure what was said in the lecture so are even more bewildered about expectations. The small-group work takes 30 minutes instead of 20 and so the allotted 90 minutes are over before questions and comments can be entertained by the speakers.

Teachers begin leaving the small groups early because they have car pools to catch, children to pick up, and work to do for tomorrow. The speakers are willing to stay later if people have questions, and three or four people remain. The rest depart quickly.

This scenario probably is familiar to every teacher and administrator. As educators we forget to practice on adults what we know about teaching. We forget about assessing needs, readiness, and prior knowledge. We forget about physical needs for comfort and security. We forget about motivation and what we know about adult development and adult learning, about practice and coaching, about modeling and administrative support. The personal and organizational needs of adult learners must be considered whenever professional development plans are made.

Considering the Organizational Environment

Sergiovanni and Carver (1980) have drawn extensively on the work of Maslow (1960) and Herzberg (with Mausner and Snyderman, 1959) in analyzing motivational and incentive factors important in a school climate. Their modified version of Maslow's hierarchy of needs shown in Figure 1-4 emphasizes the importance of establishing security for teachers in the form of money, benefits, tenure, and role consolidation before concerns switch to social need satisfaction (affiliation), self-esteem, autonomy, and self-actualization. The basic premise behind this approach is that the needs at a given level must be met before one can proceed to the next level, but once a need level is satisfied, it no longer serves as a motivator and attention proceeds to the next set of concerns. The addition of need for autonomy is an adaptation of special note. Sergiovanni and Carver argue that the need for professional independence in decision making is a very high-order need for teachers, surpassed only by self-actualization.

The work of Herzberg (1959) also can be applied to teacher motivation and incentives as described in Figure 1-5. Herzberg's two-factor theory delineates between "hygiene factors" and "motivational factors." The former refer to lower-level needs such as salary, growth possibilities, status, working conditions, policy and administration, and job security. These hygiene factors are considered "dissatisfiers" because their absence will lead to a decreased level of performance that does not meet minimally acceptable standards. The presence of adequate hygiene factors will lead to "a fair day's work for a fair day's pay," but not much more. Increasing the level of hygiene factors, according to Herzberg and Sergiovanni, will not result in increases above this basic level of performance because needs that are met no longer serve as motivators. In order to create a climate that encourages higher levels of performance, motivational factors must be present. These include higher-level needs such as achievement, recognition, the work itself, responsibility, and advancement. Satisfaction derived from these factors will lead to performance that exceeds "a fair day's work for a fair day's pay," but removing them will not reduce performance below that level.

Sergiovanni and Carver (1980) and Sergiovanni and Starratt (1983) have played an important role in demonstrating the interrelationships between Maslow and Herzberg and in applying these ideas to teacher needs and motivation. As indicated in Figure 1-6, Sergiovanni and Carver relate Herzberg's hygiene factors to Maslow's lower level needs and motivational factors to higher-level needs. Building a climate that emphasizes the higher-level motivational factors, they argue, creates an enriched environment conducive to teacher growth and professional development.

Considering Motivators

The *Metropolitan Life Survey of Former Teachers in America* (1985) confirms the importance of hygiene motivational factors discussed in the previous section. The report indicates:

FIGURE 1-4 • *Sergiovanni and Carver's Modified Hierarchy of Needs*

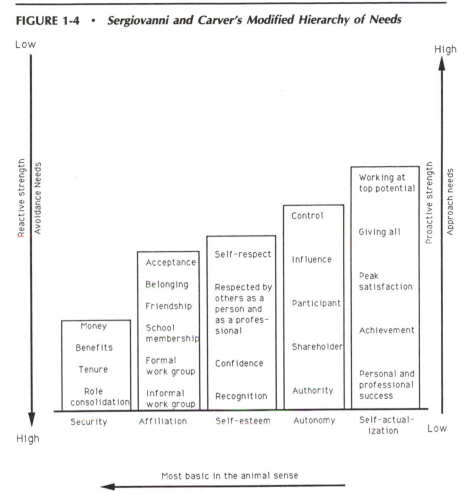

Source: Thomas Sergiovanni and Fred Carver. *The New School Executive.* Copyright © 1973 by Harper & Row, Publishers, Inc. Reproduced by permission of HarperCollins Publishers.

FIGURE 1-5 • *Herzberg's Motivation and Hygiene Factors*

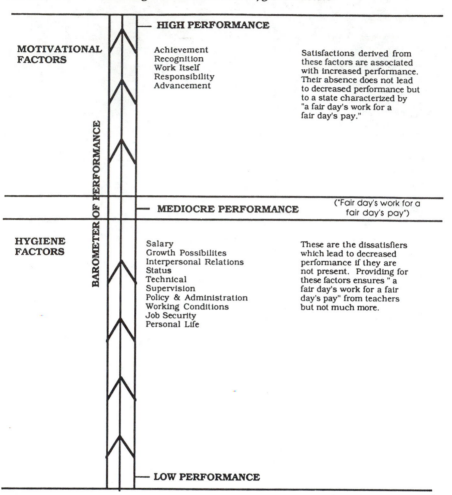

Adapted from F Herzberg et al. (1959), *The Motivation to Work*. New York: John Wiley & Sons, and from Sergiovanni, T. (1975), Human resources supervision. In Sergiovanni, T. (Ed.) (1975) *Professional Supervision for Professional Teachers* (1975) Washington D.C., Association for Suoervision and Curriculum Development, p. 18.

Sixty percent of former teachers cite poor salaries as the chief reason [for leaving]. Another 36 percent name such poor working conditions as too much paperwork, too many non-teaching duties, and lack of input about their jobs. . . . Sixty-four percent say that their professional prestige was worse than they had expected it would be. (pp. 4–5)

FIGURE 1-6 • *Interplay of Hygiene Factors and Hierarchical Needs and Motivation*

Motivation seekers focus here ——————

Hygiene seekers focus here

1. These are higher-order needs—most basic in a humanistic sense—which are best met on the job by advancing the satisfiers. Examples of these are: achievement, recognition, responsibility, advancement, and work itself.

2. Extraordinary performance is stimulated by providing for these needs, but performance does not decrease if they are absent.

3. Closure seekers seek satisfaction of these needs through motivational channels characterized by work success and individual achievement.

4. Responsibility seekers seek satisfaction of these needs through motivational channels which give them supervisory responsibility over others.

1. These are lower-order needs—most basic in an animalistic sense—which are best met on the job by eliminating the dissatisfiers. Examples of these are: supervision, salary, policy and administration, benefits, interpersonal relationship, working conditions, and personal life.

2. Extraordinary performance is not stimulated by fulfilling these needs, but performance decreases as dissatisfaction increases.

3. Instrumentalists with motivational potential focus here by choice and seek higher levels of satisfaction off the job.

4. Instrumentalists without motivational potential are failure-avoiders and are fixated at lower need levels. This is a symptom of poor mental health.

S.A.*
Autonomy
Esteem
Social
Security

*Self-actualization

Source: T. Sergiovanni and F. Carver, *The New School Executive.* Copyright © 1973 by Harper & Row, Publishers, Inc. Reproduced by permission of Harper Collins Publishers.

Retention of teachers was also addressed in this study. Eighty percent of both current and former teachers agreed that decent salaries, increased respect for teachers, increased financial support for schools, and more motivated students would allow teachers to perform as professionals and increase job satisfaction.

Teacher empowerment is a term that is used to indicate that teachers are more in control of their professional lives. Maeroff (1988) contends that three prerequisites to teacher empowerment are status, knowledge, and access to decision making. This message is echoed by teachers in the *Metropolitan Life Survey* (1986), of whom 97 percent think that school districts should have a team approach to school management.

Boyer (1988), in a state-by-state study of teacher involvement in decision making, found that teachers have little influence in education procedures. "While most teachers help select textbooks and shape curriculum, the majority do not help select teachers and administrators at their schools nor are they asked to participate in such crucial matters as teacher evaluation, staff development, budget, student placement, promotion and retention policies, and standards of student conduct" (p. 1).

Indeed, many teachers do not want to be involved in the latter topics. They feel these are areas for administrators to handle and would avoid involvement.

The notion of restructuring schools presents options to teachers but often is difficult to have accepted and implemented. Merit pay plans are strongly opposed by teachers. Career ladders receive mixed reviews, as do specialty certification boards.

The evaluation of the career-ladder concept shows three types currently in use:

1. *Performance-based ladders* are those where progress up the rungs is based on evidence of increased competence at progressively more difficult and/or complex levels of professional performance.
2. *Job-enlargement ladders* are based on differentiated job roles and responsibilities that serve the needs of students and the school beyond the teacher's own classroom. These job-enlargement activities include such duties as supervising beginning teachers, serving as a teacher representative to the administrative staff, and/or developing new or updated curriculum.
3. *Professional-development ladders* determine advancement based on the completion of qualifying staff development activities, coursework, and/or advanced degrees, similar to ways that teachers are now paid. (Furtwengler 1989)

The career-ladder programs have met with mixed success when it comes time for funding. It is often the state legislature that must decide on the fate of a career-ladder program rather than a district or local school.

A national survey indicated that programs such as teacher mentors, induction programs, and special teacher development and incentive programs have been funded in seventeen states (Cornett 1988). There are other states with pilot programs and local initiatives underway.

Teachers' roles are changing, and the recognition of the changing needs of professionals is forcing decision makers to offer a wider range of incentives. The need to attract and retain the best possible teachers has created an emphasis on providing incentives appropriate for teachers with a wide range of experience. Cresap, McCormick, and Paget (1984) divide incentives into five categories, which include compensation plans, career options, enhanced professional responsibilities, nonmonetary recognition (such as praise and awards), and improved working conditions.

A number of studies on incentives have been conducted in the past few years (Bartell 1987; Collegial Research Consortium 1987; Dorman & Bartell 1988; Dorman & Fulford 1989; Furtwengler 1989; Murphy, Hart, & Walters 1989; Rhodes 1989). The studies represent evaluations of career-ladder plans, teacher satisfaction with redesigned structures, types of incentives preferred by teachers at various career stages, availability of incentives, and teacher efficacy in light of reform measures. Suggestions for incentives appropriate by career stage will be explored in detail in subsequent chapters.

Considering Personalized Professional Development

As we learn more about adult and organization development, motivational theories, and incentives to promote increased job satisfaction and productivity, our concepts of staff development must change to reflect the best possible practices. Changing demographics in society and in the work place will also influence decisions about the best ways to meet professional needs in the schools. The need to tailor staff development opportunities to individual needs has been stressed in the literature and in the field (Krupp 1981, 1982; Levine 1989). The question of how to do it within the current structure of the school has created a dilemma. The restructuring efforts raised by career-ladder plans and principles for differentiated roles endorsed by teachers' organizations open doors for implementing individualized programs. The plans could incorporate assessment or be totally removed from the evaluation process. Fessler and Burke (1988) describe a model of staff development that incorporates the use of teacher assessment. In the model they stress the need for agreement between teacher and supervisor perceptions of the teacher's performance. Once agreement is reached, a plan for a growth program is decided upon by the teacher and supervisors. The personalized program needs to be appropriate, systematic, and continuous.

An alternative that does not necessarily tie staff development to assessment is the Career Lattice Model (Christensen, McDonnell, & Price 1988). This model pulls together research on teaching roles, differentiated staffing, career ladders, and incentives and presents a structure for developing personalized professional development plans.

The model in Figure 1-7 outlines the relationship of the various components. The teaching responsibilities include areas in which all teachers generally are involved. The teaching cycle of diagnosis, planning, curriculum development, choosing instructional strategies, and evaluation is foremost in the responsibilities listed. Also included are related areas of classroom management; discipline; creating a classroom and/or school climate; communication with students, colleagues, parents, and community; maintaining professionalism; co-curricular activities related to school functions such as coaching, drama club, newspaper, yearbook, and so forth.

FIGURE 1-7 • *The Career Lattice Model*

Career Lattice Role Options

Teaching Responsibilities	Learners	Knowledge Producers	Coaches	Teacher Educators	Mentors	Leaders
Student Evaluation						
Planning						
Curriculum						
Instructional Strategies						
Materials						
Classroom Management						
Discipline						
Climate (School/Classroom)						
Communication						
Professionalism						
Co-Curricular						

Source: From J. Christensen, J. H. McDonnell, and J. Price, *Personalizing Staff Development: The Career Lattice Model* (Bloomington, IN: Phi Delta Kappa Educational Foundation, 1988), p. 20.

The role-option categories illustrate possible roles teachers can assume throughout their careers. The role definitions include:

- *Learners*. In this role the teacher is learning new skills or content to use in the classroom or to share with others in some way. For example, a school might need someone with expertise in computer education and a teacher is selected to become the "resident expert." Coursework and classroom visits might be the professional development plan for this teacher as he/she learns new skills. Later he/she could serve in a leadership role within the school as a future professional development goal.
- *Knowledge Producers*. This role involves the teacher in collaborative or action research in the classroom or in the development of new materials and techniques. It might involve writing new curriculum or teaching units.
- *Coaches*. This role is often reserved for an administrator. However, it could be peer coaching for staff development purposes rather than retention purposes.
- *Teacher Educators*. The role of teacher educator is to teach other teachers. It might be in a collaborative role with a college or university with preservice teachers, or it might be sharing knowledge with other experienced teachers.
- *Mentors*. In mentoring, the teacher assumes a role supportive of some or all areas of teaching responsibilities. A teacher could be a mentor for a beginning teacher or for any other teacher in need of support.
- *Leaders*. This category can take many forms. It can involve leadership at a grade level or in a content area, in curriculum development at a local school district level, or even within a professional organization.

In this model, teachers can develop a personalized program that could be initiated by themselves, by administrators, by students, parents, or others. For example, if students want to start a student government, they could request a faculty sponsor, and a faculty member could take on a leadership role in this capacity. Another example might be a school board mandate to have a reading specialist in each school. This action could require a faculty member to become a learner first by taking some courses in reading. The teacher could then become involved in teaching other teachers (teacher educator role) or coaching other teachers in new ways to teach reading to students. Teachers can become empowered to assume these role options in a variety of ways. College or university courses, workshops, visitation of other classrooms, reading, professional organization work, and alternative job experiences are among some of the alternatives.

The Career Lattice Model could provide for teachers' individual professional needs but may require some role changes with the school structure. Roles traditionally held by teachers, principals, and central office personnel might shift. Budget allocations might also need some reconsideration if this model were implemented. A variety of ways the model could be implemented will be discussed in subsequent chapters.

Summary

The complex nature of a career cannot be addressed with a 2-hour workshop three times a year or an inspirational speech at the beginning of the year. As the teaching profession attempts to attract and retain excellent teachers, it is imperative that teachers' needs are viewed as dynamic and individual. The literature reviewed in this chapter highlights the developmental needs of adults and the need for changes in the organization to help meet these ever-changing needs. Throughout the careers of teachers, new challenges emerge. Some of these challenges come from the changing conditions in the work environment and some from changes in personal needs and conditions. An appropriate and responsive program of teacher development is sensitive to these changes as they occur and provides appropriate support systems to assist teachers in adjusting to their new circumstances. This should be as true for teachers with ten or twenty years of experience as it is for a beginning teacher.

The focus of this book is to examine the teacher career cycle and to consider incentives and support systems appropriate at each stage. In Chapter 2 a model describing various stages of the teacher career cycle is presented. Subsequent chapters provide detailed descriptors of the various stages, as well as implications for differentiating incentives and support systems.

CHAPTER TWO

The Teacher Career Cycle

RALPH FESSLER

The major premise of this book is that teacher development is a dynamic, career long process. In Chapter 1, the rationale for this approach was presented. This chapter continues the theme of career long teacher development by presenting a model of that process that will serve as the framework of analysis for subsequent chapters. In the following sections, a selected review of previous attempts to analyze teacher career stages is presented, as is a description of the process of model building that was used to develop the Teacher Career Cycle Model.

Previous Views of the Teacher Career Cycle

A number of individual studies and previous attempts at model building have influenced the development of the Teacher Career Cycle Model. The following contributions have had the greatest impact on the model building process reported in this chapter.

Pioneer Contributions

Much of the research available on the stages of teachers' career development has its roots in the work of Frances Fuller (1969), who was interested in planning meaningful preservice programs for education students at the University of Texas. Her Teacher Concerns Questionnaire, which was a product of extensive interviews, literature reviews, and refined checklists, has yielded the following categories or clusters of concerns of individuals at various stages in the process of becoming a teacher (Fuller & Bown 1975):

- *Preteaching concerns,* where education students are deeply involved in the pupil role and are often very critical or even hostile toward classroom teachers they observe.

- *Early concerns about survival* arise when preservice teachers first come in contact with actual teaching. Now their concerns are with their own survival in teaching and control, mastery of content, and supervisor evaluations. Stress in this period is great.
- *Teaching situations concerns* incorporate both the survival concerns and concerns about all the demands and limitations of teaching and trying to transfer their learning to a teaching situation.
- *Concerns about pupils* are expressed by preservice teachers, but they are often unable to respond to pupils' needs until they learn to cope with their own survival needs.

Through these stages, Fuller noted that the focus of those becoming teachers seemed to progress from concerns for *self,* to concerns for teaching *tasks,* to, finally, concerns for the *impact* they were having on students.

Hall, Wallace, and Dossett (1973) expanded the Fuller model by developing instruments to diagnose teacher needs and provide relevant staff development activities. Their Stages of Concern Questionnaire (SoCQ), reported by Hall and Loucks (1978), was designed to measure where concerns appeared when innovation was being instituted. The results of this research correspond to Fuller's initial findings that a person's concerns progress through the stages of self, to task, to impact.

In an effort to meet the professional development needs of individuals involved in the innovation adoption process, a conceptual structure called the Concerns Based Adoption Model (CBAM) was adopted. This model is important to the review of teachers' career stages since it is a formal recognition of the fact that needs must be addressed on an individual basis depending on the stage of development. Hall and Loucks (1978) report that the Concerns-Based Adoption Model is an aid in planning and evaluating staff development activities.

Observations from the 1970s

During the 1970s, several authors presented schemata of teacher development that were based primarily on their own observations and anecdotal reflections. Although these contributions did not have much hard data to substantiate their views, they did provide the beginning of a framework for further analysis.

Unruh and Turner (1970) were among the first to propose the notion of career stages. Their periods included:

- *The initial teaching period,* which may run from one to five or six years. This period is characterized by problems with management, organization, new curriculum developments, and being accepted by the rest of the staff.

- *The period of building security* covers roughly six to fifteen years of service. Teachers here find satisfaction in a career and "know what they are doing." They seek ways to improve their background and knowledge and take additional courses and advanced degrees both to qualify for salary increases and to improve their teaching.
- *The maturing period* is characterized by security in professional life and involvement in outside interests (politics, art, literature, music, etcetera). The secure attitude of teachers at this stage allows them to see change as a process and not a threat. They look for verification of new ideas and thrive on new concepts.

Gregorc (1973) reported on observations of teachers at University High School in Urbana, Illinois, and described the following four stages of teacher development:

- A person in the *becoming stage* demonstrates an ambivalent commitment to teaching and is beginning to develop initial concepts about the purposes of education, the nature of teaching, the role expectations in the educational process, and the role of the school as a social organization.
- A person in the *growing stage* demonstrates the attainment of a stage of development in which the level of commitment tends to be based on the individual's minimal expectations of the school and those that the school has of the individual. The basic concepts and stereotypes of the educational process and of personal discipline and responsibilities are forming.
- A person in the *maturing stage* has made a strong commitment to education and functions beyond the minimum expectations and draws upon, and contributes to, the varied resources of the school. In this stage, the individual tests concepts about education, self, others, subject matter, and the environment.
- A person in the *fully functioning* professional *stage* has made a definite commitment to the education profession. Immersed in the process of education, the person is trying to realize full potential as an individual teacher and as a contributing member of the profession. Concepts and beliefs are constantly undergoing testing and restructuring.

Katz (1972) described the following four developmental stages of pre-school teachers and the training needs necessary at each of the stages.

- *Stage 1 (Survival)* lasts about one to two years and requires technical, on-site support.
- *Stage 2 (Consolidation)* lasts into the third year and requires on-site assistance, access to specialists, and advice of colleagues and consultants.

- *Stage 3 (Renewal)* lasts through year four. Strategies prescribed to meet professional training needs include conferences, professional organizations, visits to demonstration projects, teacher centers, and professional journals.

- *Stage 4 (Maturity)* extends through the fifth year and beyond. Appropriate professional development activities here include seminars, institutes, courses, degree programs, books, conferences, and journals.

The views posited by Unruh and Turner, Gregorc, and Katz provided valuable insight into the notion of differentiated stages of teacher development. A major limitation of these early attempts at model building is that they tended to "lump" all mature teachers together without further differentiation. The view that experienced, mature teachers continue to grow and change was not present in the works of these early theorists.

The Ohio State Studies

Kevin Ryan, with Flora, Burden, Newman, and Peterson, (1979) directed a series of qualitative studies on teacher career development at Ohio State University. These studies were based on structured interviews of teachers at various phases of their careers. Included were teachers at the following levels of experience:

- First year teachers (Flora)
- Early and middle experience—4 to 20 years of experience (Burden)
- Experienced teachers—20 to 30 years (Newman)
- Retired teachers (Peterson)

Key findings in these studies are summarized in Figures 2-1 and 2-2.
The Ohio State studies are significant in the literature about teachers' career stages because they are based on structured interviews and provide a beginning of a research driven database. Much of the previous work was based primarily on perceptions, personal observations, and some anecdotal references. Other studies of the same genre include Hange (1982), Invarson and Greenway (1981), and Newman, Burden, and Applegate (1980). A limitation of these studies lies in the small number of people interviewed and the limited geographical areas represented.

Observations from the 1980s

Several researchers have synthesized the work of others to present frameworks of teacher career cycles. Of particular note here is Burden's (1982) synthesis, which provided refinement in the labeling and characteristics of teacher careers. Burden's framework was:

FIGURE 2-1 • *Summary of Ohio State Studies Using Personal Interview Technique*

QUESTIONS	FIRST YEAR TEACHER STUDY (R. Flora) (1 year study; 18 teachers)	EARLY & MIDDLE EXPERIENCE (P. Burden) (4-20+ years of experience) 15 teachers (average 12 years) of grades K-6

What are the personal concerns of the teachers in your study?	Type I
	   Forming new identity as teacher/ new community/marriage, etc.
	
	Type II
	   (Job related) How to have a good life considering all demands of teaching.
		Teachers in the first years felt they were not confident, not very flexible, non-assertive, more dependent.

What are the professional concerns of the teachers?	1. Teaching performance quality, i.e., inadequate record keeping, planning, instruction, etc. 2. Relationships with students. 3. Discipline & control (want respect & students to like them). 4. Colleagues & parents - want positive impression. 5. Becoming part of the school. 6. Being successful, not just survive. 7. Self as teacher - lack of confidence in their images & balance.	1. Changed from subject-centered to child-centered. 2. More insightful. 3. More organized and capable to deal with demands of job. 4. More confident.
What changes have they gone through or are they going through?	1. Became either more or less comfortable in teaching. 2. Became either more negative or more positive in attitudes toward students. 3. Discipline became easier for most first year teachers. 4. Planning for instruction became easier for most. 5. Personal & professional lives became easier to separate.	1. More warm, willing to try new things, happier, like themselves more than when first year teachers. 2. As they had more experience, they had more time & pursued their own interests.
What are the implications for staff development?	1. Orientation & initial programs should address management, organization, etc. 2. School-wide programs should be reasonable (i.e., new programs, etc.). 3. Clear criteria for acceptable performance. 4. Need for support from non-judgmental person who knows them and their situations.	1. Needed information on technical skills as first year teachers. 2. As they had more experience, needs changed to larger issues; tension accountability. 3. Ways to teach more creatively and to use different methods. 4. Curriculum/committee work seen as good inservice.

Source: From P. Burke, R. Fessler, & J. Christensen, *Teacher Life-span Development: An Instrument to Identify Stages of Teacher Growth* (Montreal: American Educational Research Association, 1983). Taken from original source material: Newman, Burden, and Applegate (1980a,b); Peterson (1979); Ryan, Flora, Newman, Peterson, and Burden (1979).

Stage 1—Survival Stage. Included the first year of teaching. Teachers were concerned about their adequacy in maintaining classroom control, teaching the subject, improving their teaching skills, and knowing what to teach (lesson and unit planning, organizing materials, etc.).

Stage 2—Adjustment Stage. Included years two, three, and four. Teachers were more knowledgeable about teaching and were more relaxed. They started to see complexities of children and sought new training techniques to meet the wider range of needs. Teachers became more open and genuine with children and felt they were meeting children's needs more capably.

FIGURE 2-2 • Summary of Ohio State Studies Using Age Categories

QUESTIONS	EXPERIENCED TEACHERS (K. Newman)	RETIRED TEACHERS (A. Peterson) 20-30 years experience 20 secondary school teachers 10 teachers -- elementary & secondary level (average age of 72)	
Throughout their careers what differences did teachers identify by age categories?	In 20's & 30's they tried to find a district, school. Saw 20's as good time in teaching. 30's made reaffirmation of career. Age 40 fell in a rut, discouraged and took steps to get out (change). Dissatisfaction in teaching. 40's and 50's wanted to quit but felt guilty.	20-29	completed education, joined educational association, (marriage, coached, etc.)
		30's	had own children; 2nd job necessary for men; community/organization; master's degrees; joined other professional organizations; happiest time of career; concluded all education.
		40's	some married women widowed; curriculum innovations.
		50's	change in finances (children gone); more time for hobbies; officers of professional organizations; some revitalization.
		55	tired of teaching; wind down in career.
		60's	prepared for retirement.
What changes have teachers seen in themselves?	More weary, less energy. More flexible with students. More personal.	Age 20-40	(Stage I) career development.
		Age 40-55	(Stage II) optimal career performance (most productive, influential)
		Age 55-60's	(Stage III) career maintenance and conclusions to career.
What are the implications for staff development?	1. Need to recognize changes in student and teacher roles over lives of teachers. 2. Teachers need to learn about stages of adult development and know what is happening to their lives (i.e., guilt with loss of idealism, etc.)	Stage I	Teacher as consumer.
		Stage II	Teachers as producers of staff development.
		Stage III	Need to have reduced responsibility and have a different staffing pattern, etc.

Source: From P. Burke, R. Fessler, & J. Christensen, *Teacher Life-span Development: An Instrument to Identify Stages of Teacher Growth* (Montreal: American Educational Research Association, 1983). Taken from original source material: Newman, Burden, and Applegate (1980a,b); Peterson (1979); Ryan, Flora, Newman, Peterson, and Burden (1979).

Stage 3—Mature Stage. Included the fifth year and beyond. When teachers were comfortable with teaching activities and understood the teaching environment, they felt secure and that they could handle anything that happened in their teaching. They were continually trying new techniques and were concerned with meeting the needs of children and their relationship to the children.

Burden's model helped to sharpen the view of career stages through a synthesis of interview data. While an important contribution, this view of teacher career stages continued to combine all "mature" teachers into one homogeneous group. Further differentiation among mature teachers was not explored.

Feiman and Floden (1980), in their review of research findings, identified three approaches to teacher development. The first approach described stages in teachers' careers that included: (1) survival, (2) consolidation, (3) renewal, and (4) maturity. They also described approaches concerned with the personal development of teachers (ego, moral, and cognitive development) and approaches to support teacher development through programs of professional inservice.

The first version of the Teacher Career Cycle Model, which serves as the framework for this book, appeared in 1984 (Burke, Fessler, & Christensen 1984), and subsequent versions followed shortly thereafter (Fessler 1985; Burke et al. 1987). The basic notion underlying this model was that the teacher career cycle is influenced by external environmental factors, some from the teacher's personal environment, others from the organizational environment. Rather than a linear progression from one step to the next, the model presented the view that environmental influences create a dynamic ebb and flow, and teachers respond by moving up, down, and through various stages. The model also presented differentiation among "mature" teachers. Specific stages of the cycle included:

- Preservice
- Induction
- Competency Building
- Enthusiastic and Growing
- Career Frustration
- Stable and Stagnant
- Career Wind-Down
- Career Exit

A more detailed presentation of the model is found later in this chapter.

European Models of Teacher Career Development

Recently, two models of teacher career development have emerged from European researchers (Vonk 1989; Huberman 1989). These views provide schemata that differentiate among career teachers and, further, introduce the notion of alternative career options experienced by teachers at various stages.

Vonk (1989) has developed a model of teachers' professional development that is based on a review of the literature and on his series of case studies of teachers (Vonk 1984). His framework provides for the following stages:

- *Preprofessional phase* reflects the period of initial education and training, during which time the prospective teacher is preparing for the role of teacher and exploring various role options.
- *Threshold phase* describes the first year of teaching, when much activity is centered around attempting to get a handle on the job and gaining acceptance by students, peers, and administrators.
- *The phase of growing into the profession,* usually between the second and seventh years of teaching, during which time the attention is focused on improving teaching skills and competencies.
- *The first professional phase,* when the teacher demonstrates the accomplishments, skills, and mastery of an accomplished professional.
- *The phase of reorientation to oneself and the profession,* during which time the teacher may question and doubt his/her commitment to teaching. This is sometimes associated with midlife crises. Some teachers may drop out of teaching at this point; others may continue but with less energy and enthusiasm than before.
- *The second professional phase,* when some teachers reenergize themselves and continue on to further professional accomplishments.
- *The phase of running down,* which is the period before retirement.

Finally, Huberman (1989) has developed several models of teacher career stages that describe a series of paths or options that occur during teachers' careers. The first Huberman model (Figure 2-3) is unique in that it is based on data collected among a population of women with five to ten years of experience.

Huberman's career trajectory for women includes:

- First, a period of *career launching and initial commitment,* which may occur between years one and six. Some teachers at this stage experience *easy beginnings,* good contacts with manageable students, and a comfortable adjustment to teaching. These teachers are enthusiastic about teaching. Other novice teachers experience *painful beginnings,* where they feel overwhelmed and anxious, have difficult students, strict supervision, and experience isolation from their peers.
- Second, a period of *stabilizing and final commitment,* generally between four and eight years of teaching. Both easy beginning teachers and those painful beginning teachers who have at least partially resolved their problems enter into this stage. During this period there is frequently formal

FIGURE 2-3 • *Huberman's Career Trajectory for Women*

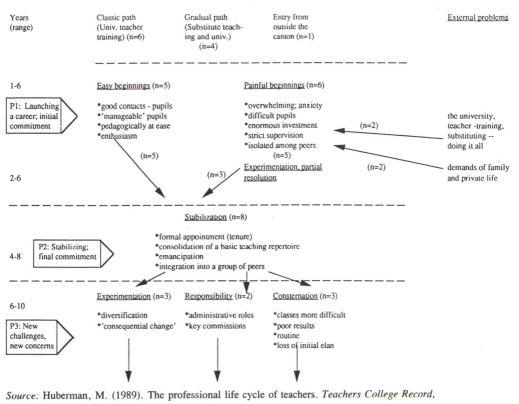

Source: Huberman, M. (1989). The professional life cycle of teachers. *Teachers College Record, 91*(1), 41.

appointment (tenure), consolidation of a basic teaching repertoire, emancipation (autonomy), and integration into a group of peers.

- The third stage is *new challenges, new concerns*. During this period, "stabilization" teachers enter into one of three tracks: (1) *experimentation,* with emphasis on diversification and consequential change; (2) *responsibility,* with an emphasis on assuming administrative roles and appointments; and (3) *consternation,* where their results and feelings about teaching are more negative.

Huberman also presents a more generic model of the teacher career cycle (see Figure 2-4), in which teachers between years one and three experience a common set of concerns about *survival* and *discovery* and then move to a period of *stabilization*. At this point, there are multiple streams, with some teachers following a path to *experimentation/diversification* and others moving to *stocktaking/integration*. Further options for each of these tracks are pictured in

FIGURE 2-4 • *Huberman's Model Sequences of the Teacher Career Cycle*

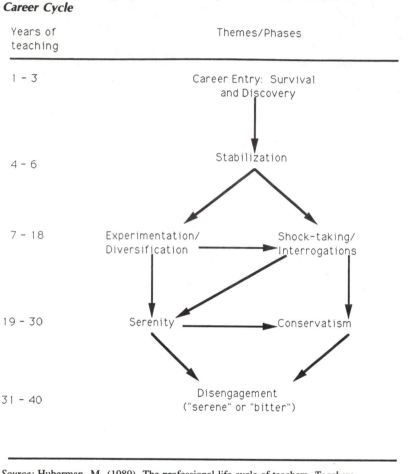

Years of teaching	Themes/Phases
1 – 3	Career Entry: Survival and Discovery
4 – 6	Stabilization
7 – 18	Experimentation/ Diversification Shock-taking/ Interrogations
19 – 30	Serenity Conservatism
31 – 40	Disengagement ("serene" or "bitter")

Source: Huberman, M. (1989). The professional life cycle of teachers. *Teachers College Record, 91*(1), 37.

Figure 2-4, including routes leading to late career *serenity* or *conservativism*. Finally, all paths merge again at career end or *disengagement*. This exit may be viewed as "serene" or "bitter."

Both Vonk and Huberman present sophisticated, multifaceted views of the teacher career cycle. Their notion of alternative career paths is more complex than those of earlier theorists who presented more linear, unidimensional views.

Summary of Literature Review

The adult development research reviewed in Chapter 1 has provided a strong theoretical base for educators to examine the development of teachers throughout their careers. The literature reviewed in this section yielded many "first attempts" at analyzing the career cycles of teachers and uncovered some suggestions, trends, and weaknesses. Many of the studies conducted have had limited samples; therefore, their results have limited generalizability. Reports exist where stages are based on observations and "feelings," but there is no research base to verify the stages. Some extensive research studies have been conducted in specific areas such as stages of concern about innovations, and a qualitative database on teachers' careers is beginning to emerge. The recent works of Vonk and Huberman provide some fresh insights into a career-long approach to teacher development and the notion of alternative paths or options.

The Teacher Career Cycle Model

The Process of Model Building

The process of model building that was utilized in this project is described in Figure 2-5. The first step in the process is to gather data that present a view of the "real world." For this project, this observation refers to an observation of the world of teachers' careers. Data sources used to develop this view included observing common practice, interviewing teachers, conducting case studies, and reviewing the literature. All of these methods were utilized in the development of the teacher career cycle model, including interviews of 160 teachers (Miller 1983) and a comprehensive literature review of adult development and life stages (see Chapter 1 and previous section of this chapter, as well as Christensen, et al. 1983). In addition, the literature related to teachers' career stages reviewed earlier in this chapter influenced the building of the model. The impact of these sources on specific components of the career cycle model are summarized in Figure 2-6.

Based on a synthesis of data collected, an explanation of the real world of teacher careers was hypothesized into a working model. Early versions of this model have been presented elsewhere (Burke, Fessler, & Christensen 1984; Fessler 1985; Burke et al. 1987).

This model-building phase of theory development requires the synthesis and expansion of prior knowledge into a framework that adds new insights and structures for analysis. The working model developed at this stage should not be viewed as fixed, but rather as a tentative paradigm that offers the current best explanation of existing data. Subsequent data gathered should be cycled back into the model to make modifications and refinements. The Teacher Career Cycle Model presented in the next section of this chapter is the latest version of a model that has evolved and been modified as new data and analyses have emerged.

Given the dynamic nature of model building described above, the working

FIGURE 2-5   •   *Model Building*

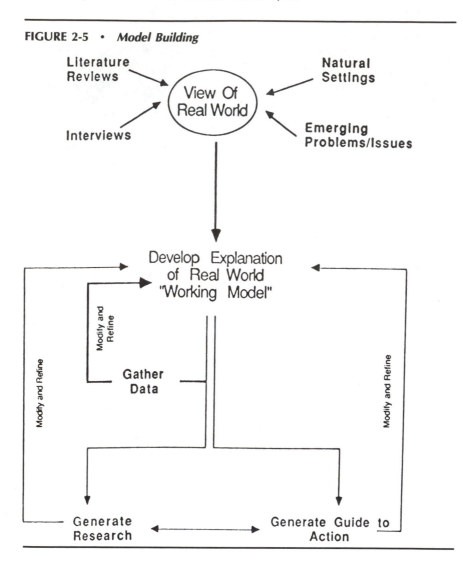

model should serve the dual purpose of providing guidelines for action and a structure for future research. This "guide to action" function provides a framework for practitioners to use the model constructs as a guide in decision making, planning, and policy formation. A number of such practical implications and applications exist for the career cycle model, and these will be presented in subsequent chapters.

For the researcher, the working model offers a framework for research and further analysis. Model constructs suggest interrelationships among complex

FIGURE 2-6 • *Career Cycle: Contributing Sources*

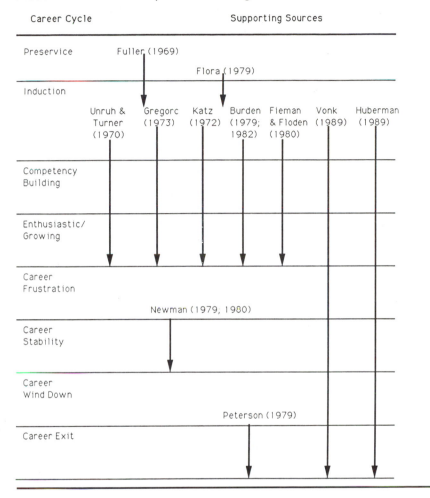

phenomena and hypotheses about additional relationships. This provides a scheme to systematically drive research and add to the knowledge base and body of theory in a systematic and interactive way. The Career Cycle Model has served as the framework for the design of instrumentation, the generation of research questions, and the formation of research designs (Burke, Christensen, & Fessler 1983; Price 1986; Burke et al. 1987).

As indicated in Figure 2-5, both the "guide to action" and the "research generation" components of a model should be fed back into the model constructs to provide necessary refinements and modifications. It is through this constant feedback that the knowledge base supporting a model can be expanded and the model itself can be maintained as an evolving framework that is responsive to new data.

Research Base for Career Cycle Model

The Career Cycle Model was developed through the model-building process just described. The working model generated from the synthesis of the literature and interviews was used as a basis for designing a federally funded research project that investigated the constructs of the specific career stages and, for each stage, personal and organizational environmental influences, appropriate incentives, and appropriate professional development delivery modes. The current version of the Career Cycle Model described below was influenced by the data derived from this project. In addition, subsequent chapters of this book devoted to the various stages of the model include sections that draw on these data to describe the personal and organizational environmental influences, as well as appropriate incentives and professional development activities for each stage.

The authors of this book made the decision that it would not be a technical report of research findings, but rather a practical guide to understanding the career stages experienced by teachers and the implications for teacher development and professional growth. Where specific research is cited, appropriate documentation is provided. First and foremost, the career cycle model should be viewed as a convenient framework for understanding and planning for the professional growth of teachers. For those readers interested in pursuing the research reports that serve as the foundation for the Career Cycle Model, the following specific sources are recommended:

- Paper presented to the American Educational Research Association describing the model development and research report (Burke et al. 1987)
- Report of the federally funded research project on career cycles (Christensen 1985)
- Report on interviews that led to the working model (Miller 1983)
- Technical Report of the Development of Instruments used in the Career Cycle Research (Price 1986)
- Detailed presentation of data related to incentives for teachers at various stages of the career cycle (Collegial Research Consortium 1987; McDonnell, Christensen, & Price, 1989)

Model Components

The Teacher Career Cycle Model enlarges upon previous work by offering a comprehensive and expanded picture of the career cycle and by placing the career cycle concept into the context of influences from personal and organizational factors. This approach, which borrows heavily from social systems theory (Getzels et al. 1968; Hoy & Miskel 1991), presents a view of teacher career cycles that is dynamic and flexible, rather than static and fixed.

The model presented in Figure 2-7 describes the dynamics of the teacher career cycle. The model offers a view of the career progression process that reflects influences from environmental factors (both personal and organizational). The career cycle itself progresses through stages not in a lock-step, linear fashion, but rather in a dynamic manner reflecting responses to the personal and organizational environmental factors.

The teacher career cycle responds to environmental conditions. A supportive, nurturing, reinforcing environment can assist a teacher in the pursuit of a rewarding, positive career progression. Environmental interference and pressures, on the other hand, can impact negatively on the career cycle. The environmental factors are often interactive, making it difficult to sort out specific influences that affect the cycle. In an attempt to sort out the variables, however, the influences can be separated into the broad categories of *personal environment* and *organizational environment*.

Personal Environment

The personal environment of the teacher includes a number of interactive yet mutually identifiable facets. Among the variables from the individual personal environment that impact upon the career cycle are family support structures, positive critical incidents, life crises, individual dispositions, avocational outlets, and the developmental life stages experienced by teachers. These facets may make an impact singularly or in combination, and during periods of intensive importance to individuals, they may become the driving force in influencing job behavior and the career cycle. Positive, nurturing, and reinforcing support from the personal environment that does not foster conflict with career-related responsibilities will likely have favorable impact upon the career cycle. Conversely, a negative, crisis-ridden, conflict-oriented personal environment will likely have a negative impact upon the teacher's world of work. The following discussion illustrates potential concerns in each of the facets noted above.

Family

The family life of a teacher is a key environmental component. The internal support systems can be supportive or negative. Parents who encourage and support the decision of a young adult to become a teacher will likely have a positive impact during preservice and early career experiences. Displeasure with this career choice will likely make it more difficult to meet the challenges of becoming a teacher. These internal support systems also carry over into the teacher's own primary family unit, as choice of mate, having children, and related family events may have a great impact on career activities.

FIGURE 2-7 • *Dynamics of the Teacher Career Cycle*

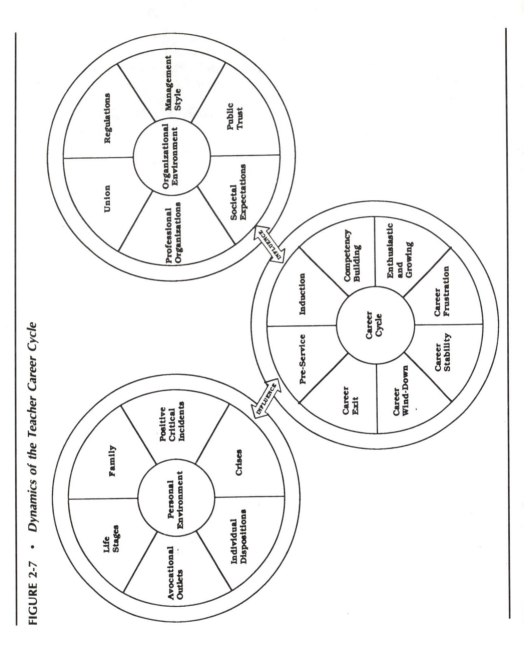

The various family roles that a teacher is expected to assume may also affect the career cycle. If the mate of a female teacher expects her to perform all traditional homemaking and parenting roles in addition to the demanding activities of teaching, there may be great strain on the career. Alternatively, a mate who shares in homemaking and parenting responsibilities will facilitate career enrichment.

Other family factors that may affect the teacher's career include birth of children, financial conditions, and the health and welfare of other family members. These may take the form of positive critical incidents and crises.

Positive Critical Incidents

Positive critical incidents may take many forms, including marriage, birth of children, and religious experiences. Such positive events in one's life may provide the foundation for security and support that will carry over into career activities. Interaction with "significant others" may also include mentors or others who have had positive impacts on choices and life decisions.

Crises

Personal or family crises may have a dramatic impact on job related activities. The illness of a loved one, death of a close relative, personal illness, financial loss, marital difficulties, and legal problems are all examples of crises that may turn a teacher's priorities away from teaching. Chemical abuse problems of a family member, a particularly difficult problem to cope with, have been increasing greatly in incidence in recent years.

Teachers presented with crises of these kinds frequently find it difficult to cope with career expectations and pressures. Many teachers experience job-related difficulties during periods of crises. Some, however, are able to rechannel their energies into their jobs as a way of escaping from their problems.

Individual Dispositions

Each person is unique, with behavioral traits, cumulative experiences, aspirations and goals, and personal values that combine to define the individual's personality. These factors influence career decisions and directions. Personal aspirations and goals may have influenced a decision made in young adulthood about selecting teaching as a career. Through experience and changing needs, priorities are sometimes reassessed in later years, perhaps resulting in career changes or career frustration. In other cases, maturity may help one be a more reflective, professional teacher, primed for continued growth and development.

Avocational Interests

Avocational interests may provide opportunities for continued growth that may be channeled back into teaching activities. In addition, they may provide outlets for fulfillment, achievement, and recognition that may supplement rewards received from teaching. For some teachers, these are outlets for needs not found in their teaching. Examples of avocational interests frequently available to teachers include hobbies, volunteerism, religious experiences, travel, and sports and exercise.

Life Stages

The life-stages literature, popularized by Sheehy (1976) and Levinson and colleagues (1978), identify personal factors that may have an important impact on the career cycle. During various adult life stages, there is often questioning and reflection about career, family, life goals, and personal priorities. This is particularly true during the period of mid-life crises, when individuals are sometimes preoccupied with questions about what they want to do with the rest of their lives. Periods of intense questioning and reassessment may have considerable impact on job performance and career options.

It should be noted that the list and description of facets of the personal environment are not all inclusive. What we are presenting here is a description of some key components in the personal environment that impact upon the career cycle.

Organizational Environment

The organizational environment of schools and school systems is a second major category of influences upon the career cycle. Among the variables impacting here are school regulations, the management style of administrators and supervisors, the atmosphere of public trust present in a community, the expectations a community places upon its educational system, the activities of professional organizations and associations, and the union atmosphere present in the system. A supportive posture from these organizational components will reinforce, reward, and encourage teachers as they progress through their career cycles. Alternatively, an atmosphere of mistrust and suspicion will likely have a negative impact. The following reflects some of the concerns in these organizational facets.

School Regulations

Teachers are subject to numerous regulations from school, district, state, and national sources. These regulations often provide order and structure to the school and reflect the goals and values of the system, community, and nation. At other times, however, regulations may result in bureaucratic layering that may have negative impacts on teachers. Examples of school regulations include curriculum requirements, development of individual education plans for special education students, and mandates about student testing or evaluation. Each of these may be perceived by teachers as positive or negative, depending on how they affect their classrooms and careers.

Management Style

The management style of the school principal may have a dramatic impact on individual teachers' career cycles. If a principal has established an atmosphere of trust and support, with opportunities for teacher empowerment and leadership, the response of teachers is likely to be positive. A less trusting, more inspection-oriented approach to management and supervision will likely yield less enthusiasm from teachers. The literature on motivation and management styles, reviewed in Chapter 1, illuminates the important role of this factor.

New leadership may result in changes in management styles and in teacher responses. It is not uncommon for frustrated teachers to be recharged by new leadership that gives them a fresh start and opportunities for renewed growth. Conversely, a new principal with a more controlling orientation may result in problems for teachers accustomed to greater autonomy.

Public Trust

The atmosphere of public trust may have a profound impact on teachers' careers and job performance. A positive atmosphere, where confidence is expressed in teachers and schools, will result in high teacher esteem and a positive outlook on teaching as a career. Conversely, a steady bombardment or criticism of schools and teachers is bound to have a negative impact on the way teachers see themselves. These external climates also are reflected in the financial support provided to schools.

The recent intense criticism of schools and teachers, especially those in urban settings, has resulted in low morale and frustration among many teachers. Daily press coverage of the woes of the schools, with teachers' competency and commitment often the central theme, has left some teachers wondering about the future of education and their future as teachers.

Alternative approaches to the problems of large city schools, such as school-business partnerships and plans to move toward school-based management, provide a more positive, proactive environment for teachers. Opportunities for renewal and growth provide structures for teachers to view their careers in more positive terms.

Societal Expectations

In addition to issues of trust, societal expectations for schools take many forms that impact on teachers and their career cycles. Community goals, ethics, values, expectations, and aspirations all play an important role, as do the views of special-interest groups and national and regional reports about schools and teachers. All of these factors help to define the external climate that teachers and schools find themselves in, and the dynamics of a given community may have a dramatic impact on the way teachers see themselves and on the expectations for their roles.

One aspect of these external expectations takes the form of financial support for school activities. This may be reflected in the level of budgetary support for school operations and needed reforms, the extent of support for school construction needs, and the support manifested in funds from the private sector through school partnerships and volunteerism.

Professional Organizations

Teachers often receive opportunities for leadership and growth from professional organizations, such as the International Reading Association, National Science Teachers Association, National Council of Teachers of Mathematics, National Council of Teachers of English, National Council for the Social Studies, Association of Teacher Educators, Association of Supervision and Curriculum Development, and the National Staff Development Council. These national groups, along with their state affiliates, offer opportunities for teacher renewal, growth and leadership.

Unions

The atmosphere of teacher empowerment in the United States has been enhanced by the two major teacher unions—the National Education Association and the American Federation of Teachers. This concern for the professional growth of teachers has evolved in recent years from an earlier period of confrontation and mistrust between the unions and management. The specific climate still varies greatly from community to community, and teachers' views of their jobs and careers are influenced by the atmosphere and agenda of teachers' unions. A positive climate promoting teacher growth and empowerment can lead to feelings of pride and accomplishment, while an atmosphere of mistrust between the union and management can lead to teachers' feelings of negativism.

Again, it should be noted that the preceding discussion is not all-inclusive, but rather illustrates key organizational factors that impact upon the career cycle.

Career Stages

The stages in the career cycle represent the "picture of reality" that was derived from the data collection and model-building process described earlier in this chapter. These stages represent "norms" based on aggregate data and serve as a valuable way both for thinking about career stages in the abstract and for assessing practical applications in school settings. Eight components of the Career Cycle Model are described briefly below. These descriptions and practical applications are expanded as separate chapters of this book, beginning with preservice in Chapter 3 and running through career exit in Chapter 10.

Preservice

The preservice phase is the period of preparation for a specific professional role. Typically, this would be the period of initial preparation in a college or university. It might also include retraining for a new role or assignment, either by attending a higher education institution or as part of staff development within the work setting.

Induction

The induction stage is generally defined as the first few years of employment when the teacher is socialized into the system. It is a period when a new teacher strives for acceptance by students, peers, and supervisors and attempts to achieve a comfort and security level in dealing with everyday problems and issues. Teachers may also experience induction when shifting to another grade level, another building, or when changing districts completely.

Competency Building

During this phase of the career cycle, the teacher is striving to improve teaching skills and abilities. The teacher seeks out new materials, methods, and strategies. Teachers at this stage are receptive to new ideas, attend workshops and conferences willingly, and enroll in graduate programs through their own initiative. Their job is seen as challenging, and they are eager to improve their repertoire of skills.

Enthusiastic and Growing

At this stage, teachers have reached a high level of competence in their jobs but continue to progress as professionals. Enthusiastic and growing teachers love their jobs, look forward to going to school and to the interaction with their students, and constantly seek new ways to enrich their teaching. Key ingredients here are enthusiasm and high levels of job satisfaction. These teachers are often supportive and helpful in identifying appropriate inservice education activities for their schools.

Career Frustration

This period is characterized by frustration and disillusionment with teaching. Job satisfaction is waning, and teachers begin to question why they are doing this work. Much of what is described in the literature as teacher burn-out occurs in this stage. While this sense of frustration tends to occur most often during a mid-point in one's career, there is an increasing incidence of such feelings among teachers in relatively early years of their careers. This is particularly true of those new staff who face the continual threat of reduction in force under a policy of "last hired/first fired."

Stability

Stable teachers have plateaued in their careers. Some have become stagnant and have resigned themselves to putting in "a fair day's work for a fair day's pay." These teachers are doing what is expected of them, but little more. They may be doing an acceptable job, but they are not committed to the pursuit of excellence and growth. These teachers are often going through the motions to fulfill their terms of contract. Others at this stable stage can be characterized as maintaining, with selective enthusiasm for teaching. Teachers at this stable stage are in the process of disengaging from their commitment to teaching.

Career Wind-Down

This is the stage when a teacher is preparing to leave the profession. For some, it may be a pleasant period in which they reflect on the many positive experiences they have had and look forward to a career change or retirement. For others, it may be a bitter period, one in which a teacher resents the forced job termination or, perhaps, cannot wait to leave an unrewarding job. A person may spend several years in this stage, or it may occur only during a matter of weeks or months.

Career Exit

The exiting stage of a teacher's career represents the period of time after the teacher leaves the job, but includes circumstances other than simply retirement after many years of service. It could be a period of unemployment after involuntary or elective job termination or a temporary career exit for child rearing. It could also be a time of alternative career exploration or of moving to a nonteaching position in education such as administration.

The Dynamic Nature of the Career Cycle

At first glance there is a tendency to view the career cycle as a linear process, with an individual entering at the preservice level and progressing through the various stages. While there is a certain logic to this view, it is hypothesized here that this is not necessarily an accurate picture of the process. Rather, a dynamic ebb and flow is postulated, with teachers moving in and out of stages in response to environmental influences from both the personal and organizational dimensions. The following scenarios are presented to demonstrate this view.

Scenario I

Consider the teacher who exhibits classic characteristics of "enthusiastic and growing." She loves her job and is constantly seeking new ways to make her classroom an exciting and lively learning environment. At the height of this climate of enthusiasm, however, she is informed that her job is about to be terminated (organization influence—budgetary cutbacks). After perhaps moving through a period of career frustration, this once enthusiastic teacher will be entering career wind-down and career exit. It is possible she will find herself in a new preservice stage as she prepares for a career change.

Scenario II

Consider a second enthusiastic and growing teacher who learns that his son has a severe chemical abuse problem (personal environment—family crisis). The trauma of this experience may well drain his resources and cause him to reorder his priorities. Such a teacher may settle into a stability stage in order to devote more attention to his family problem.

Scenario III

A third case might be one in which a teacher has resigned himself to a "fair day's work for a fair day's pay." This "stable" individual may have great talent, but views teaching as a job and not a commitment to excellence. Enter on this scene a very sensitive and supportive supervisor (organizational environment) who accurately assesses this situation and works with the teacher to rekindle enthusiasm for teaching. Strategies might include giving the teacher greater input into decisions affecting him, modifying assignments to maximize strengths, and reinforcing positive actions through verbal praise and positive evaluations. Many teachers will respond to such actions with renewed "enthusiasm and growth."

Scenario IV

Finally, consider the career wind-down teacher who is about to leave the profession. Very unexpectedly, her husband dies (personal environment— crisis). This dramatic change in her personal life may result in a reassessment of this career wind-down decision. Depending on the nature of additional personal and organizational environmental conditions, this teacher may renew a commitment to teaching and enter an enthusiastic and growing phase or may fall back into a period of stability.

Summary

The model outlined here reflects the authors' synthesis and integration of the existing available data into an explanation of the "real world" of teacher careers. It presents a series of structures that can be further studied and developed. As suggested in the model-building process described earlier and outlined in Figure 2-5, the Career Stage Model should not be viewed as fixed, but rather as a dynamic, working explanation of the real world that must be subjected to refinement and modification as new data is fed back into the process.

The Teacher Career Cycle Model serves as the framework for the remainder of this book. Each of the eight stages of the model is the focus of a subsequent chapter, beginning with Chapter 3—Preservice; followed by Chapter 4—Induction; Chapter 5—Competency Building; Chapter 6—Enthusiastic and Growing; Chapter 7—Frustration; Chapter 8—Stability; Chapter 9—Wind-Down; and Chapter 10—Exit. In each case, the chapter author relates the specific stage to the total Teacher Career Cycle Model, including an analysis of the influences from the personal and organization environments and an assessment of appropriate incentives and staff development approaches for teachers at that stage. To facilitate this analysis, vignettes are used to illustrate the application of model components. While these scenarios are based on interviews with real teachers, names and other identifying characteristics have been changed.

The final chapter of this book, Chapter 11, presents a summary and synthesis of the Teacher Career Cycle Model, as well as guidelines for applications in school settings.

CHAPTER THREE

Preservice Education

JUDITH CHRISTENSEN

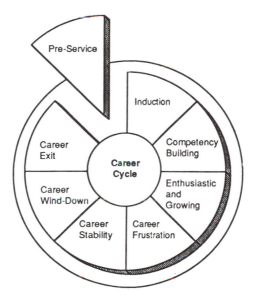

The preservice stage is the period of preparation for a specific professional role. Typically, this would be the period of initial preparation in a college or university. It might also include retraining for a new role or assignment either by attending a higher-education institution or as part of staff development within the work setting.

The preservice stage is the starting point of a career cycle. Traditionally, as people change positions within a profession or change professions completely, they will find themselves back in the preservice phase of their careers. Thus, this stage is as unrelated to age and time as any of the others. In this chapter, an examination is made of the personal, social, and organizational influences on teachers at the preservice stage. An overview of some of the research on preservice education and recent issues in our society that influence education will precede the discussion of the stage and portraits of two very different people who are in the stage. Finally, the chapter will address professional development needs and incentives appropriate for people at this point in their careers.

Research and Recent Issues

The recent interest in teachers' careers stems from a variety of sources. Educational reform movements across the country sparked the interest of politicians and the general public in the quality of education and the preparation of teachers. Work in adult developmental psychology coincided with population bulges of the maturing "baby boomers" and focused attention on needs of adults at various life stages. The "graying" of the current teaching profession and lack of turnover in school staffs created interest in teachers' career paths. Decreasing numbers of college students entering the teaching profession served as another impetus for taking a critical look at teachers' careers. Lortie's (1975) study of teachers and teaching pointed to teaching as "career-less" because there were so few of the potential upward steps often found in other types of middle-class work. He stressed that there were few differences between the status and role of a young tenured teacher and of a highly experienced teacher. This seminal work helped focus a number of future studies on the needs of teachers.

About the same time Lortie was studying teachers, Fuller (1969; Fuller & Bown 1975) was examining the development of preservice teachers. As Fuller looked at concerns of teachers at various points in their preparation programs, she identified some clusters of concerns throughout the early experiences of learning to teach. Fuller labeled the clusters or stages (1) preteaching concerns, (2) early concerns about survival, and (3) concerns about pupils. A description of each of these phases was outlined in Chapter 2.

These studies helped teacher educators think about the individual needs of the preservice learner. The need to address the concerns of preservice teachers is critical if we are to attract and retain bright, capable students in education. Students are attracted to teaching for a variety of reasons. Lortie's (1975) study showed enjoyment in working with young people; pride in performing important public service; ease of entry, exit, and reentry; time compatibility; some modest materials benefits; and psychic rewards emanating from student achievement as the significant reasons for choosing teaching as a profession. A 1987 study conducted by the American Association of Colleges for Teacher Education (AACTE) cited the following as reasons why students chose teaching as a career: "helping children grow and learn (90%); seems like a challenging field (63%); like work conditions, e.g., market, calendar, security (54%); inspired by favorite teachers (53%); sense of vocation and honor of teaching (52%)" (p. 43). A comparison of the reasons for teaching in 1987 do not look dramatically different than they were in 1975. However, Lanier and Little (1986) cite the work of Sykes, who characterizes the diminishing returns of teaching. He questions how prospective teachers can maintain optimism when there is

> decreased enjoyment from work with less responsive and appreciative young people, a deteriorating public image of teaching as an important service, a major reduction in lateral school mobility for women and upward school mobility for men, the erosion of material benefits, reduced psychic rewards from less regular student achievement, and teaching environments that all too often are disruptive, dangerous, and bureaucratic to the point of frustration. (p. 544)

The problems described by Sykes contribute to the frustrations encountered in the beginning years of teaching and even in the practice teaching experience. The high rate of teachers who leave the field early in their careers can be attributed, in part, to the reality shock of first assignments. If the profession is going to attract good teachers and keep them, it is imperative that induction programs are planned to help new graduates. This is especially true for minority teachers, of whom 40 percent say they are likely to leave teaching within five years compared to 25 percent of nonminority teachers (Metropolitan Life 1988). The need for induction programs is discussed in greater depth in Chapter 4.

The need for teachers is growing, and the numbers of students entering teacher education programs has increased steadily over the past few years. College students are deciding on teaching careers, and people in other careers are deciding on career changes to enter teaching. The two preservice teachers you will meet in this chapter reflect both these subsets.

Teacher Profiles

Sarah

Sarah is 21 years old and has transferred schools during her junior year so she could be closer to her fiancee. She has moved back home to live with her parents after completing three years at a large midwestern university. She will complete her program within the year at a private college in a midwestern metropolitan area. Currently, Sarah is in the second of a two-part student teaching experience. She is planning on moving after graduation to Florida, where her future husband will be setting up a business, and she will look for a teaching position. Sarah would like to teach primary-age children without "horrible home problems." She feels she can deal well with teaching, but if children come to school with so many problems, it is difficult to deal with them in a large group setting. At some point in her career, Sarah sees herself setting up a private practice to work as a counselor with troubled children.

When asked about stages she has been through, Sarah replied:

> When I was first in the education program, I loved all of my classes. When I got into methods classes, I felt I knew the material already and it was frustrating. I just wanted to get out and teach. Now that I'm student teaching again it's exciting and I'm enjoying it a lot more.

Sarah's greatest concern about teaching is burn-out or that she will decide she does not want children of her own. She feels strongly that, when she does have children, she will stay at home with them until they are in school.

Karen

Karen is a 40-year-old African American single female who is changing careers after a variety of experience in business and theater arts. To make the change, she enrolled in a Master of Arts in Teaching program (MAT) in a private college. Karen began her college years as a physics major at a private college in a large urban setting. She did not finish her degree until about fifteen years later, when she graduated with a degree in computer science. In the intervening years Karen worked as an executive secretary and became involved in theater work. She became what she describes as an "arts and education specialist." She formed her own children's theater company, which she operated for three years. Funding sources were difficult to find to maintain the company, so Karen decided to "become her own patron." She took a job as a systems analyst for a real estate company to make enough money to run the children's theater. She moved up in the company until she ran a department of twenty. During this time, she did not have time for much involvement in theater, but she had time to go through "a gestation period of my own philosophy of where art fits into society." She became interested in African history and aesthetics. After four years in business, Karen became "very disenchanted with making a lot of money for people I didn't respect." She left the company to study African history but ended up traveling and living in Europe and Africa for a year. She returned to America when her mother became ill.

Karen decided to go into education "because I realized what I missed most was interaction with children. Their enthusiasm validates mine; it is one time in my life when I can be as excited about finding out about something new or as full of wonder as I want to be without ever having to justify it."

When asked about stages she has had in her preservice program, Karen told about a time in the middle of student teaching when she had serious doubts about teaching. She said she wanted to work with the first-grade low math class like a lab.

> I wanted them to play with numbers and get a good sense of numbers. My cooperating teacher and the other members of the team were appalled. They thought it would be crazy and totally detrimental to the children. They said, "How dare you. We won't be doing it this way. Here are the workbooks. We do these workbook pages." They said kids would play with manipulatives all day but still would make no connections. They interpreted my arguments as an attack. They saw me as someone walking in off the streets, saying they don't know how to teach. I said that these are new ideas and are new approaches that go along with problem solving and that I just wanted to try a different approach. It was totally rejected, so I had to spend time teaching children in a way and with materials that I truly did not believe in. It was painful for me.

When asked what she sees herself doing in five years, she expressed an interest in further study, in creating a boarding school in the district for children with exceptional needs, and in creating materials (including computer programs) for use in classrooms.

Influences from the Personal Environment

As the profiles of Sarah and Karen indicate, the dynamics from the personal environment have a significant impact on a person in the preservice stage. Elements from the personal environment can help or hinder individuals seeking teaching as a career whether they are following the "traditional" or "nontraditional" entry into the profession.

Family Influences

The family plays an important part in supporting the preservice teacher, both financially and psychologically. The student who enters college directly from high school often receives financial support from the family. Family members can be influential in encouraging or discouraging the preservice teacher. Many students, such as Sarah, have parents who are or have been teachers. In Sarah's case, her mother had been a teacher and convinced her not to go into education when she entered college. Her mother felt it was hard work for low pay and that other careers were better. Sarah spent three years as a television broadcast major and worked part-time at a cable television station where she felt women were treated unfairly. She decided to enter education because of her love for children, and now her mother is fully supportive of her career choice. Sarah's engagement and support from her fiancee are also positive influences on her preservice experiences.

Karen's family influences came from her mother and sister, who sent her "care packages" during her graduate program and encouraged her to keep going. She did not receive financial support from her family, which is often the case with nontraditional students. They are on their own and must borrow money to pay for their career change. In addition, they are often supporting a family while going to school, which creates an extra burden.

Critical Incidents and Crises

These two areas certainly influence the lives of students in the preservice stage. For a traditional student, becoming engaged to be married can be a positive support, as in Sarah's case. The marriage can also cause a crisis when relocating happens during the student's program. Sarah has pressures to plan a wedding, prepare to move away from family and friends, and try to find a job several thousand miles away while trying to student teach.

Nontraditional students face similar problems plus concerns about relocating to new jobs with a spouse, births of children, and caring for children or aging parents. Another crisis often occurs when a person leaves a career in which he/she is established in leadership roles and enters a new career at the "bottom rung." This was part of the frustration Karen felt in her student teaching experience, which added to her feeling of "powerlessness."

Adult Development and Individual Disposition

Preservice teachers vary greatly in their stages of adult development. A 20-year-old and a 40-year-old student will have different life experiences, expectations, and goals. Twenty-year-olds are in the early adult transition stage (Levinson et al. 1978), while 40-year-olds are entering the midlife transition stage. Their view of the world is influenced by their own experiences, as are their expectations of children.

Sarah did not like her methods courses; she felt she knew the information and just wanted people to "let her do it." She was frustrated in classes and was much happier in student teaching.

Karen, on the other hand, had a very different perception of her coursework. She states: "People coming into the program when they're a little older have much different expectations. As a whole, we wanted more reading. We wanted to know who else we could read about. It was very stimulating!"

Karen's disappointment came in student teaching when she could not try out everything she had learned and experienced in her previous work with children. These differences could be attributed, at least partially, to life stages and individual dispositions.

Avocational Outlets

Preservice students in a traditional college setting have many avocational opportunities. Organization work, student government, sports, theater, music, and art are only a few of the resources and activities available. Many preservice students will begin an avocation in college that they will maintain through life. Sarah enjoys writing and literature and hopes someday to write children's books. Karen's interest in computers allowed her to incorporate them into her teaching program. Her interest in theater was directly applicable to her classroom activities and to the whole school in their year-end dramatic production, which she helped direct.

Many nontraditional preservice students find that their avocational interests bring them into teaching. Teaching religion classes, serving as scout leaders, PTA involvement, and volunteer work at schools are common ways of realizing the rewards of working with children.

Influences from the Organizational Environment

The organizational environment for preservice students includes not only the K–12 school where observation and student teaching experiences occur, but also higher-education organizations. This combination sets up a complex and often competing environment that creates many conflicts for preservice students. The socialization of preservice teachers into the teaching profession can be viewed in a variety of ways. Certainly, it is an interactive process that is not easily changed. Zeichner and Gore (1990) provide an excellent review of the literature on teacher socialization and state: "One consequence of viewing teacher socialization as an interactive process is that teachers influence and shape that into which they are being socialized at the same time that they are being shaped by a variety of forces at many levels" (p. 341).

With this idea in mind, some of the pieces of the organizational environment will be examined through the experiences of Sarah and Karen.

Higher-Educational and K–12 Organizational Influences

An organizational influence at the higher-education level was mentioned in the preceding section. It is worth discussing again because it is often noticed as a difference between traditional and nontraditional students. That influence is in the perceived importance of theory and methods courses. Sarah's point of view to "just let me get out there and do it" represents the view of many traditional students. On the other hand, Karen's enthusiasm for coursework, exploring ideas with professors and other students, and reading is in contrast to Sarah's feelings.

Karen also found her personal support at the college. She immersed herself in the program "twenty-four hours a day" because she had to finish in a year. Studying, work, and other students became her whole life. She says, "The program attracts bright, interesting, energetic people. There were some wonderful people in the program that I got to be around. It was a joy to work with them."

The college made sure Karen received a tuition fellowship and financial aid. She felt supported by faculty too: "There were professors I didn't have for courses, who I just met that I could go and talk to."

The K–12 organization also influences the preservice teacher. As Zeichner points out, the process is interactive and dynamic and can be encouraging or frustrating to student teachers. In Sarah's case, student teaching was supporting and encouraging. She enjoyed working with the children and found that her cooperating teacher let her take on many teaching responsibilities. She was comfortable with the management and teaching style of her teacher and was able to fit into the existing structure comfortably.

Karen was not so encouraged. She felt student teaching was a "traumatic experience." When asked why it was so she said,

> I think it was because that experience let me realize how little power teachers actually have. It was frightening to me to think that team members will keep you from using strategies that you know are right, that you truly believe in your heart that this is the way to go.
>
> I was coming in not a young girl so I had really internalized a lot of philosophies I had been taught. I came full of enthusiasm for new techniques and said let's try it this way! I found a lot of resentment and resistance to this. We've been doing it this way for twenty years and the children have been doing very well.

Karen felt discouraged by her experience but said she just kept telling herself over and over that this would soon be over and that when she had her own class she would do what she wanted.

The principal also played a role in Karen's feeling of powerlessness. She states, "The accountability factor seems to rely on the 'tried and true'—the worksheets. The principal knows these children are learning something because she can walk in at any time and see some worksheets. You can see how many they have right and know these children are doing something."

Karen has learned that one cannot go into a school or class and make a lot of changes—especially as a student or even first-year teacher. She says you have to "maintain bits and pieces" and implement changes slowly. One needs to learn what makes "peers and superiors happy on one hand, and what makes parents happy on the other hand, but will allow me to make the progress I know can be made."

Societal Expectations

The influence of society at large is felt at the preservice stage of the prospective teacher's career. The problems of society as well as the importance of teaching in the eyes of the public will have an impact on preservice teachers. Sarah and Karen provide specific examples. Sarah's mother was a teacher and encouraged her not to go into education. She convinced Sarah that "the money was too low, it was very hard work with few rewards." Sarah's concern about dealing with children who have a poor home life and many physical as well as emotional needs is not an uncommon one for beginning teachers. Sarah is already concerned about burn-out if she has to deal with many problem children. However, her concern about children with problems causes her to contemplate a private counseling practice sometime in the future.

Karen's interest in children's needs outside the classroom started with her theater work and continues to extend to after-school and Saturday experiences with children. She has a commitment to help children wherever possible. For example,

> These children have not had the experience of going to a museum—no one takes them so we do. The teachers tell her that it is not her responsibility but rather a "job that belongs to parents"—I should not be doing that. . . . When I take a child off the playground because he is getting in trouble and have him work at a computer while I eat my lunch, teachers say "That's duty-free time. The union fought for years not to have to do this."

Karen says she has to ask herself what she is willing to sacrifice in her personal life and personal time to aid her professional time. She feels, "For people to think that they can be done at five o'clock and be in a profession is unrealistic. Yes, with children there are different demands, but a profession requires that of us in this society. That's how we define a profession as opposed to a job."

Just as Sarah had expectations that in the future she might change to a counseling career to help children with special needs, Karen also looks at a possibility of starting a boarding school—either private or part of a district—to help children who come from deprived backgrounds. The commitments of both these women match the reasons for teaching described earlier in this chapter.

Professional Organizations and Unions

The preservice stage of teaching is not heavily influenced by professional organizations or teachers' unions. There is an awareness level as college students are introduced to the organizations affiliated with various content areas. Students become acquainted with how organizations influence curriculum and legislation as well as recent research in specific content areas. Professional journals are used in courses, and students are familiarized with the tools teachers have available to remain current in their professional knowledge. Teaching organizations have student units to introduce preservice students to the services available through the national organizations. Students usually learn about local teacher organizations in seminars held concurrently with student teaching. Sometimes students are directly involved in disputes (strikes, slowdowns, etcetera) in their student teaching experience, but more often there is very little involvement. Karen noticed some influence of staunch organization supporters when she worked extra time with students during her lunch break and after school.

As teachers leave the preservice stage, they change from an awareness level to a level of use and involvement and various organizations. They turn to journals for ideas and materials and to unions for services and, most likely, salary and benefits negotiations.

The role of the organizational structure for the preservice teacher is extremely complex as a student moves from the college level into the K–12 institution. There are no easy transitions when the rules of operation change so drastically and one tries to live in both worlds. It is the responsibility of both institutions to make the transition as smooth as possible for the preservice student.

Support Systems and Incentives

If the support structures for preservice teachers must come from both levels of institutions, what are appropriate roles for each? Who are the appropriate people to be involved? What is the best time for each institution to be involved?

Figure 3-1 represents the parties involved in the process of becoming a teacher from the initiation through the end of a teaching career. The arrows indicate an elaborate interactive process at every stage. Ideally, the communication is open and helps the process evolve throughout a teacher's career. The roles of the people involved should be interactive with continual communication taking place. The current emphasis on clinical sites in the K–12 schools, teachers taking on some roles within the university structure, and university personnel becoming more directly involved in the K–12 school points to the implementation of an interactive model.

The specific tasks or functions of the various institutions will change as the student progresses through the preservice stage and moves into inservice. It is

FIGURE 3-1 • *Factors Involved in Becoming a Teacher*

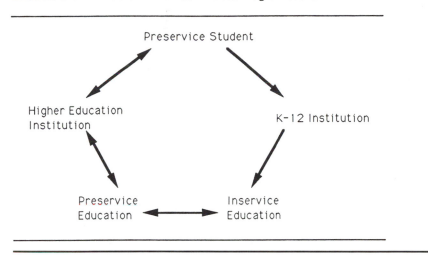

Preservice Student

Higher Education
Institution

K-12 Institution

Preservice
Education

Inservice
Education

likely that sometime during a teacher's career he/she will end up back in the preservice stage preparing for a different role in education or an entirely different career. Figure 3-2 outlines possible tasks for each institution.

Each institution may or may not have parallel roles but there is a continuum of responsibilities for both throughout the preservice stage and the inservice stages as described in subsequent chapters. The impact of support from each institution on Sarah and Karen was described in detail in the previous section. The element of incentives which are important to preservice teachers provides more information about institutional support and beyond. Research on appropriate incentives for preservice and beginning teachers indicates some pronounced differences mainly in the area of monetary needs (Collegial Research Consortium 1987; McDonnell, Christensen, & Price 1988). Prospective teachers and beginning teachers view loans and loan forgiveness as a highly appropriate incentive. Non-traditional students like Karen who are giving up jobs to return to school need extensive financial support to maintain essential living conditions for themselves and often families as well. Traditional students also have a need for financial aid and work opportunities to support longer preparation programs. Sarah helped finance her undergraduate program by transferring schools so she could live at home and bring college costs down. Unlike Karen, she did receive help from her parents.

Once on the job, loan forgiveness is seen as an attractive incentive. Both Sarah and Karen agree that it will be difficult to repay loans on a beginning teacher's salary. Sarah's husband will be starting a new business and she does not want to burden him with more loan expenses. Karen and other career change teachers feel the pinch of taking pay cuts from their former careers and would

FIGURE 3-2 • *Organizational Supports*

Higher Education	K-12 Institution
Orientation & financial aid Early advising and mentoring	
Early exposure to schools and children	Gradual involvement in classrooms w/pupils On-site personnel to orient students to local school/ district
Integration of theory, methods and practical experience Seminars to accompany practical experience with children Cohort or support groups of students	On-site personnel to provide demonstration lessons and conduct seminars with university personnel Provide placement of several student teachers in one site
Formal and informal contact with professors	Informal and formal contact with teachers, principal, support staff
Introduction to professional organizations	Teachers' organization orientation for preservice teachers
Professional seminars to accompany student teaching	On-site personnel trained in observation, feedback, evaluation
Formal observation, evaluation work with K-12 schools to provide training for teachers in these skills	On-site seminars during student teaching
Professional seminars available to new teachers	Induction programs to help beginning teachers
Advanced degree options or course work related to role changes	Inservice education to help keep teachers current and extend knowledge

welcome loan forgiveness help from the government or from the school district. Karen, in particular, was willing to teach in the inner city if loan forgiveness was included as an incentive. This is an important idea to consider as teacher shortages occur in particular areas.

Another incentive tied to money is that of higher salaries. Sarah was particularly concerned with this and thought the importance of teaching needed to be rewarded with higher salaries. Her mother had discouraged her from teaching initially because she felt it was very hard work for little monetary reward. Many prospective teachers are lured into other fields because of higher salaries when they really feel they would rather teach. A common reason career changers give for coming into teaching is that they know the money is not good but they want to "do something that is worthwhile." As mentioned earlier, Karen summarizes this feeling when she says, "I was disenchanted with making a lot of money for people I didn't respect. . . . I realized what I missed most was interaction with children, that their enthusiasm validated mine." Higher salaries would make teaching more attractive to both traditional and nontraditional students. Many would be willing to work twelve-month contracts to increase their base salaries. This incentive is much more attractive to preservice and beginning teachers than it is to teachers at other career stages.

An incentive not related to money is recognition of the importance of teaching. Preservice and beginning teachers are acutely aware of the poor image of teaching and want their chosen profession to receive the recognition it deserves from society at large. Sarah feels strongly that "society needs to recognize the importance of teaching. There is a terrible imbalance between teaching and such things as sports and sports figures."

Professional Growth

The preservice stage is a time of learning. The role of teacher as learner is the strongest here and in the induction stage. Survival is utmost in the mind of student teacher and beginning teacher, and professional development is linked directly to immediate use in the classroom. Sarah indicated she had been invited to a staff development day in her district and "could not understand why the teachers were so unhappy about attending. I found all the ideas presented were interesting and exciting and I couldn't wait to use them with my class." Sarah did not take into consideration the fact that most of the teachers had at least fifteen to twenty years of experience and probably were not hearing anything new!

Sarah hopes that in her first year of teaching she will have a mentor assigned to her and that she will be allowed to observe other teachers as part of her professional development program.

Karen has some strong feelings about professional development. She says,

> I don't want to become an 8-year-old. I want to be stimulated in-
> tellectually. I want my colleagues to work together on solving problems in
> the school. I would like to work with groups of teachers, parents and
> administrators to sit down honestly and brainstorm ways to improve
> schools. . . . I would like to see discussions about *why* some of the
> activities presented in sessions will work. . . . I think they should treat
> teachers as intellectual beings as opposed to third-graders.

The comments from Sarah and Karen illustrate a wide variety of appropriate professional development activities for preservice and beginning teachers. It is not accurate to assume needs are similar because people are at the beginning of their careers.

Summary

The need to treat teachers as individuals is as apparent at the preservice stage as in any other of the career stages. It is impossible to ignore the influences of the preservice teacher's personal or organizational environment. The organizational structure is extremely complicated at this stage when both the higher education and K–12 institution exert pressure on the preservice student. The cases of Sarah, a traditional student, and Karen, a nontraditional student, point out a number of critical differences in students and their expectations. Just as teachers must consider the individual needs of students, so must higher education and school systems support the diverse needs of the people within their ranks.

CHAPTER FOUR

Induction

ESTHER LETVEN

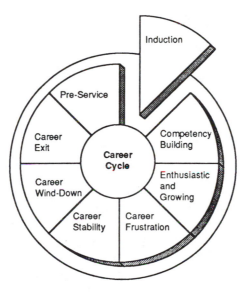

During this stage of the career cycle, the teacher is socialized into the system. It is a period when a new teacher strives for acceptance by students, peers, and supervisors and attempts to achieve a comfort and security level in dealing with everyday problems and issues. Teachers may also experience induction when shifting to another grade level, another building, or when changing districts completely.

For the person new to teaching, induction is a period of integration into the professional and social fabric of the school, district, and community. All teachers enter the profession at a point of inexperience. This is a crucial transition period from student teaching to classroom instructional leader.

Preservice preparation can, at best, prepare teachers to a point of readiness to enter the profession. Not even the best teacher education program, however, can accurately represent the reality of full-time teaching (Odell 1987). Cruickshank and Callahan (1983) note that while "the distance between a student's desk and a teacher's desk is short in linear feet, it is probably the longest psychological distance that these young adults have traveled in such a brief time" (pp. 251–252). Teachers often report they are not prepared for their first job since the experience of being fully in charge of a class is very different even from student teaching. The folk wisdom among teachers is that you learn to teach by teaching; most do not mention college education courses as having much influence on their teaching performance (Featherstone 1988).

The potential for failure is real in the minds of many beginning teachers. It is likely that at no other time in their teaching careers will teachers be so unsure of their own competence than during their first years of teaching. School districts assume beginning teachers have the ability to adapt to new situations, and teacher training programs verify that their students have the skills to teach. The only ones who know the real truth about the disparity between what they know and what they need to know are the new teachers themselves (Lind 1990). They are often concerned about their ability to be successful and may find themselves in settings and with responsibilities for which they feel unprepared. When they do encounter problems, they may be unsure of where to turn for help.

Veteran teachers making a position, level, or subject change also experience an induction period. Self-doubt, anxiety, and stress are common during this period of change. Questions of competence surface, particularly when a change in position requires leaving the familiar and forging new relationships with colleagues and supervisors.

In this chapter, personal and organizational factors are examined that influence teachers at this transitional stage, including those new to the profession and those who are making a significant change in work assignment.

Views of Induction Stage

This early period in a teacher's development is often referred to as a "survival" stage by educational researchers and stage theorists. Induction-stage teachers are concerned about surviving from day to day. Questions such as "Does it get better?" or "Will I make it to the end of the week?" or "How do I do a good job and still have a life outside of teaching?" are common among new teachers (Odell & Loughlin 1986). Scheduling and organizing the day, functioning within the school system, maintaining classroom discipline, and finding teaching re-sources and materials are other important concerns of new teachers (Veenman 1984). During this period, teachers experience a series of adjustment phases and stages of concerns regarding their work.

Phases of Survival

Embedded within the initial survival stage are different phases. Kramer's (1974) study of the socialization of beginning nurses parallels the experience of many beginning teachers. Kramer describes three phases of reality shock includ-ing a honeymoon period, a time when shock and rejection are felt, and finally, a period of recovery. The honeymoon phase with its fascination, excitement, and rosy view of the situation is quickly followed by shock and rejection as in-duction-stage nurses teachers encounter conflicting values in the hospital/school setting or tasks for which they feel unprepared. Following Kramer's model, beginning teachers, during the third or recovery stage, are frequently able to see the amusing side of things and are able to respond more objectively to situations and demands of teaching.

Levine's (1989) work describes periods of adjustment faced by newcomers to a setting. Beginners entering new situations are consumed by the events of getting settled and have little time for reflection. Once the confusion subsides, a period of disillusionment or disorganization sets in. The searching phase is a long period in which life choices are examined in a more reflective way. After resolving these issues, newcomers reach the point of adaptation and integration.

Stages of Concern

The work of Fuller (1969) and her colleagues (Fuller & Bown 1975) recognized how uniquely different the concerns of beginning teachers are from those of their experienced colleagues. They describe three distinguishable stages of concerns that are characteristic of induction-stage teachers. The first stage involves survival concerns that focus on one's adequacy and survival as a teacher, such as class control, being liked by students, and being evaluated. Fuller believed that to advance to more mature stages (concerns about teaching strategies and concerns about learner outcomes), beginning teachers must first resolve concerns related to adequacy and survival.

Another framework, a socialization approach to the process of becoming a teacher, examines how beginning teachers adapt to the roles of teacher, give meaning to their beliefs, and adapt to the beliefs of others. Needs such as security, affiliation, and self-esteem must be satisfied before beginning teachers can act as autonomous or self-actualized persons able to respond more adequate-ly to the realities of their circumstances (Veenman 1984).

This chapter focuses on the growth and development of teachers in the induction stage of the teacher career cycle. Influences from both the personal environment and organizational environment that have a strong impact upon teachers in this stage are identified and discussed. Specific programs to meet growth needs are listed for this stage, along with appropriate incentives for teachers. Valuable support systems for induction-stage teachers are also identified.

The following section is an introduction to "Mark," "Tammy," and "Lee," three teacher exemplars woven into this chapter to illustrate the induction stage of the teacher career cycle.

Teacher Profiles

Mark

Mark is 24 years old, married, and has one 2-year-old child. He is a first-year speech therapist working at both the elementary and junior high levels in a city with a population of approximately 75,000. The community is undergoing a diversification of its economic base due to losing its automotive industry, which was the major employer in the immediate area. The school district has twenty-three elementary schools, five junior high schools, and three high schools. Most of Mark's time is spent in an elementary school of 300 students that is adjacent to a junior high where he spends 10 hours a week. The working-class neighborhood surrounding these schools has been particularly hard hit by the closing of the automotive plant.

Mark received his bachelor of science degree and a master of arts degree from the same midwestern regional university. After completing his undergraduate degree in communicative disorders, he continued as a student until he finished his masters program two years later in speech and language pathology. While an undergraduate student he received the Chancellor's Leadership Award for service to the community and the university. After completing his graduate degree, Mark accepted his current teaching position and moved his family to a new community.

Professional memberships include the local, state, and National Education Association. He currently is serving as a member of his community's Cerebral Palsy board of directors. Outside interests include photography, antiques, and travel.

While only three months into his first teaching position, Mark recognizes the phases of adjustment he has already experienced.

> . . . a lot of phases—the first phase was just being overwhelmed. Speaking of special education, there's a lot of paper work—a lot of legal forms you

have to fill out and the process of learning—making sure you meet deadlines. So I guess my first phase was being overwhelmed with everything. I think I'm at the stage right now where I've finally got a handle . . . on how things are running. Now it's just a matter of using it, and I'm not looking at my procedures manual as much anymore. The first three months, the majority of it was just being overwhelmed. I'm feeling a little bit more comfortable now.

Mark is comfortable in his interactions with the students and enjoys the therapy part of his work. He is still struggling with how to organize the management tasks.

The things that discourage me are . . . the caseloads and the paperwork. If you have five kids that are referred at the same time, then all of those cases have to be done within 60 days by state law. The district would like you to have it done within 50 days. Doing therapy and planning therapy, you have to find time to get those different tasks done—that's the part I don't like.

Mark is realistic about his feelings of insecurity and understands the developmental nature of his induction into the profession.

I have to gain more confidence personally. I think I'll gain more confidence professionally when I know the procedures and what is expected of me. . . . I think I'm competent in knowing what the kids need [but] when it gets to diagnostic things . . . [when] you can't put your finger on the problem, that shakes your confidence and being just a first-year teacher not having the real practical experience in what to look for—I would like to get more confident and learn the procedures.

Tammy

Tammy is a 24-year-old, unmarried, junior high school Spanish teacher in the same school district as Mark (see previous section for description of school district). The junior high school where she teaches serves about 350 students, primarily from working-class families.

Tammy's bachelor of science degree is from the large flagship campus of the state university system. She majored in political science and Spanish. After completing her undergraduate education, she returned home and completed the certification requirements for her teaching license at the regional campus of the state university system. She is still living with her parents during this first year of teaching.

Tammy is the oldest child of a working-class family. Her parents tried to discourage her from going into teaching, but her experiences teaching English while studying for a year at the University of Madrid influenced her decision to teach.

Tammy is an intense, achievement-oriented young woman. Her student teaching experiences helped her understand the pressure she puts on herself.

> Because I was always a straight "A" student, when I first attempted to student teach it was hard. I made the mistake of going back to my own high school to student teach, and I put too many expectations on myself, and I was there for about three weeks and had a breakdown. I had to go to the hospital. That was really awful, and I didn't think I would go back into teaching. When you are teaching, so much is expected of you. You know what you want to do, and you can't. Then in my second placement, it was wonderful. I had some wonderful teachers, and they really got me to a stage where I realized I can't do everything that I want to do and that I have to go home and at a certain times say . . . that's it, no more papers and no more lesson plans.

Three months into her teaching career, Tammy is uncertain about her future. Now she's wondering . . .

> Is this what I want to do the rest of my life? I was laughing when they called me about this interview because I said it will depend upon what time of day it is—how I'm perceiving teaching. Some days I go home and I love it and can't think of doing anything else, and some days I do have doubts. One of my options is leaving teaching.

Lee

Lee is a 40-year-old wife and mother of three. She has 17 years of teaching experience in an urban school system. After receiving her undergraduate degree in special education, Lee taught secondary, educable mentally retarded (EMR) students for 16½ years; the immediate past four and one-half years in the same high school. For the 7 years prior to her high school assignment, Lee placed EMR students in vocational settings.

Lee was at a career frustration stage and was seriously considering leaving the profession when an opportunity for change presented itself. In mid-year Lee applied for and received a diagnostic teaching position working with students who had physical handicaps. This new position opened in December as a response to heavy caseloads in the department. They needed Lee at full capacity quickly, which meant little time was available for orientation or to learn the new role (which involved a lot of medical knowledge).

Accepting this position meant several changes for Lee. She went from one exceptionality to another, from classroom teacher to district diagnostic (itinerant) teacher, and from high-school age to pre-school through 21 years. Since she received no advance training, she is facing many challenges.

> Scoring and analyzing the tests, working with different ages, mental levels and physical involvements . . . the report writing, the medical research— these were all new areas for me. . . . Everyday I'm on a different M-team—in school I was only on one. I felt overwhelmed at first; it's like being thrown into med school.

Lee changed positions to escape a top-down managed program that provided her little autonomy or room to grow. Lee explains why she left the MR program:

> It wasn't the students or the school. It was the lack of support on the part of the program administration. There was a lack of concern, recognition, and reinforcement. It was a numbers game—that's all it became. Calls for help went unanswered or belittled. Their philosophy was to put your people down and keep them down—always critical. I wanted out of MR at any cost. In the MR department, all decisions are made at the top—we made no decisions.

Even though she is glad she made the change, there have been some anxious moments. "In M-team staffings I've felt some anxiety about incompetence, about making a mistake. I didn't want to let my co-workers down; I wanted to show them that I was capable."

Personal Environmental Influences

Teachers in the induction stage of their careers are experiencing all the dilemmas of being newcomers. As they seek to clarify their professional identities, they struggle with doubts about professional competencies. Their personal environments often influence how easily they travel this path of occupational entry or role change.

Family Influences

The family is a critical internal support system for these beginners. Their search for comfort is often marked by confusion and disillusionment, which often affects family relationships. Each day is a new adventure waiting to be shared with anyone who will listen. Patient, understanding family members can do much to ease anxiety, stress, and feelings of self-doubt.

Those living with parents can be easily influenced by parental attitudes about teaching as a profession. Parents who convey doubts about career choices can negatively influence the adjustment of new teachers. On the other hand, encouragement and stories of their own adjustment struggles can ease anxiety and build a positive support system.

During this period an inordinate amount of time is spent on school-related activities. For those who are married, the time demands of this adjustment phase can cause conflict centered around the difficulty of fulfilling household responsibilities. Finding acceptable living accommodations, for example, is important if induction-stage teachers, regardless of age, are to have the time and emotional energy to navigate this adjustment period.

Adult and Developmental Influences

In addition to being an initiation into the profession, the first year of teaching is frequently a time of transitioning into the adult world and all its responsibilities. In a study of teachers' personal and organizational concerns and influences (Burke et al. 1987), the concept of personal needs and goals proved to be one of the discriminating functions for the induction stage. Beginning teachers move from the freedom of student life to the restrictions and responsibilities of professional life (McDonald & Elias 1983; Ryan 1970, 1980), making the first year a period of intensive learning.

If entering the profession at the traditional college graduate age, all the normal developmental tasks of young adulthood occur simultaneously with career entry. This is a time of exploration and discovery. Optimism and idealism give them the energy and enthusiasm to adjust to the changes in their life situations. Career stage research describes induction-stage teachers as enthusiastic about teaching, energetic, able to admit they have much to learn, and striving to improve their teaching skills (Burke et al. 1987).

Separating from the past and developing adult identities may mean living on one's own for the first time and becoming financially independent from parents. If moving to a new community, one must develop new roles and build new social relationships. This often means leaving behind a network of friends and support systems and moving into a world of strangers.

Resolving Erikson's (1959) young adulthood conflict of intimacy versus isolation may take on added significance if novices are struggling to survive in a world of strangers. Adults in schools often feel isolated. While constantly surrounded by students, they are frequently cut off from other adults. Seeking personal relationships with their colleagues may be part of their search for mentors (Levinson et al. 1978).

Those who enter the profession later in life may be fulfilling a generativity need to contribute to the social good (Erikson 1959). Having family and friends affirm this career choice as worthy is important during this period of adjustment.

Making a career or role change may occur at several life junctures. Advancing in the work place and assuming some degree of authority are natural objectives during early adulthood, while changing careers later in life may be an attempt to modify the dream of early adulthood (Levinson et al. 1978). An expanded set of life experiences does influence the induction stage. While anxiety and self-doubt are still present, it helps to have a history of past success.

Critical Incidents and Crises

Any change, positive or otherwise, can create a crisis response for beginners since induction is a period of high stress and self-doubt about one's competence. Higher than normal anxiety levels may cause an overreaction to even the smallest incidents in their personal lives. They need stability in their world, and school may not be the place to find it right now. Moving to a new community, becoming financially independent, getting married, or beginning new relationships takes energy, most of which is used up trying to gain acceptance and comfort in the school environment.

Individual Disposition

Personal values are frequently tested during periods of transition. Feeling insecure about their competence, beginners often question their own values as they search for solutions. Those who find themselves in school environments where the belief structures are different from their own must resolve these discrepancies. Searching for acceptance by students, peers, parents, and supervisors requires an understanding of how one's personal value system fits with the work environment. In a study of teachers' personal and organizational concerns and influences, induction-stage teachers reported higher positive levels of influence for personal needs and goals, acceptance, and importance of support organizations (Burke et al. 1987).

Since the level of uncertainty is inherently high during the induction stage, clear aspirations and goals are useful. Keeping a clear vision of why they chose education as a career or why they made a move to a new position helps strengthen the resolve to be successful regardless of the obstacles.

For beginning teachers who enter the profession later in life after raising children, cumulative experiences with schools can shape their attitudes and behaviors. The great discovery for a parent-turned-teacher is the view from the other side of the desk. Acquiring a new role in the educational enterprise requires flexibility and perspective. Caring about the welfare of a group of students is very different from being an advocate for one's own child.

To understand why some teachers navigate this induction period more easily than others, a number of studies have tried to relate the problems of beginning teachers to personal and situational variables. Griffin (1983) found that new teachers with lower levels of idealism felt more capable of handling classroom problems than those with higher levels of idealism. Not unexpectedly, teachers with higher concern levels about self and teaching tasks reported more severe problems in teaching (Adams & Martray 1980, 1981). Anxious teachers with strong needs for acceptance, certainty, and an orderly environment perceived more problems with discipline and time management (Myers, Kennedy & Cruickshank 1979).

Cognitive development theory helps explain individual differences among beginning teachers and why some teachers experience more problems than others (Glassberg 1980). This approach addresses teachers as adult learners and describes a progression in new teachers' levels of conceptual development from stages marked by simplistic and noncreative thinking to more advanced stages of analytic and flexible thinking (Glassberg 1979; Hunt & Joyce 1981; Sprinthall & Thies-Sprinthall 1983). The more advanced in their development, the more adaptable induction-stage teachers are to the challenges confronting them every day.

Avocational Interests

During this period of adjustment, time is a precious commodity. In making choices about how to use their time, those activities and interests that do not directly affect their new roles are frequently eliminated or tabled. Previous hobbies or other activities that might provide healthy outlets are often considered extra and time-consuming. Finding a balance between work and pleasure is a struggle for most induction-stage teachers.

Impact of Personal Environment on Mark, Tammy, and Lee

Mark

Mark is comfortable with his career choice, but he is concerned about the impact his schooling has had on his young family. His wife, who delayed her education, is very supportive. While they face all the developmental tasks of young adulthood, they remain optimistic about the future.

> I felt bad about my wife having to give up her college career to stay home to take care of the baby, and so she's a bit behind, and now we have bills to pay. The positive thing is that it's really nice to come home to somebody and have support. She is going to be a teacher too, so that's another positive thing—I can relate real-life experiences in school to someone.

Mark still has questions about personal security issues. Caring for his young family is a natural concern of early adulthood. Commenting on his district's orientation program, Mark says: ". . . knowing nothing about insurance—I wish they could have spent more time on that and just sat down and arranged it so we could ask any question we wanted—claims? percentages? I still don't know. Spending more time on pertinent real-life things that are very important."

Developing a social life in their new community has been a struggle; balancing the demands of home and work has absorbed most of his time and energy. Some friendships are forming at school. "We haven't really made a lot of friends yet—the positive thing is that being in school I'm meeting a lot of people—a lot of contacts, getting to know about the city. With a child and school work, there's not much of a social life."

While time to socialize is limited, community involvement is important to Mark since it gains him both professional and personal contacts.

> I'm also on the board of directors for Cerebral Palsy Organization. Another one of my goals was to be involved in some kind of community activity because I feel like we will be here for a while, and I don't want to be isolated again—I want to know people.

While very busy with school and community activities, Mark has found a healthy balance between work and pleasure. "I like to have the weekends to do things with my family—that's the time we need to spend together. I like to go to new places—museums and things like that. I'm into my own personal regime of exercise—I like to swim and bike."

Tammy

Tammy lacks confidence in her teaching abilities and worries about the impact she's having on her students. Anxiety and self-doubt accompany her home each day. "I sometimes wonder about my discipline tactics. I go home thinking what should I have done here instead, and how should I approach this tomorrow? Should I forget about this incident and let it be gone, or should I bring it back up and try to deal with it?"

Tammy is still living with her parents. While they are supportive, Tammy is aware of their attitudes toward her career choice.

> My family did not want me to go into teaching. They wanted me to go into law. Now they are supportive but they are real union people. They can't understand why I bring so much work home. That is against their mind-set—when you punch out the clock, when you come in that door you shouldn't have to bring that much work home. They don't understand this

way of life, and they try to, and they are supportive. I think sometimes they prefer that I was in something else making more money.

Tammy's social world is limited right now. She relies on her friendships from high school even though they have little in common anymore.

Weekends I go out with friends, but some days on the weekends I'm correcting papers all day, My friends kind of felt the same way as my family did about my teaching. Because I had done well in school, and they went into business and they are making a lot more money than I am now. But now that I have funny stories to tell—they just love to hear about it, and I think sometimes they are a little envious of the change of clientele. I don't see the same people every day, and I don't get into the rut that they do.

Feeling overwhelmed by the tasks of teaching, Tammy has done little to expand her personal horizons.

I'm not a churchgoer, and sometimes I think I should be. This is my first year, and it's so hard for me to organize everything that I don't have a lot of time to do things, and that's one reason you have a lot of people leave—because [of] so many time demands at school, extracurricular things I have to do.

Tammy's high level of concern about herself and her teaching performance is illustrated by this reflection on her past emotional breakdown.

I didn't think I had any right to call myself an authority. But the way I view teaching now is the way I have to view it to survive—I have to keep learning and the kids keep learning. If I know everything then that would take half the fun out of the job. When you look at someone who has been there for ten years . . . I can't compare myself to that person because, of course, they have learned more than I have.

Lee

Lee's past professional experiences have made this induction period easier than a "first time" beginner's. Even so, Lee reports that this adjustment period is being noticed by her family. "I used to come home miserable every day when I was in the classroom. Now I come home more energetic and enthusiastic. I'm feeling much better about myself. I feel like I'm actually accomplishing something. My family can't understand why I'm spending so much more time on my work."

Organizational Environmental Influences

The missionary ideals formed during teacher training are quickly tempered by the harsh and rude reality of everyday classroom life referred to by many as "reality shock" (Veenman 1984). The extent of this shock experienced by induction-stage teachers is influenced by such situational factors as administrators, colleagues, task requirements, and resources. A positive, supportive organizational environment will move newcomers through the stages of adjustment more quickly than will an atmosphere of mistrust or isolation.

Public Trust and Societal Expectations

The status of teaching as an occupation is an important influence on induction-stage teachers. During this period of self-doubt and uncertainty, new teachers need assurance that their chosen profession is valued and that schools are doing a good job. Career stage research confirms the influence that societal expectations have on induction-stage teachers (Burke et al. 1987). The widespread public concern about the nature and quality of schooling is often focused on improving the quality of teaching in the classroom, which puts the spotlight on teachers. Consequently, surviving from day to day is played out within the context of society's expectations of retaining only competent teachers.

When working with their students' parents, exhibiting competence is important to beginning teachers. First experiences with parents are often frightening since competence is being tested by those with a significant stake in their performance. Inexperience makes them vulnerable to the influences of assertive parents and special-interest groups.

School Regulations

During this time of natural uncertainty, it becomes critical that induction-stage teachers understand, in concrete terms, the rules and regulations of schools and districts. This is not a time to operate outside the norms. Orienting newcomers to both procedural and curricular information provides a sense of security since they understand the boundaries they must respect.

Formal procedures and standards are difficult enough to grasp, but even more difficult to understand is the unwritten culture of the "way we do things around here." Any strategies for reducing uncertainty will add stability to new teachers' professional lives.

Management Style

Management's assignment of responsibilities to newcomers has great impact on role comfort. Unrealistic job assignments hinder new teachers' progress.

Their assigned classroom responsibilities are often the same, or more difficult, than their veteran colleagues, which causes them to fear they will be judged incompetent when compared to more experienced teachers. Lortie (1975) reminds us that teaching is a profession where beginners are fully responsible from the first working day and must perform the same tasks as their colleagues with twenty-five years of experience. Extracurricular assignments, if given at all during the first year, should take into account the strengths and abilities of beginners; they should not be assigned leftovers.

Induction-stage teachers report higher levels of influence for principal support (Burke et al. 1987). Sensitivity on the part of principals to the anxieties and needs of newcomers is crucial if they are to feel a part of a larger team. Since time is precious, having sufficient supplies and materials can reduce time-consuming searching. Inadequacy of curriculum and instructional materials adds an additional burden to teachers who have a limited reservoir of experience.

Principals are challenged to forge professional relationships that provide support while still maintaining the administrative responsibilities of supervision and evaluation of probationary teachers. New teachers need to understand what indicators will be used to determine their success as teachers. Needing to survive and believing that principals judge competence on their ability to keep order in the classroom, many beginning teachers embrace any routine or strategy that keeps the kids in their seats. In their search for competence, any strategy that "works" is added to their repertoires. Since principals are viewed as seeking data to make decisions about future employability, beginning teachers often avoid their principals and, consequently, lose them as useful professional resources. The evaluative nature of this induction period encourages a guarded, best-foot-forward attitude, which may deny induction-stage teachers the assistance they may need.

Relationships and communication between beginning and experienced teachers are complicated by the professional isolation in which teachers work. This may explain why induction-stage teachers express, at relatively high levels, that they are discouraged by the academic climate, are not so optimistic about teaching, and are not as comfortable or secure as a result of their experiences (Burke et al. 1987). Rarely do new teachers have chances to observe their experienced colleagues teach. Opportunities for collegial interaction about teaching are also rare (Johnson 1985). Those new to a profession or role have many questions about procedures and curriculum. They need positive role models who will provide in-classroom assistance. They need ready access to colleagues who can answer simple questions and provide practical "how to" assistance.

Professional Organizations and Unions

Professional organizations and unions have less influence on induction-stage teachers than do their immediate school environments since the organizations are too far removed from day-to-day survival needs. However, induction-stage teachers do report that the relationship between union and management is important (Burke et al. 1987), which might indicate their search for security, certainty, and professional respect.

Impact of Organizational Environments on Mark, Tammy, and Lee

Mark

Mark is successfully navigating his way through his organizational environment. As a speech therapist in two different buildings, he interacts frequently with other professionals, although he is the only speech therapist among them. Mark, after observing the other teachers in his two buildings, expresses the common concerns of an induction-year teacher.

> I feel like I haven't fit into the group yet. I'm new and these teachers have been there eight to fourteen years. . . . I feel like a lot of those teachers have almost an attitude of "I just want to do my work and that's it." I don't want to get like that, and I'm sure when they started they had their ideas—I don't know what it is—different work, policies, or what.

Seeking colleagueship from his peers in speech and language therapy has been difficult due to time constraints, but their support and modeling have been important to Mark.

> I don't know all of them yet. Because of time limits, we don't have the time to get together at a meeting and socialize because you have to get other stuff done. I don't really like that part of it . . . but I think as an overall group, they've been so helpful to me, knowing I'm the new kid on the block and knowing that I'm going through the same thing that they went through. Even the ones that are in their second year . . . I look at them and think I'm going through so much pain and trouble here and frustrated, and this is your second year, and you look so competent, you look so at ease. I hope that I'm half that competent and feel that comfortable at that time.

Following the rules and regulations for an exceptional-education teacher can be frustrating due to all the paperwork necessary for compliance with state and federal laws. Unlike some of his more veteran colleagues, Mark accepts the policies at face value. He's not experienced enough to make any value judgments, so he gladly complies.

> A lot of people feel that there are just too many policies. . . . I just have to follow state laws. I think the state laws are pretty fair—the time that we

have to have things in—they are somewhat flexible and you can always get extensions. . . . I'm just like the new kid on the block—whatever you tell me, I'll do. I don't know whether I have the right stand.

Mark is fortunate to be working with a very supportive building principal. Her understanding of the reality shock faced by new teachers has eased some of Mark's anxieties.

At the elementary school I have a really good principal. She's real progressive—keeps encouraging me to be better. I don't think they really prepare you for the real world. She knows how it is—she's real approachable, very realistic. She brings a lot of practical knowledge, telling me about her first year.

Mark is aware of the local teacher association, but as a first-year teacher, the union has had little influence on him.

I guess another goal of mine is to be more involved with the union. But being my first year, I have other priorities. . . . So far I'm happy with them—I think they keep us abreast—the people are pretty competent. I like to give them the benefit of the doubt. I think they are working for me.

Tammy
Unlike Mark, Tammy has found her teaching colleagues to be her prime source of support.

Within the school itself, I'd have to say the staff is positive; they have been wonderful to me, and there were two new teachers this year. There isn't a day that goes by that someone doesn't pop into my room and say, how are you doing? If it wasn't for that I would feel alone, just caged with these kids.

On the other hand, she does not trust the relationship with her principal since she is concerned about how he will evaluate her.

He's really into PR, which really bothers me because I'm going to be evaluated this year. I've looked at the form and half of the evaluation is on my extracurricular activities and about one-fourth of it is what I actually do in the classroom, and that is what I think I'm there for, and that's what I feel is the most important. According to his evaluation form, what I think is of least importance.

Some of Tammy's fears about her performance evaluation stem from the dissonance between her image of a good principal and the behavior of her supervisor.

> Also, his announcements in the morning are awful. He just has really bad English and that just bothers me to have the kids listening to it. I can't help it because that's how I view people. If you speak poorly then I'm going to think that you are not very well educated. A man in his position should be more careful.

Tammy's closeness to her colleagues has already influenced her response to district policies. District textbook selection procedures, designed for maximum teacher input, have added an additional time burden to their professional lives. Tammy is focusing on the burden instead of the opportunity.

> There is one policy that irritates me a little bit. We have to evaluate our books. We put a lot of time in the school during the day and to evaluate a book takes a lot of time. . . . By the time I'm done with the day of teaching to go over there and evaluate maybe twenty-five books, it seems like murder. Teachers are trying to get some time off during the day when we can all go there in just one day to look at them and that wouldn't even be sufficient.

Like Mark, Tammy has felt little influence from the teacher association.

> I would like to get involved in our union. My perception of it so far is that it is not that strong . . . When I first came and they had dinner for us and tried to get the dues and explained everything. But other than that, I can't say that they have done much for me that hasn't already been done by somebody before.

Lee

Lee admits that leaving her former colleagues was difficult and that she has not yet had the time or opportunity to develop new relationships. On the other hand, she finds the change "refreshing."

> I'm much busier now. I don't have as many opportunities for social interaction. But I enjoy the autonomy I have now. It's not like working in a school with the same people where the talk in the lounge is more about your personal life. Now I'm working more on my own; the interaction with colleagues is now more professional.

Lee found the move from classroom position to itinerant position gave her the autonomy she wanted.

> At first I was very lonely. Instead of belonging to a school, I was on my own since I was traveling throughout the district. I felt like a new teacher walking into her classroom for the first time. But I found I was actually treated like a professional for the first time in seventeen years. I was able to make decisions for myself—before, I was not allowed to do that.

This position change added the spark to Lee's career that had been missing for so long. "I work with such a variety of people—in and out of education, all over the city, with degrees in different areas. It's a lot more stimulating than the classroom. It's like going back to school; I'm learning every day. There's no mundane routine."

Professional Growth Needs

Research on Role Functions and Concerns

A synthesis of the literature identifies several role functions for teachers, such as teachers as learners, knowledge producers, coaches, teacher educators, mentors, and leaders (Christensen, McDonnell, & Price 1988). Induction-stage teachers function primarily in the role of learners.

The major task confronting new teachers is learning to think and behave in ways appropriate to the demands of teaching. During their teacher preparation programs, they become knowledgeable of the general cases, the theories, or the rules, but are unaware of how these ideas are worked out in practice. Yinger (1987) postulates that beginning teachers are exposed to a "language of schooling" as part of their teacher preparation that may be in conflict with the actual demands of practice. The "language of practice" cannot be acquired until they are actually engaged in teaching.

The reality of everyday classroom life causes a relatively stable core of beginning teacher concerns frequently identified in the literature. These concerns or areas of professional growth needs are generally classified into such categories as classroom management and discipline, pupil instruction, relations with parents and the community, relations with administrators, and relations with teacher colleagues (Johnson & Ryan 1983). However, not all beginning teachers experience the same problems at the same time or in the same way. Fuller's (1969) work reminds us how developmental in nature their concerns are. Induction-stage teachers will not be ready to address the learning needs of pupils if they are still focusing on their own feelings of adequacy and survival as teachers. The real challenge is how to find satisfactory ways to help beginning teachers meet the day-to-day demands of teaching while also helping them acquire an ever expanding view of their role as teachers.

In Arend's (1983) study, beginning teachers varied greatly in the type and amount of learning in which they participated. The types of learning experiences that received the most favorable responses were highly individualized (one-to-one technical assistance and observations of other teachers) or very practical (solving particular problems and developing classroom materials in clinics and workshops). The beginning teachers rated most competent were also the most avid participants in learning experiences. Beginning teachers who might have gained most from additional learning did not participate. Since beginning teachers' learning curves are individually determined, the challenge is finding ways to help passive learners without destroying the patterns of beginning teachers who already attend to their own learning needs.

Since the conditions and concerns of beginning teachers are extremely diverse, professional development opportunities must vary. Induction-stage teachers enter with different needs based on a multiple of variables such as life experiences, preparations, and matches between job placement and training. An individualized, situation-specific, developmental approach is the most effective strategy to help newcomers learn and grow.

Professional Growth Needs of Mark, Tammy, and Lee

Mark
To help him grow into his new role, Mark relies heavily upon his assigned mentor. She is able to answer his specific questions on a timely basis. "They help you when you have problems with ideas; just for anything, you just ask—like I don't know where to find this material, or I don't know how to handle this parent."

For Mark, workshops are only useful if they are relevant to the problems he is experiencing right now.

> It has to be really pertinent to me at that time. Just to go to workshops to get your contract renewed, a lot of teachers just sit there and look for something easy. . . . You need workshops on how to prepare for your first parent-teacher conferences, on motivational skills. . . . There's a few that—yeah—I think they are good when you need them.

Tammy
While Tammy values workshops and inservice programs more highly than Mark does, she uses these occasions to socialize and learn from her colleagues.

I have already gone to a few workshops for foreign languages. Every time I come back from one of them, I'm always excited about teaching again, and I have these great ideas. Maybe I'll go to the classroom with them and fail, but still it's nice to be with the other people and be excited about teaching. And also somebody will have the simplest solution to one of your major problems. I've had that happen at some of those. . . . Inservice sessions are important. It's important to get together with other people in the building when everyone is not on this tight schedule.

As for a continuing education plan, Tammy wants to improve her Spanish. Based on her previous preservice experience, she sees little value in formal pedagogical coursework, however.

I think I should take some more education courses, but I don't want to get my masters in education. All the education courses . . . drove me insane; they were monotonous. I need to get my masters in Spanish because I want to be the best in that area. I want to know my content inside out, even though what I know now is far more than I need to know at this level.

Lee

All the new technical information needed by Lee to perform her responsibilities forced her to learn quickly and in a variety of ways.

I did a lot of reading at home. I sat with all the manuals and studied them at home. I also followed my colleagues around and watched them test and score. I studied their reports to pick the styles I liked for my own reports. As I had a need, I asked for help from my colleagues. One of my colleagues is still asking questions and learning even after being in this position for fourteen years. It's like solving a puzzle . . . you have all these separate pieces and when they fit together, it's great.

Like Mark and Tammy, Lee does not find formalized workshops worth her time unless they meet her specific needs.

District workshops are a waste of time. If they are specific to what I need, then they are okay. I've only attended one that had information I could use. I would love to go to inservices on alcohol and cocaine abuse because I need that for my job. But I don't want to go to inservices on "collaboration versus cooperation."

Incentives for Induction Teachers

Incentives important to teachers at different career stages (McDonnell, Christensen, & Price 1987) can be separated into security items that support needs in the personal environment and professional items that support needs in the organizational environment. Security incentives such as loan forgiveness, attractive insurance benefits, and job protection and security provide beginning teachers with personal comfort that enables them to focus their energies on the work of teaching.

In examining the school as a work place, Rosenholtz (1987b) identified several conditions that affect teachers' productive commitment to schools. Incentives that provide psychic rewards, task autonomy and discretion, opportunities for learning, and efficacy about their work provide beginning teachers with the self-esteem needed at this uncertain time in their professional lives.

Psychic Rewards

Knowledge of success is important for work to be motivating (Hackman & Oldham 1980; Kanter 1977). Knowledge of performance is directly related to the amount of positive feedback received from doing work (Rosenholtz 1987b). Induction-stage teachers look for positive relationships with individual students and seek recognition from colleagues, parents, and principals. Since most teaching occurs in settings that are isolated from peers, approval from students is often heightened for beginning teachers.

Task Autonomy and Discretion

Rosenholtz (1987b) asserts that people want to experience work as meaningful—that is, important to their personal values and beliefs. Beginning teachers should feel personal responsibility for the outcomes of their teaching; they need to believe that their performance is attributable directly to their own efforts and not to some outside factors such as having "good" or "bad" classes. "Jobs that give people more autonomy and discretion require that they exercise judgment and choice; in doing so, they become aware of themselves as causal agents in their own performance—the feeling of making things happen with intentional striving" (Rosenholtz 1987b, p. 17).

Career stage research (Burke et al. 1987) affirms this autonomy and discretion sought by induction-stage teachers. Highly rated incentives included control of instructional decisions, choice of teaching assignments, and flexible work days. Having autonomy and discretion builds the self-esteem critical during this induction stage.

Opportunity for Learning

Feedback from colleagues and principals help induction-stage teachers become aware of the areas in which they need to improve. Without this feedback, beginning teachers rely almost entirely on trial-and-error learning, relying on their own abilities to diagnose problems and develop solutions. "With little access to role models among their peers, they rely on memories of good teachers they recall from their own student experiences instead of gaining substantive knowledge from their more expert or experienced colleagues" (Rosenholtz 1987b, p. 18).

Efficacy about Work

Since those who choose to teach often explain their decisions to enter the profession by citing the importance of working with children and helping them learn, then it is understandable why new teachers strive to feel confident about their classroom practices, believe student learning outcomes are possible to achieve, and feel they are making a significant difference in the lives of their students (Rosenholtz 1987b). Positive feedback from parents, colleagues, and principals helps beginning teachers believe the work they are doing is important.

Incentives for Mark, Tammy, and Lee

Mark
For Mark, working with and helping children is a greater incentive to teach than money. Even though he is the primary caretaker of his family, money is secondary.

> Money is good to survive, but I don't really see it as an incentive for me to teach. I don't think they pay enough really. I could have gone into clinical work in hospitals with adults. I did have experience in that, and I didn't like it. I like the kids. Money would probably rank about 6 in a scale from 1 to 10.

Like most induction-stage teachers, Mark wants positive feedback about his performance. However, he recognizes empty recognition and does not value it.

> The first-year praise is really important, but it has to be praise that's worthwhile or appropriate. Like you hear "oh, you're doing fine, a good job." But be more specific—you know, such as, "you did group really well," "I could see where you were going," or "you write your IEPs perfectly."

Time is a precious commodity for beginning teachers. Mark values control over the use of his discretionary time. "We don't schedule kids on Wednesday afternoon, which is basically our time to do diagnostic testing, report writing, and our meetings. I think if we didn't have that, I would not be real happy. An incentive is giving more time to the teachers to do preps, etc."

Interacting with colleagues is a greater incentive for learning than attending workshops or courses. Mark comments: "It would be nice to team teach. That would be a real incentive if things could work out that way."

Workshops are not an incentive to him unless "It is something I'm really interested in, and they tell me what they are going to offer. Then it would be an incentive."

Tammy

While Tammy did not enter the teaching profession for financial gain, she does expect to be adequately compensated, especially during this period when she is building her classroom resources.

> Money is important, but it can't be that important or I wouldn't be here. I wouldn't be teaching. I could be making thousands more dollars in the business field, translating. But I want enough where I can live comfortably. . . . In my first year I see all of these things I need, bulletin boards, etc. I have to go out and buy things—so money is important in that respect because a lot of the money I make goes into my classroom.

Recognizing that junior high school students are not likely to express praise openly for a teacher, Tammy relies on the positive feedback she receives from their parents.

> Praise from parents means a lot to me. I've had parents call me up and tell me good things and that means the world to me. They will say something before their kids will a lot of times. The kids are too embarrassed to say that they like something in the class; they don't want their peers to see that they might have enjoyed something.

On the other hand, she does not respect recognition from her administrator because it is not congruent with her teaching values.

> Administrators—I guess I view that praise as false praise—I don't know. We have these evaluations on our grading system and what it basically was, was a computer printout on how many people were passing or failing on courses. If over 25% of your kids were failing, then you got this bad little note from the principal. It happened that less than that were failing in my class so I got this good note. I was one of the rare teachers in the building that got it. I just looked at it, and it didn't mean anything to me because if over 25% aren't doing the work, I'll fail them whether he gives me that note or not.

Tammy would like to work collegially with her peers in designing integrated curriculum projects. She is feeling the isolation of being the only teacher in her discipline. "I don't have an opportunity to work with teachers and try to come up with some cooperative lessons. I would like to do that. I could fit mine into social studies so easily—even math. I feel as though we are kind of left out by ourselves."

It is important to Tammy to have an impact on her students. She draws a correlation between their success and her teaching performance.

> Specifically, when students that I saw were doing very poorly at the beginning of the year or are doing poorly in other classes do well in my class, then I attribute that to my class. That's when I feel best of all. Then again, sometimes those kids will start to fall and that's upsetting. When you think you have done something and then it is demolished in a day or in 5 minutes.

Lee

Positive feedback from her students' parents and her supervisor are psychic rewards motivating Lee.

> The respect and trust of my supervisor is important to me. I don't feel like I have to punch in and out. It's very self-satisfying. I'd do anything for her in return; therefore, I work harder. . . . I get immediate feedback from parents. They are so thankful and appreciative of anything that is done for their children. These parents are incredible at stroking you.

In Lee's mind, the increased autonomy and discretion are the major advantages of her job change. "This position gives me the sense of being a professional, of being responsible. No one is looking over your shoulder or slapping your hand. You're responsible for your own decisions."

For a long time Lee could not see the difference she was making. Now she has a renewed sense of efficacy about her work.

> When I go into agencies and schools, I'm looked at as the expert. They want advice. I feel I am important because people are depending on me, which causes me to go home and study more so I do have answers. Physically handicapped is such a new field and so medically oriented that most people don't know much about it. It makes me feel that maybe I'm doing something important.

Support Systems for Induction Teachers

New teachers ought to be inducted into the profession in a thoughtful and humane fashion. This can be a time of cementing bad habits rather than a time of professional growth unless proper support and assistance are provided. When left on their own to develop expertise as teachers, they often learn by trial and error. When left to rely on their own limited resources, new teachers develop "survival techniques" that may crystallize and harden into teaching styles that ultimately prevent them from becoming effective teachers.

The needs of beginning teachers are so well recognized that numerous state departments of education are concentrating on the induction of new teachers. Nearly three-fourths of the states are developing statewide beginning teacher assistance programs. These programs consist of some combination of assistance and assessment that addresses the most frequently mentioned problems of discipline and class control, time management, finding and using materials, evaluation of students, and isolation and insecurity.

While all induction-stage teachers require some form of assistance, these needs vary from individual to individual. In a survey of inservice support for first-year teachers, Grant and Zeichner (1981) concluded that the problems and concerns of beginning teachers are extremely diverse. The implication of this and other studies (Ryan 1980) is that induction or support programs should be individualized and developmental. The needs of teachers just entering the profession may be markedly different from those who are changing grade levels or returning to the profession after significant absences. The needs of a 22-year-old beginning teacher will be different from those of a 43-year-old. Support for induction-stage teachers must be sensitive to this variability of needs.

While the needs may vary, most agree that the initiation of teachers into the profession requires more than handing over keys to a classroom. Beginning teachers need orientation to the culture and climate of the school if they are to become a part of it; they need to learn the explicit as well as the unwritten expectations of performance. They face questions in practice they have only addressed in theory. They need to develop support systems to help sustain energy and commitment to their new profession. Most induction programs, therefore, contain an ongoing orientation component, an assigned support teacher or mentor, periodic support and sharing sessions, structured observations and feedback, and opportunities to observe other experienced teachers (Lind 1990).

Induction Alternatives

Principals are key actors in helping induction-stage teachers adjust to their new settings. Textbooks and materials should be provided as early as possible, and teaching assignments should be reasonable. Job-embedded support such as released time to observe other teachers, reduced class sizes, and exemptions from nonteaching responsibilities are within the jurisdiction of principals. By assigning support teachers/mentors to induction-stage teachers, principals encourage in-classroom assistance and ensure daily nurturing of the newcomers.

First-year teachers preoccupied with survival spend little time pursuing assistance or counsel unless time or support is offered directly to them. They are cautious about seeking assistance for fear it might raise questions about their competence (Newberry 1977). Assigning support teachers to beginners sends the message that it is all right to ask for help. Mentors assist with daily questions while also helping to socialize newcomers into their work environments. Mentors should be competent professionals who have the personal skills and desire to help induction-stage teachers succeed in the profession. They serve as guides, supporters, advisers, and coaches.

Induction alternatives should be designed and offered so that beginning teachers can choose different assistance to meet their individual needs. Some beginning teachers may decide not to take advantage of mentor relationships; others might be interested in support groups or workshops on solving problems related to the work of teaching or coping with personal concerns such as finances or time management. Some induction-stage teachers will want curricular or instructional assistance before the year begins; others will find this help more relevant after the first grading period; others will never feel a need for this kind of assistance. Support programs should be sensitive to the divergence of needs and flexible enough to respond with appropriate and effective assistance.

Support Systems for Mark, Tammy, and Lee

Mark and Tammy are both receiving support from their school districts' induction programs, which assign mentors to new teachers and offer after-school support seminars. Lee, however, is not part of any formalized support program.

Mark

Not wanting to be a burden on anyone, Mark is relieved that he was assigned a mentor—someone who agreed in advance to help him through his induction period.

At first when I got here I thought about the mentor program—oh geez, what are they going to do? Seems silly, but the program itself and having all the resources really amazed me. I'm sure that even if you didn't have the mentor program, I have twenty other speech therapists that I could call. But being assigned a mentor, that's the mentor's purpose, and I don't feel as though I'm asking too many questions.

Tammy

Like Mark, Tammy feels her mentor gives her the individual, daily support she needs.

The mentor program saved my life. I'm the only Spanish teacher. The woman next door teaches French and she is my mentor, which is really nice because we are in the same area at least. When I'm down, she's there, and when I'm up, she's there. It's just nice to have someone say I don't have to be perfect. She thought the same thing when she was a first-year teacher. I don't know if I'd still be there if it wasn't for her.

Tammy also finds the seminars to be a valuable source of peer support. "We come here and they teach us new things. It's nice to meet with the other new teachers; you're going through the same thing with them."

Lee

Unlike Mark and Tammy, Lee is not in a formalized support program. Since she is not new to the profession, she already knows how to work within the system. She has the experience and professional confidence to guide her through this induction period. Her questions are best answered as they arise. In her case, her colleagues and supervisor are her support system.

At first I felt very insecure and unqualified. But there was a sense of excitement because I was actually learning and growing. I've had real guidance from my supervisor. I don't feel put down or that I can't do it. There's lots of reinforcement and concern. For example, I gave all the tests to a student but I didn't know how to interpret them. I went to my supervisor, and she helped me understand the connections.

Summary

Beginning teachers follow one of two paths. Some enter a competency-building stage in which they demonstrate a lively, open, continuous desire to learn more and become more proficient. Others remain static, resistant to change, and unenthusiastic about continuing their professional development.

A painful induction year can leave permanent scars. In analyzing interviews with over 100 veteran teachers in and around Geneva, Switzerland, Michael Huberman of the University of Geneva found that those who remembered an unpleasant first year were considerably less satisfied with their profession today than those who recalled an easy induction. It seems that those who faced the largest problems in their first job never developed into the teachers they could have been (Huberman 1989).

Fear, habit, and institutional inertia keep most people from changing much once they have developed a style that works. Thus it seems that the induction year may actually shape whole professional careers (Featherstone 1988). A successful induction period should pave the way for the competency-building stage, when beginning teachers seek to improve their teaching skills and abilities. By the end of the induction stage, teachers should view themselves as learners who see their jobs as challenging and who are eager to improve their repertoire of skills.

During their induction stages, Mark, Tammy and Lee envisioned their professional futures. Each, in his/her own way, recognizes the competency building still ahead of them.

Mark says:

I don't think I'm going to be a speech therapist the rest of my life. I think I will be dealing in the area of special education. I think I will go back to school and get an administrative license—maybe. That's how I feel now; I don't know how long down the road it will be. It won't be in a couple of years, but . . .

Tammy says:

At this point I want to stay in the classroom because I see so many areas where I need to improve. I don't think I will want to move out of the classroom until I feel that I've reached my peak, and I'm doing the very best that I can. I don't see that for a few years. Once I reach that point then, yes, I think I'd like to move maybe out of the classroom. I can't see myself moving out of the classroom forever, because I like it too much.

Lee says:

Everyone should be forced to make a career change. There's too many stagnant people. They may know their jobs and do them well, but for themselves . . . I think it's healthy to change. Otherwise you get like couch potatoes—you get so comfortable, you don't want to move.

The induction stage is a crucial period of transition from being a student to becoming a teacher. The complex tasks associated with the responsibilities of full-time teaching may seem overwhelming to some, and there is a need to provide support from both the personal and organizational environments. Supportive influences from family and friends are particularly important, as are the developmental influences associated with concerns of early adulthood. For those entering teaching later in life, career transition experiences and changes in values and priorities must be considered. From the organizational environment, crucial influences include the management style and support systems provided by the administration. Induction teachers need personalized professional growth activities that take into consideration their individual needs. Principals and supervisors must be aware of the special needs of induction teachers and must play a key role in establishing a positive climate that will enable novices to master survival skills and move on to competency building and enthusiastic and growing stages.

CHAPTER FIVE

Competency Building

PETER J. BURKE   JOHN H. MCDONNELL

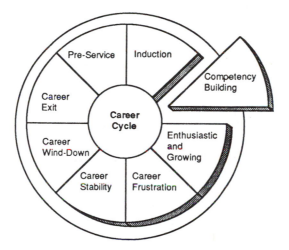

During this stage of the career cycle, the teacher is striving to improve teaching skills and abilities. The teacher seeks out new materials, methods, and strategies. Teachers at this stage are receptive to new ideas, attend workshops and conferences willingly, and enroll in graduate programs through their own initiative. Their job is seen as challenging, and they are eager to improve their repertoire of skills.

The competency-building stage in the career growth process is a time of adding expertise and testing new techniques. This stage quite often follows the reality shock, described in the previous chapter, that is often associated with the induction stage. Competency building is a time of "grabbing the handles" of teaching and developing a feeling of comfort in the profession. This stage, like induction, is a critical time for teachers. It is a time of "make it or go broke." The expertise that teachers are adding is crucial to their success. This stage, more than any other, serves as a conduit to nearly all of the other stages.

A teacher who builds appropriate competencies during this stage should be able to move gradually into the enthusiastic stage described in the next chapter. If, however, teachers are unable to develop the appropriate expertise—never able to build their professional repertoire to an acceptable level of competence—they may move to any of the several other stages. One could redefine one's professional goals and enter a new phase of preservice training, such as counseling or administration. Alternatively, one could stabilize at a level of expertise short of being fully sufficient, for instance, a secondary teacher who never masters questioning and group discussion skills and therefore prefers to lecture every class. Or, one could become frustrated in the profession and actually regress in skill and build walls against any effort to develop or gain new expertise. The inability to develop expertise could, in the end, push a teacher to exit the profession and look for another career.

Views of the Competency-Building Stage

The competency-building stage in the teacher career cycle can be compared to the stage structures of several educational researchers and theorists. Burden (1982b) designed a three-stage approach to a teacher's career. The survival stage was identified as the first year of teaching, and Burden identified many of the characteristics that were discussed in the induction chapter of this book as components of this period. Burden's second stage, adjustment, was hypothesized to last from the second to the fourth year of teaching experience. Once teachers were able to develop the necessary and sufficient components or characteristics of being a teacher during this adjustment stage, they moved into a stage Burden called mastery.

The adjustment stage from Burden's work—that is, the second, third, and fourth years of teaching—can be compared to the competency-building facet of the teacher career cycle. Teachers "survive" their induction year, develop their expertise during later years, and, optimally, reach a mastery of the teaching profession. While the adjustment stage for Burden has specific time parameters that are not identified in the career cycle competency-building stage, the teacher characteristics of growth and development are similar for both conceptualizations.

Feiman and Floden (1980) theorized four stages to make up the career development of teachers. They suggested that most teachers go through the stages of survival, consolidation, renewal, and maturity. Survival, like Burden's first stage, deal with the very beginning of one's experience and can be compared to the characteristics in the induction facet discussed in Chapter 4. The Feiman and Floden stage of consolidation, like Burden's adjustment, can be compared to the career cycle facet of competency building. Unlike Burden, Feiman and Floden did not lock the development in the consolidation stage into a strict time frame.

Other researchers who identified stages in teacher growth (Krupp 1981, 1989; Gregorc 1973) concur with those mentioned here in the existence of a stage or phase of teacher growth between initial teaching experience and full competence as a classroom teacher. By whatever name—adjustment, consolidation, or competency building—the structure is clear. Needs for the individual must be identified; growth programs to meet the identified needs must be designed; and the programs, either in their original design or in some modified form, must be carried out to help the teacher grow and develop professionally.

This chapter concentrates on the growth and development of a teacher in the competency-building stage of the teacher career cycle. Influences from both the personal environment and the organizational environment that have a strong impact upon teachers in this stage are identified and discussed. Specific programs to meet growth needs are listed for this stage, along with appropriate incentives for the teachers. Valuable support systems for competency-building teachers are identified as well.

In keeping with this book's theme of integrating theory with concrete illustrations, two teacher exemplars are woven into this chapter to better illustrate the stage conceptualizations. The following section is an introduction to "Greg" and "Willie," the two exemplars selected for the competency-building stage of the teacher career cycle.

Teacher Profiles

Greg

Greg is 25 years of age, single, with no children. This is his third year of teaching—all in the same position for the three years. Greg teaches in a union high school district that consists of one high school in a small midwest community consisting of farms, low-income, small town residents, and a growing suburban area. The school has an enrollment of 1200 students. Greg teaches U.S. history, U.S. government, and consumer education. He received his bachelor of arts degree from a midwestern liberal arts college and is currently working on his master's degree in education at the same institution. His undergraduate degree was history; he is also certified to teach in the area of broad field social studies. Upon his graduation from college, he received the education department's award for meritorious service. Professional memberships include the state Association of Teacher Educators, the local, state and National Education Association, and the National Council for Social Studies. Outside interests center on athletics.

Greg is clearly in the competency-building stage. He finds his teaching life never boring given his current teaching responsibility of four sections of U.S. history and one section of U.S. government. He also has study hall during the day and is head coach for both men's and women's soccer. In general, he finds life quite busy.

Greg clearly sees the difference between the induction stage and his current outlook on his teaching.

> You learn in college about education and school environment, but you really don't get a good feel of it until you are actually in the classroom. For my initial term, I was very challenged. It was difficult, but I enjoyed what I was doing. The second year is so much easier. It's such a relaxing feeling plus my confidence level has just grown so much in the classroom, and that makes all the difference in the world. There definitely is a stage. You are excited to start teaching the first year, but I think for a lot of people there is a tremendous shock in that you don't really anticipate the amount of work that you have to do or some of the problems you have inside the classroom. I think once you have finished that first year and started your second year, it just might be a boost to yourself in terms of confidence. I am now relieved actually and very confident, looking ahead. I'm really excited about what the next couple of years has to offer.

Greg also used his induction phase to build rapport with students. Now that he has accomplished that, he feels a

> . . . closer relationship whether they are in the classrooms, in the hallway, or on the athletic field. I think I have developed a much more positive relationship with many students. I feel much more confident in the classroom as a result. I am willing to take on a little bit more, knowing that I will be successful.

While well into the competency-building stage, Greg also indicates some anxiety in the area of student learning.

> You always want students to strive and learn as much as possible, and sometimes you expect a student to reach a certain point, and it doesn't

happen. He doesn't achieve the goal I have, but that might be my problem; perhaps I set my goals too high. Expecting excellence in academics is something I am a little disappointed in.

Willie

Willie is 37 years of age, married, without children. He has been teaching for three years. This is the second year of his current assignment. He teaches eighth-grade physical science and ninth-grade earth science at a junior high school in an industrial, blue-collar, middle-sized midwestern community. There are approximately 700 students in the school. His education includes undergraduate work at an East Coast university, transferring to a liberal arts college in the Midwest where he graduated with a B.A. in English literature. He then took additional coursework in environmental toxicology at a major university in the Midwest where he had planned to receive a Ph.D. The degree is currently unfinished, and he plans on its remaining that way. With this chemistry background, he returned to the liberal arts college and earned certification for teaching chemistry. He belongs to the local, state and National Education Associations as well as the national Association of Science Teachers. Because of his age and circuitous route to becoming a teacher, his outlook is somewhat different from Greg's. His long trek to find the appropriate niche certainly has had an effect on his view of teaching.

> When I first began to look for work in teaching, two and one-half years ago, I was pretty much going to take what I could get. I was trained as a chemistry teacher, and that is what I wanted to do, but those jobs are few and far between so I decided that as long as it was in science, I would take it. I began to get desperate when I couldn't find a job in science, so I started looking at English. At the very last second, I got a job as a one-semester contract teacher at a junior high school teaching eighth-grade physical science. When that ended, I was asked to come back as a long-term sub for nine weeks, as a reading specialist, and teach remedial English courses. I then went through a period of general substitute teaching in the district. At this point I felt like I was making deposits in the bank—that I was going to withdraw sooner or later, and sure enough, after spending a fruitless summer sending out hundreds of letters looking for teaching jobs and having several good interviews which amounted to naught, on the very last day, the very last second, I called up the personnel office, and they asked me if I would like a permanent position at my current junior high school teaching earth science. Unfortunately, that is not my area of expertise—I am no geologist for sure. I still have my ear to the ground looking for a chemistry position.

Because he is not in his first choice of fields, Willie sees himself in a transitory position. "It's a steppingstone where I intend to remain for a while, but I do intend ending up teaching chemistry somewhere or another. If I wait long enough, positions are bound to become open before I'm too old—I would like to stay in the district."

Although his induction phase was marred by the problems of finding an appropriate position, it is clear that in his competency-building phase Willie is committed to staying in the profession. Clearly in this stage, he is able to be reflective about his teaching.

> I think the things that make me feel the best are the things I do the best. What I do the best is motivate and engage, especially students who are otherwise unmotivated and disengaged. The thing I probably do worst is classroom management, and I am learning. I learn something about that every day. Last year I was much worse than I am now, and I'm sure that next year I will be better at it than I am now. It's a matter of acquired techniques. I think that motivating and engaging students is a positive technique in classroom management.

The career stage teachers are in can be influenced by many events occurring in their personal lives and in the organizational environment. The following sections expand on some of the influences of particular importance to competency-building teachers.

Personal Environmental Influences

Teachers who are in the competency-building stage of their careers have unique influences from their personal environment that distinguish them from teachers in other stages of development. Their family, their personal growth stage, and positive critical incidents all have a role in shaping the physical and psychological make-up of a teacher who is building competency in the profession. To a lesser extent, the categories of cumulative experience, crises, and avocational interests also play a part in influencing teachers in the competency-building stage.

Family Influences

The family plays a critical role in the lives of teachers who are building their repertoire of teaching skills. Family members must form an internal support system for the teacher who is undergoing careful self-analysis and self-evaluation of the teacher role. Spouses at this stage must adjust to the prioritization of professional growth being a near equal to family concerns and endeavors. Vacation time is often scheduled for growth experiences such as summer school or workshop attendance. Financial resources, often limited for teachers' families at this stage, may be budgeted to include college or university tuition for advanced study, seminar or workshop fees, and travel to attend professional growth activities. Tools of the trade, such as professional books or instructional materials, are budgeted for as well.

Special needs of family members must be balanced with professional growth needs. Most frequently, the competency-building teacher has established a measure of independence from the family of orientation (parents and siblings). These family members must provide support and encouragement to the teacher and not create situations or circumstances that will divert the teacher from meeting growth needs. Most important from the family of orientation is the absence of critical or negative influence on schools, education, or the profession of teaching. Too often noneducator—or even educator—parents do not consider teaching an appropriate profession for their children. This negative influence might not only thwart the necessary competency development; it could also push a promising teacher out of the profession.

Teachers at this stage are very often planning or beginning their own families. Planning for and having children, being attentive to their care and needs, and balancing the demands of the profession are complicating factors for competency-building teachers. Teachers are the most frequent observers of good and bad parenting techniques. These observations cause stress in developing and implementing their own parenting style.

Adult and Developmental Influences

Much has been written about personal growth and development of adults. Teachers in the competency-building stage are influenced by their own personal dispositions just as they are by family members. Having dedicated themselves to a career in education, they aspire to develop the necessary competencies to fulfill this life goal. In a study of teachers' personal and organizational concerns and influences (Burke et al. 1987), the concept of personal needs and goals proved to be one of the discriminating functions for the competency-building stage. One of the most useful characteristics noted in the adult development literature for teachers at this stage is the search for a mentor in their professional life (Krupp 1981). A fellow teacher, a former teacher, an administrator, or an acquaintance in another profession could serve as mentor. The key to mentoring is the provision of a positive model for growth and development.

Another adult growth characteristic that influences teachers in this stage concerns the realization of a personal value system. Moral or values education has developed into an important component of schooling. Whether through modeling or through direct instruction, teachers must transmit a consistent and positive value system to students. Teachers in the competency-building phase need to first recognize their personal values and then integrate their values into their professional development plans.

If a teacher is not able to define her or his life priorities, or does not recognize the integration of personal values with professional growth, then there may develop a dysfunctional relationship between the personal environment and movement through the career cycle. Adult growth in the psychological category must be consistent with professional development. Interpersonal relationships, personal values, life goals, and personal aspirations add to the development of an individual into a career teacher.

Positive Critical Incidents

Positive critical incidents are essential as a part of a developing teacher's personal environment to support growth into a competent teacher. The family, as mentioned before, can create positive support. Their care, support, and willingness to participate in plans that lead to growth are all important. Communities can contribute to the realization of positive critical incidents as well. The positive acceptance by administration and communities is a second function that research found to identify the competency-building stage (Burke et al. 1987). Status and respect for teachers and for education can create the positive circumstance that will keep teachers in a growth mode.

All people need to share successes and have others help celebrate positive happenings. Marriage, birth of children, completion of an advanced degree, or other incidents can create positive feelings that need to be shared and supported in an individual's personal environment. Positive support linked to these incidents can result in a renewed attitude on the part of the teacher as she/he anticipates growth needs and experience.

Crises

Just as people need to share positive incidents, there is a need for support should crises occur. Illness, death, divorce, or other negative circumstances could have a negative influence on the professional development of a teacher. These circumstances are especially critical for teachers in the competency-building stage. Time and effort must be expended to work through crises, and, at the same time, professional development goals must be kept in sight. Too often, promising teachers lose track of their goals due to a crisis and are not able to get back on track following resolve of the issue.

Cumulative Experiences and Avocational Interests

Cumulative experiences and avocational outlets are likely to have moderate influence for teachers in the competency-building stage. Teachers are just beginning to relate their own educational background to the education they are providing for their students. They are relating any previous experiences with children, along with their preservice and induction experiences, to the techniques that create success in their classrooms. The experiences that are a part of the competency-building phase become those life experiences for future stage development.

Hobbies or avocational outlets often take a back seat to professional endeavors during this stage. Teachers concentrate their efforts on the activities and practices that will make them better teachers. In some cases, these hobbies can be brought into the classroom in an instructional way, or some teachers can coach or direct an activity that is one of their own hobbies. For the most part, however, hobbies play a more important role for teachers at other stages.

In summary, the personal environmental influences of family, life-stage, and positive critical incidents play a key role in the development of a teacher in the competency-building stage. To a lesser extent, crises, cumulative experience, and avocational interests influence the life and, therefore, the career of teachers in this stage. The next section takes examples from our teachers Greg and Willie, linking characteristics from their personal sphere of influence to their teaching and to their professional growth needs.

Impact of Personal Environmental Influences on Greg and Willie

Greg

Greg is still searching for that appropriate relationship between high expectations and current capabilities. In this stage of his career, he is confident that he can reach it. The personal environment is very important for Greg in his teaching. His longtime interest in athletics takes center stage here.

> I think the thing for me about coaching is the fact that I get to see a student in a social environment, doing a different activity. I think in a lot of ways it helps me understand students a lot better, not seeing them with a book or pencil in their hand or notebook in a contained situation, but out on the athletic field. It has helped me understand students a lot more. For me personally, it is a good release. Athletics are a lot of work, especially if you want to be successful, and it takes many extra hours, obviously. But it is something I really enjoy doing. It's a good release from the classroom.

Greg has clearly related a personal interest to a professional interest to support him in his competency-building stage. While Greg is unmarried, his family and friends have been significant in supporting him in his career in education. He reports:

> Education was always something my father encouraged me to go into. I was very lucky that my family situation was one that they were not going to hinder me or stop me from doing what I wanted to do. In my case, they have been very supportive of my involvement in education, and they encourage me to continue in it.

Other aspects of his personal life have also been supportive of his chosen career, including his peers and his church.

> Many of my friends went into education so I sometimes talk with them and compare notes—different experiences that they are having. Even in institutions such as the church, there has been support. I think anytime you are dealing with young people in an institution such as education, I don't think too many people are going to knock it. With me, everybody has been totally supportive. My father didn't tell me I'd better become a lawyer, etc. I was pretty lucky.

Greg understands the importance of this personal support.

> In terms of support, had my family taken the opposite viewpoint, had there been some concerns, it would have made me feel a lot more insecure, especially going into education or any type of profession that is people oriented. I would have been concerned if people did not like the fact that I wanted to be involved in that.

In looking back at previous stages of his professional career, Greg focuses on the importance of student teaching in his preservice stage. "One of the most important things that has helped me, and I wish I had done more of it, is simply that student teaching time; having a chance to be in the classroom helped me tremendously. Maybe we should require more of that."

Greg is clearly well into his career. He is busy, building competencies and personal support.

> I don't want to sack my career, but you know when you are in education there is really not a whole lot of time to do much; you live for the weekends, and I think most people do in my job, and I don't mean that in a negative sense. I do look forward to free time.

Willie

Willie's personal environment has been positive in terms of pursuing a teaching career. "At times I tend to emulate my father in the classroom, especially when things begin to get a little hairy. He is a good male role model to fall back upon."

This is often the case in teaching. In Willie's case, it seems to run in the family, and he has the unique opportunity to have his father as a mentor. His current family is also supportive. "My wife enabled me to be a teacher because she was the one who worked while I was going to school. Now she is reaping the benefits—she watches me grade papers until 2 a.m.!"

On the other hand, at times Willie's friends and peers make him doubt his profession.

> If anything, they have probably made me doubt why I became a teacher and why I remain a teacher because I do see, especially, a number of my friends with whom I was in graduate school. They persevered where I could not and went on and got their Ph.D.'s, and they are now sitting pretty. They have gotten their research fellowships. That was not for me. I thought that was a dead end for me. It was too sterile.

This is certainly not a positive support for teaching, yet thus far Willie has persevered.

> I wouldn't say that teaching is a dead end at all. I was just interviewed for the school newspaper here, and the eighth-grader who was interviewing me looked at me with those big, blue eyes. She said, "Mr. Willie, why did you become a teacher?" and I thought about giving her some flip response— giving her the rap, you know, philosophical nature, and then I said, "Because every other job I've ever had has bored me to tears and this one doesn't."

Willie is still excited about teaching in his competency-building stage. His future support and professional growth and his ability to manage the personal influences will determine if he maintains that state of mind.

Organizational Environmental Influences

Just as there are unique influences from the personal environment of teachers who are in the competency-building stage of their career cycle, so, too, are there specific components of the organization that influence these teachers. Public trust and societal expectations play a key role in the development of competency-building teachers, as do school regulations and management style. Profession-

al organizations and unions are secondary influences for teachers in the competency-building stage.

Public Trust

Public trust in education is exhibited in a number of ways. Just as the
family is an important support mechanism for competency-building teachers
from the personal environment, the public is a necessary support device for
teachers in this stage as well. The atmosphere of support from the public includes
a public confidence in the schools, financial support, and individual participation
in school activities.

Public support has its beginning at the local board of school directors or
school board. School board members are most often lay people who are elected
to represent a segment of the community or the community as a whole in the
directing of the schools. The policies set by the board, their funding priorities,
and the goals they set for the district all play a part in the lives of all teachers.

These school board activities play an especially important role in the career
of a competency-building teacher. The central focus of board support is the
budget assigned to teacher development. Competency-building teachers, perhaps
more than any other group, have the need for financial support for professional
development activities. Reimbursement for coursework, support to attend workshops, travel expenses for seminars, and money to purchase professional materials are all components of this support.

Educational goals established by a local board of education give direction
to the development of competency-building teachers. These teachers should
establish their personal goals in line with the goals of the district. This could be
developing a new reading program or designing a new competency test in
mathematics or implementing a new gifted and talented project or any other of a
myriad of educational endeavors. Teachers who are building competency must
identify with the district goals and develop their professional expertise to help the
district successfully meet the established goals (Fessler & Burke 1988).

A second important component of public trust for competency-building
teachers is the trust of the parents in the community. Beyond trust, there should
be active support and participation by parents in school activities. Just as parents
desire reinforcement that their children are growing intellectually, teachers need
parental reinforcement that they have trust and confidence in what they are trying
to accomplish. This confidence will bolster teaching dedication to gain competence and continue to grow professionally.

Societal Expectations

Societal expectations are an expansion outside of the local district of the
same type of influence exhibited by the local public. The national reports on the

status of teaching and learning influence how teachers feel about their work. Influence from special-interest groups, from the National Geographic Society to the National Rifle Association, permeates the classrooms. Competency-building teachers must analyze and synthesize the information from these groups and determine its value for the classroom. The information from any special-interest group can create an influence for a developing teacher.

School Regulations and Management Style

Probably the most immediate influences from the organization, at least for the competency-building teacher, come from school regulations and the management style of the building administrator. Teachers in this stage have survived the first year or two of their experience. Personnel policies and tenure decisions, however, still have a direct impact on their professional lives. They may still be untenured and have the need to display their skills in a positive and effective way.

A crucial component of this category is the need on the part of the teacher to experiment with innovative instruction techniques while, at the same time, proving to be a valuable member of the staff. Regulations may win out over innovative designs for teaching. Class assignment may be a complicating factor in the development of innovative teaching practices. Teachers in the competency-building stage may not have the seniority to be in control of teaching assignments. An elementary teacher who would like to experiment with primary reading instruction might be assigned to an intermediate grade level. A high school math teacher who would like to experiment with new techniques of teaching geometry might be assigned to all remedial courses. Either of these assignments might thwart development activities by teachers.

Administrative management style could be a complicating factor for competency-building teacher development as well. The primary criterion is an atmosphere of trust. If a building manager, a principal, operates from a basis of distrust, the development of a competency building teacher could be hindered. One commonly accepted principle of school administration is that the management style of a principal, be it autocratic, democratic, *laissez faire,* or a combination, should match the teacher's style if growth is to occur. Career stage research confirms the importance of administrative acceptance to competency-building teachers (Burke et al. 1987).

Teachers in the competency-building stage need the support of the administration. There should be open communication and philosophical agreement. Just as there should be district goals for the educative program, each school building should have improvement goals and objectives. These goals also should give direction to the development activities of competency-building teachers. Within the building, the principal should have control of the teacher's assignment and of the resources available for development. Wise allocation of these resources could play a crucial role in the professional development of teachers.

Professional Organizations and Unions

Professional organizations and unions generally play a lesser role in the influence of a competency-building teacher. Professional organizations do play a role in the development efforts through journals, publications, seminars, workshops, or conventions. Too often, teachers in this stage do not have the time or resources to take advantage of the opportunities offered by professional groups. Interaction with these organizations is often reserved for teachers in other stages in the career cycle.

Unions, while extremely important to the security of the developing teachers, usually play a minor role in influencing their professional growth. Teachers in the competency-building stage need the protection of their union, where one exists, but look to college or university classes or other seminars for their growth and development. Teachers in this stage have not gained the expertise necessary to take leadership roles in the union, nor do they have the time necessary to devote to such activities. They rely on the union to give them the opportunity to grow and develop in the profession while maintaining a comfortable personal life.

Organizational influences, then, include administrative support and other extrinsic support mechanisms such as colleague or community feedback or professional organizations. This chapter's exemplars outline specific instances of these support categories.

Impact of Organizational Environmental Influences on Greg and Willie

Greg

The organizational environment has a considerable influence on Greg's work in the schools. His colleagues clearly stand out in this area.

> Teachers maintain a very close relationship with one another. Coming in as a first-year teacher, I was gratified to know that everybody was willing to help me. It made me become more comfortable with the new environment a lot sooner than I thought. There is a very close relationship I feel in the school with teachers and administrators.

Other factors that have affected this organizational environment are the ties between the reform movement and its emphasis on accountability with his own emphasis on teacher autonomy. This area comes in for some severe critique, especially from his position as a relatively new competency-building teacher.

> Some of the new policies the administration is implementing have created more work for the teachers, not necessarily for a better ultimate end.

Speaking specifically, making the teacher outline objectives within their classes, written objectives which have to be turned in; written lesson plans have to be turned in, and the list goes on and on.

He further states:

I think accountability in the beginning will have a negative effect on people. Maybe negative isn't the right word; the type of performance changes that are taking place right now in terms of what the administration wants done aren't necessarily appropriate. I think what's more appropriate for both faculty and administration is to sit down and say what can we do now to make ourselves more accountable.

Even at this competency stage, Greg is looking at the issues of accountability, autonomy, and professionalism. He seems to be exploring the area of teacher empowerment.

Unions are an ever present phenomenon in most environments of teachers. As a competency-building teacher, however, unions have little effect on Greg.

In our school I think there are only four or five people who didn't join the union. I felt some pressure to join; however, I don't feel that unions are bad so it didn't bother me to join. It would have bothered me if I felt it would not have been useful.

Other areas from the organizational environment that affect Greg as a competency-building teacher are local and state regulations.

The regulations are getting tighter. They are expecting more out of schools, and I think rightly so. They should, especially in this day and age when we are living in an environment that is so much more complex. One needs to know a lot more just to be successful. There are a lot more regulations being handed down.

Community support is also evident in Greg's situation. He speaks to the importance of it well.

In terms of our own community, I think we've been very lucky. We have been successful with the school board, not only in negotiation of teacher contracts, but reaching ultimate goals. Certainly, if there is a problem in society or community, one of the first places people are going to point the finger is at the schools. We have tremendous community support here—I think we need to become more involved in the community.

Willie

Personal and organizational influences came together for Willie in a positive way when he decided to become a teacher. As is often the case, teachers as role models led Willie into the profession.

> I had several teachers in high school whom I considered to be excellent teachers. They took me and pushed me into academia. I did not originally plan to go to college, and they strong-armed me into it—especially my eleventh grade English teacher—a great big guy. He forced me to apply to college. I was going to sit back and let the draft get me and go to Viet Nam because that would be the only way I would get to see the world, but he said, "Just put in one application." They accepted me at that college.

Other organizational entities that are positive for Willie are the students.

> When I do get a student who is disengaged and a kid who is not motivated, a kid who hates school, especially a kid who hates science, this is positive for me. He will say, "I've never done well in science. I hate science." I will have them for a week or two, and they will start to come around. That really warms the cockles of my heart.

The organization influences can also be negative. Willie comments on the differences between junior high and high school students now and when he was their age:

> I have to talk about the decline of the West. . . . For whatever reason you may ascribe, our children no longer have a firm moral sense, a firm ethical sense. Perhaps it has been corroded by countless hours in front of the TV; perhaps it's because we have all become so GD affluent; perhaps we've gotten away from the traditional upbringing of church and family. It's probably a little of all of those. But whatever it is, I'm seeing a lot of kids who just don't give a damn about anything, a lot of kids, I would say the vast majority, 99% of the kids I see walk through here, have zero ambition, NONE. Their big ambition is to have the bell ring at 2:40. That did not happen when I was in school. I really think we had a little more in mind.

It is clear that Willie sees education as a critical aspect to western civilization and closely connected with its decline. What he sees in the organizational environment of his junior high school and the community seems to him to have significant implications. "I think this is a very, very bad problem—serious problem in public education in America right now. If somebody doesn't do something soon, it will get out of control."

Another aspect of the organizational environment are unions. Willie states:

I'm all in favor of unions as long as they don't overreach their bounds. As long as they are still responsive to the members, and they fulfill their original purpose, then they are useful. We have several excellent union representatives here who go to great lengths to keep us informed.

During this competency-building stage, Willie sees the need for institutional support. He is concerned about keeping up with the literature in his field.

What's developing in my field—that's a lack I feel since I've grown apart from my *alma mater;* that I'm no longer up on the cutting edge of what's the latest in education. I almost feel like I'm adrift—here's your teaching package—go get 'em, that's all you're ever going to get.

Another important organizational support for Willie is the collegiality of the school.

We all develop our own support systems in our occupations, and teachers do it more than most—I think simply because they are in such a stressful occupation. There's a sort of semi-serious banter in the lounge about who's going to do what to what student for what reason. That is definitely a tension reliever; it's a good laugh—that actual adult humor certainly doesn't hurt anything during the day. It sort of helps you keep your perspective because it is awfully easy to lose it.

Administrators also figure in Willie's comments. Administrative style seems less important than support. Willie points out: "We have an extremely strong principal here. He gathers all the reins into one tight fist and, fortunately, the man is extremely competent and knows exactly what he is doing and does it very, very well. If he were less competent, it would be disastrous."

In addition to school administrators, Willie is influenced by the policies and regulations of the district.

Teachers are always at odds with their districts about policies and regulations, and I'm no different than anyone else. We just had an informal staff meeting about the new district budget, and it sounds like they have gone off the deep end—they are never going to get enough money ever again for anything, and we are going to have to fight for every penny we get—literally. It's ridiculous to expect quality education and not want to pay for it.

Certainly, this aspect of district support has a negative effect on Willie as he goes about his teaching duties.

The state also plays a role and affects Willie's school environment.

> The Department of Public Instruction keeps changing the regulations and is driving me nuts. I was one of the ones who came out and could have gotten a life license but didn't. I could have shot myself for not doing it and now I've got one of these five-year renewal jobs, and I've got to go back somehow and get in six semester hours every five years. God know how because I teach all summer also. So it's going to have to be many, many equivalency clock hours and workshops. I'm not looking forward to that, and I'm not entirely convinced it's going to make me a better teacher.

Professional Growth Needs

The needs of teachers in the competency-building stage of the teacher career cycle are as varied as there are teacher roles. One way to survey the professional growth needs of competency-building teachers, or any teachers, is to refer to the role options available to teachers (Christensen, McDonnell, & Price 1988). These role functions or options include a synthesis of teacher responsibilities taken from sources about career ladders, differentiated staffing, and master teacher plans. They include the teacher as learner, knowledge producer, coach, teacher educator, mentor, and leader. In the competency-building stage, the teacher as learner, knowledge producer, and coach are particularly important. These role options will be the focus in this section.

Teacher as Learner

The most obvious of the role options designated as a growth need for competency-building teachers is that of teacher as learner. In this role, the teacher is developing an expertise, or learning a role, either for use in the classroom or to transmit to other staff members. A professional development plan for this role option might include coursework, professional reading, workshop attendance, or school visits used to learn the skills and content essential for growth and success.

The topic for the teacher as learner could be self-selected, it could be defined by the mission or goals of the school, or it could be assigned by the administration. The topic could result from an identified deficiency in the teacher's skills, or it could grow from a special interest of the teacher. For example, a teacher with a weak preservice preparation in teaching science could self-select to learn more about science. The goal of the school to meet the needs of students who are defined as "at-risk," or potential drop-outs, could create another learning opportunity for developing teachers. A third possibility might be that a classroom observation by a principal identified a need for the teacher to gain skill in classroom management. These possibilities identify growth needs for competency-building teachers.

Knowledge Production

A second role function that relates to growth needs for competency-building teachers is that of knowledge producer. This role involves the teacher in collaboration with other experienced professional staff members in writing new curricula or developing new teaching units. Competency-building teachers are in an excellent position to help develop educational knowledge due to their realization of development needs on their own part. One method to meet the identified needs is to change the system. This might include restructuring the curriculum to accent the developing teacher's strengths or redesigning teaching methods to better utilize materials to help students achieve the instructional objectives. It is important that knowledge production be a collaborative effort for teachers in the competency-building stage since they may lack the insight to fully recognize unintended results of change efforts.

Action research could be another method of knowledge production related to growth needs for competency-building teachers. Action research, in its simplest form, is the analysis of a classroom problem or concern and the design of an experimental technique to solve the problem or resolve the concern (Oja & Smulyan 1989). Teachers in the competency-building stage might identify the problems or concerns and, with the help of teachers, administrators, or researchers from the state or higher-education institutions, design potential solutions. It would then be up to the teacher to implement the experimental technique and, again with the support of other professionals, draw conclusions about the success of the experiments. A design for the full implementation of successful programs would be one approach to satisfying growth needs of competency-building teachers.

Peer Supervision

Peer observation or peer coaching offers a third potential technique to help teachers in the competency-building stage to discover or define growth needs. In this technique, two teachers join together and serve as coaches for one another. While teachers at any stage could be paired together for this effort, two competency-building teachers could work together to implement this technique. These teachers could either help each other confirm growth needs that have been self-identified, or they could identify additional needs that may have been unrecognized. The importance of using peer teachers in this technique is to remove the evaluative stigma of administrator observation (Joyce & Showers 1983).

Thus, these three teacher role functions—the teacher as learner, knowledge producer, or peer coach—serve as an organizing vehicle for developing teachers to identify and begin to meet career growth needs. The following examples from the Greg and Willie interviews offer realistic experiences from which growth needs are derived.

Career Growth Needs for Greg and Willie

Greg

Greg looks ahead from the competency stage. He identifies and articulates a variety of professional growth needs throughout his career and talks in terms of an overall long-term program.

> I want to remain in education and am looking at how I am going to grow. I want to get more involved academically in different areas—perhaps a master's degree in history. Another thing is to build up a resource of information which will help me grow and be a better teacher. I think teaching is one of those nice professions that one can say it gets easier as one goes along. I'm going to try in terms of growth to become a lot more active when I can in terms of overall school events. If you walk away knowing that you did a little bit extra, this makes you feel good about yourself.

This combination of curricular and extracurricular goals indicates that Greg plans on maintaining himself in the profession and current relative to his students. He sees himself as a teacher/learner. From Greg's position as a competency-stage teacher, the methods of defining growth needs that are important to him are quite varied. Some are positive and some are negative! "Observation/evaluation— that's not going to give you a whole lot of incentive." Other things are much more positive for him. One would be additional course offerings and the knowledge production that comes with it.

Willie

Willie's professional development plans, however, clearly focus on the need to receive a master's degree.

> I've got to finish my chemistry degree, and I must get my master's. I would love to finish my chem degree there, but it's not possible because I've got a job. I work all day, and they don't offer courses at night or during the summer. They are not catering to the community.

Professional development plans should flow from needs identified in personal evaluation reviews and reports. Items identified as weaknesses can be concentrated upon to strengthen a teacher's repertoire. The classroom observation, as a component of teacher evaluation, can serve as a vehicle for professional development planning. Willie, however, shared an experience that may be all too typical of teachers attempting to build competence. Evaluation by administration is seldom a high point in a teacher's career. A specific evaluation in Willie's competency-building year indicates the humor and the pathos that may eventually result in success.

> Evaluations scare me to death. I've been observed twice this year and sometime within the next two weeks I've got my summative evaluation coming up. My first evaluation was okay; it wasn't great, but it wasn't bad. My second evaluation was a nightmare. I could hardly think of anything else that could have gone wrong. My observer was in a terrible mood when he walked in because he had a very bad day. I had the worst head cold of my entire life. It was the day they were taking pictures, so they are calling kids out of class—kids were coming and going and running and saying, "I gotta go now—goodbye." I am trying to do a lesson and the kids were all wound up and screaming and hollering. For some reason, I just freaked out and panicked and didn't use the assertive discipline techniques that I normally use all the time. My observer was sitting back there getting more and more angry at the techniques I was using and I was panicking because it wasn't working—the kids were getting more and more rowdy because I wasn't enforcing any sort of discipline effectively. Oh, God! I was so glad when that class was over. I felt like shooting myself—it was AWFUL. That seemed to me to be the pinnacle of my uncertainty—my insecurity when I first started. Because I went through that, I thought, "Well, geez, if I can go through that, I can go through anything." Since then, I've been much more relaxed in the classroom. I've made a real effort to slow myself down, to be more deliberate and forceful, especially with my eighth graders. It works wonders—it really does.

For a reflective teacher who is professionally committed to building competence, even a horrendous evaluation experience can be a learning experience for the identification of growth needs.

Incentives for Competency-Building Teachers

Research on incentives that are important to teachers in several of the facets of the teacher career cycle (McDonnell, Christensen, & Price 1987, 1989) can be used to identify specific incentives that are viewed as valuable by teachers in the competency-building stage. These incentives can be separated into security items that support needs in the personal environment and professional items that support needs in the organizational environment. By far, the most influential incentives for competency-building teachers are those in the professional realm. However, security needs must be met if teachers are to be able to concentrate on their professional lives.

Security Needs

Security needs identified as important and meaningful to competency-building teachers include forgiveness from educational loans, attractive insurance benefits, and job protection and security. These are incentives that combine to form a comfortable base from which a professional teacher can structure a personal life. With the possible exception of loan forgiveness, these incentives are important to teachers at all stages.

Organizational Incentives

The organizational incentives, beyond the essential monetary or fiscal incentives, can be categorized into incentives dealing with praise, incentives dealing with work conditions, and incentives dealing with future opportunities. Praise incentives are perhaps more important to this group than to any other in the career cycle, with the possible exception of teachers in the induction stage. A recent study (Collegial Research Consortium 1987) demonstrated that the first level of praise and recognition that is an incentive for competency-building teachers is written praise from a principal or supervisor. Formal memos of praise or informal notes that indicate a job was done well are viewed positively by teachers at this stage. Praise from students is another incentive for competency-building teachers. This praise is most often verbal, but may also come as a result of formal evaluations done in the classroom. Verbal praise from administrators or parents forms the third level of incentive in this category. This verbal praise is least valued, although appreciated by competency-building teachers.

Incentives that come from working conditions that are important to those in the competency-building stage include options for extra work in the summer, a flexible work day, influence in school decision making, control of instructional decisions, and a pleasant physical environment. The possibility of summer work could be linked to the security items listed previously. The extra work would mean extra pay for teachers at this stage, but, in addition, this extended year would also provide an opportunity for competency-building teachers to implement career development plans. Often, the school year is too hectic for teachers to reflect on their own professional needs and to design growth programs to meet those needs. The summer work would be a more relaxed time to put a growth program together.

The hectic school year could be another reason that a flexible work day or work year is seen as an incentive by teachers in the competency-building stage. Teachers, more than most other professionals, are locked into a monotonous and repetitive daily schedule. Part of the problem with the locked-in schedule is the custodial care responsibility expected of the schools. The children are there and must be supervised. Because of this, teachers lack the flexibility afforded in other professions to rearrange appointments or shift work hours. The ability to change the routine is viewed as an incentive to competency-building teachers.

The ability to decide about the work day leads to two other incentives related to the organizational environment. These are control over instructional decisions and influence in school decision making. Teachers at the competency-building stage may feel burdened by district policies for curriculum or administrative regulations for instruction. They may recognize the need to experiment, or they may desire flexibility that may not be in line with the policies or regulations. An important step in the development of these teachers is allowing them professional autonomy in the classroom.

Beyond classroom decision making, teachers in the competency-building stage see participation in schoolwide decisions as a valuable incentive. Much has been written about the school as the locus of control for improvement (Goodlad 1984). It is essential that all teachers have a voice in school goals and objectives and in plans to meet the objectives. This is especially true for competency-building teachers since their personal professional development will be linked closely to school goals. Group programs for school improvement can lead to individual plans for teacher development. For this reason, competency-building teachers need influence in school decision making, and they view this influence as an appropriate and valuable incentive.

A final incentive from the organizational environment that is important to competency-building teachers is the availability of a pleasant physical environment. Moving beyond the induction phase, in which any environment is an acceptable environment while the teacher is fighting for professional survival, competency-building teachers see the need for comfort as well as security in their surroundings. They are developing pride in their instruction and want to expand that pride to the place where they practice their profession. Teachers at this stage desire and deserve a pleasant physical environment. Too many teachers at this stage fight with multiple room assignments or poorly lit or inadequately ventilated rooms since they do not have the seniority that would qualify them for a better assignment. Their efforts should be concentrated on their own professional development, so any support available with facilities is seen as an incentive.

Teachers who are in the competency-building stage, therefore, see incentives in security items, praise, and organizational factors of extra work for extra pay, flexibility of schedule, and decision-making responsibility. The quotations that follow offer specific examples of how two competency-building teachers see the use of teacher incentives in their jobs.

Appropriate Incentives for Greg and Willie

Greg

One incentive for Greg would be an assignment that more properly takes advantage of his professional expertise. This is definitely an incentive that is derived from the organizational environment. He said: "To teach a course in, let's say, history, as an elective would be very meaningful to me. If the school is sensitive to areas in which I am strong in terms of contact and curriculum, I think recognizing those areas will help me quite a bit."

The importance of praise and positive feedback is also clear.

> Having positive feedback from within your department and from your department chairman helps tremendously. It's not just monetary rewards that make the difference but rather rewards within the curriculum; things such as conventions and inservices can be very positive. Inservices, to be real honest, are one of the things with which we have not had great success at the high school. More free time within one's department would be helpful. The problem is we don't meet that much as a department. Doing so would help us be more successful as a group. What is needed is more released time for teachers to work within the department.

Greg has been in the profession long enough to realize the collegial nature of good teaching and the teamwork needed. However, the lack of released time is seen as a hindrance to this goal.

The mixture of personal environment with incentives is clear in Greg's understanding why monetary incentives are not as important to him as they might be to other competency-building teachers.

> It's kind of nice now because I can spend the whole piece of pie on myself. Monetary incentives would certainly be much more important to a lot of teachers who have two or three children and a spouse. There are teachers who rely heavily on that pay. I don't have a feel for that right now because I have not reached that point. A lot of teachers now work, especially with that "free summer" they have. It's not always a free summer.

In fact, Greg is quite concerned about the interface of marriage and the profession. Perhaps reflecting a younger generation with an ever increasing later age of marriage, Greg is holding off.

> It's always a concern when you have a young faculty. People have apprehensions. They worry about the relationship with your students. Are you getting too close? The other thing is—is this person going to be destroyed professionally because he or she has found someone within the

faculty who is going to take away from his or her own individual growth as a teacher? Does he know someone from outside who is going to draw him out of the profession? I cannot really see myself married for another three to four years. I can't say that I won't meet someone tomorrow and perhaps fall in love and get married. My outlook now is probably three or four years down the road. To be really honest with you, it is a career decision, not a personal decision. I think that in order for that growth to take place, I have to be able to have freedom. So I look at it purely from a career decision basis.

This personal aspect of Greg's environment is one that he sees impinging on his professional development during this early stage of his teaching career.

Willie

As Willie considers professional growth and what he needs, some incentives make more sense than others. Merit pay makes some sense to Willie, but he sees problems. "I think it is very worthwhile as long as you have judges who can be impartial. I think it would be next to impossible to be one of the judges, but if they can do it, more power to them."

Another area that Willie sees as an important strategy for professional development are workshops. He describes one that he attended at the state teachers' convention.

It was entitled "21st Century Discipline in the Classroom." I would love to take the entire series of workshops from her because she has some extremely interesting ideas especially geared for junior high where they are a little too old to play with and too young to reason with. She has come up with some really nice techniques. I guess I should probably take a curriculum course of some kind or another in the near future.

What especially appeals to Willie are sabbaticals where he could take some time off and

. . . drift around the district and observe teachers because teachers never get a chance to observe teachers, and it's amazing the little tricks you can pick up from just sitting in on one class; they say imitation is the sincerest form of flattery. I would love to do this for a whole month.

Autonomy in the classroom is important to Willie, but he is very realistic about autonomy within the district.

In the classroom I have as much autonomy as I want as long as I stick to the curriculum. The curriculum itself is handed down from on high. Autonomy within the district—if you look at the district pyramid, we, of course, are the—call it the foundation if you like—the lowest level—it's what everybody else stands on.

Willie is clear on the importance of praise as an incentive. "I think praise is a huge incentive for everybody, but I don't think you can ever get enough of it, especially public junior high school teachers. Here at this school we get a lot of praise from our administrators."

Not only is praise important, but how well the students do. "For some reason our kids do real well on standardized tests. This reflects back favorably on us. I'm not sure the kids get a better education here than anywhere else, but it seems they get a good enough education to take standardized tests, which is not worthless."

Teacher praise is also important, although it plays an interesting role in Willie's life.

As far as teachers praising each other, I don't see much of that at all. If it's done, it's done tongue in cheek in a back-handed manner. There's sort of a macho ethic here where you are supposed to be tough enough to take it without having someone hold your hand and say you're doing a good job. That's an ethic within the teaching group. It is a negative one on one hand—it was scary for me when I first came here because this was my real permanent contract job, and you hear all of these "cocky-assed" teachers walking around as if they had a forty-five on their hip saying "WE BAD." Then I come in and go, "Oh, geez, you guys are going to blow me away, the kids are going to eat me alive, and I won't have a chance." But as I spend more time here, I realize that's a pose that is very effective in dealing with the lack of praise that we get.

The important role of the induction phase is clear here. Willie now knows what this "WE BAD" phenomenon is. As a competency-building teacher, he can take it the way it is meant and not let it bother him; yet praise is still missing.

Support Systems for
Competency-Building Teachers

Teachers in the competency-building stage of their career cycle have three major sources of support. These support systems include university or college courses, seminars and workshops conducted by regional, state, or higher-education professionals, and peer support from within the teaching profession. The key to the support provided for these developing teachers is help to fill any existing voids in their set of professional skills.

Higher Education

College courses for the most part are at the graduate level for these teachers. They are selected carefully to both round out their teaching repertoire and to fulfill requirements for an advanced degree. Teachers at this stage most often concentrate on courses in the area of curriculum planning or instructional delivery. A third area of study that is selected includes courses that help the teacher's understanding of school organization and administrative operations.

Teachers in the competency-building stage are slow to elect courses in content areas, except to fulfill degree requirements. The reason for this is an attention to specific needs of the stage. Their primary focus is on skills where they perceive themselves to be deficient. In most cases, they are confident in their content-area skills. It is organization of learning experiences for students and the tools of communicating that body of knowledge that are most meaningful to them.

Seminars and Workshops

Seminars and workshops that deliver content about organizing learning experiences and communicating knowledge are also important support systems for competency building teachers. These shorter-term learning experiences are selected for their specific content that matches the teacher's assignment. Teachers rely on the expertise of workshop leaders, and the most valuable seminars for them are those conducted by clinicians of a recognized reputation. Teachers trust that reputable seminar leaders will give them what they need to succeed. The added attraction of seminars and workshops is that teachers' needs can be met in a brief and efficient way.

Peer Support

Once new skills are identified through coursework or seminar attendance, teachers must practice the techniques to add them comfortably to their teaching repertoire. Peer support is an important component in providing guided practice for competency-building teachers. Two methods of support for these developing teachers are peer coaching or mentoring. Peer coaching was mentioned earlier as one technique to determine growth needs. This same technique might also be used to provide practice of new methods of teaching. Visitation of other classrooms within or outside of the home district is a first step in implementing a peer coaching process. If a teacher identifies valuable components in a peer's teaching, these components could be transported to his/her own setting. Having a peer observe the attempt to implement new methods and then provide feedback to the developing teacher can be a great assist in getting the technique right and in substantiating it as a part of the teacher's repertoire.

Mentors were discussed at length in the previous chapter on induction. Mentor teachers can play an equally important role for teachers in the competency-building stage. The mentor functions much like the peer coach in modeling effective techniques, assisting in materials selection or development, and guiding practice in new methods of teaching.

As competency-building teachers grow in their expertise, other support systems become more important to them. Family, administrators, professional memberships, staff meetings, and other elements from both the personal and organizational environment can play important support roles. Each teacher is an individual and, as such, has individual needs. Each teacher also has the right to a unique development program to help him/her grow. Research conducted by the Collegial Research Consortium (1987) found that teachers at the competency-building stage rated coursework or workshops, classroom visitations, conference attendance, and staff meetings as appropriate professional development modes. The exemplars who are quoted in the following section support these research findings.

Support for Greg and Willie

Greg

Greg sees a variety of strategies that he will use to accomplish his goals for his career. These include:

> Working closely with department members, specifically department chairs. Other strategies include workshops, observing different people within the schools and outside the school, and trying to look for different techniques that I can apply. Evaluations are helpful because they do tell you areas where you need to improve. Going back and looking over the material that you have taught previously and looking at these lesson plans tend to help you do this also. What went well and what didn't go well and then you try to go back and rearrange differently.

At the competency-building stage, Greg is able to reflect on his teaching as a strategy for improvement.

There are a variety of areas that support his professional growth. One of these is the faculty. "By the faculty maintaining very professional personal relationships among each other, it gives one a little more feeling about what's going on in the community and in the school."

His extracurricular work with coaching also is an important aspect.

"Coaching helps me a lot to understand kids. If they have a problem in the classroom and you can't identify that problem, it might come through on the athletic field. Sports is a good way for me to find out and be successful."

Greg does not always see administrators as being supportive. "Teachers want to know sometimes the reasons why certain decisions are made by administration. You sometimes don't know where they get the answer, and you want to hear. In fact, you feel you deserve to hear."

The physical plant is supportive to Greg in this competency-building stage. "We have a beautiful building, beautiful facilities, and the classrooms are nice. I don't have to worry about the Xerox machines. We have two of them".

Salary and athletics come together. "The salary is among the national averages for the school. My being head coach for two sports at the age of 23 is something I never expected to happen. This environment is comfortable to teach in—it makes all the difference in the world."

Greg is aware of new reforms and new structures in the profession. In fact, some of them he feels to be supportive of his career.

> I'm all for the new reforms in terms of career ladders. I think it is important for us to identify stages of teaching. So often you teach for five years and you either then get out of the profession or you go into administration or guidance, and this is especially true in the early stages of a teaching career. We need to look at these early years of teaching—identify the process—induction process, if you will, for the new teachers. I'm all for that, especially making that transition from student teacher to teacher. It's important. I think any school has three or four older teachers who kind of slide and who are kind of burned out. They've done it for fifteen-odd years and are still doing it. If a young teacher sees that, it kind of makes you wonder, "Am I going to be like that?" So I think that with young teachers as well as older teachers, we need to be very aware of the problems and have some type of career ladder and promotions.

And, finally, looking back at the earlier stage of preservice, he recalls student teaching experiences as being very positive. "I would encourage anybody to really get their feet wet early in student teaching. I'm glad that we are requiring higher education institutions to have more teaching hours and to have higher standards. I hope it keeps going this way."

Greg has reached the competency-building stage. He is beginning to talk like a teacher, identifying both strengths and weaknesses of the profession. He has a clear strategy for professional development. He has support from both his personal and organizational environment. Greg is well on his way to becoming an enthusiastic and growing teacher.

Willie

One strategy that Willie identifies to help him develop more competency is team teaching.

> I love team teaching. I have taught one team-taught class. We teach pretty well together as long as we keep it in mind that is what we are doing. I run with the ball a little too much, and I have to keep kicking myself to remind myself to let her do it because she knows more techniques—she knows better techniques to get through to these kids than I do. I know the subject and knowledge but she has the technique.

Team teaching may be an all-too-often overlooked way of working with a competency-building teacher to improve teaching strategies and techniques.
Other strategies for Willie are not yet totally clear.

> I haven't even begun to think about advancement yet. Right now, all I am thinking about is establishing myself. I am already lined up for the next three summer schools. I am going to be teaching all next summer, one thing or another. How I can do this and simultaneously finish my chemistry and master's degree I don't know. Right now I am on dead hold.

Willie still sees inservice as important but finds the support structures inadequate to bring it off.

> First, I think this mythical support group, whoever they may be, Group X, the first thing they should do is publicize those self-advancement classes, workshops, whatever, that are available. Too many times they are around but we don't hear about them. Secondly, the logistics of attending such a thing could be nailed down a little more firmly by Group X by seeking out such a group of people in a location where such a course is not given and connecting that group with someone who is willing to teach it.

As a competency-building teacher, Willie is already showing some signs of frustration when it comes to organizational environment. He look back upon his induction year and his initial job.

> When I took this job, I signed a contract which said I was to teach physical science eighth grade and earth science ninth grade. There was some question as to whether I wanted to coach or not, but I said, "I don't think so, not for the first year, not even for the second year. I don't need that kind of extra stress—not until I get my sea legs."

Willie has worked his way into the competency-building stage. On one hand he is excited about teaching; there is never an indication that he is considering leaving it. He wants an assignment that is more clearly within his level of expertise. But there are also seeds of frustration in Willie's comments. He is at that point where staff development will make a real difference as to whether he continues in competency building and becomes an enthusiastic and growing teacher or for any one of a myriad of reasons becomes stable and stagnant, career frustrated, and leaves the profession.

Summary

Competency-building teachers have survived the reality shock associated with the induction period and have channeled their attention to grabbing the handles of teaching. They are engaged in the process of attempting to develop a feeling of confidence and comfort in their teaching skills and abilities. Competency-building teachers tend to seek out ideas and suggestions that enable them to improve their repertoire of teaching strategies and tend to be receptive to appropriate workshops, inservice activities, university courses, and supportive supervision and mentoring. Important personal environmental influences during this stage include family support and the concerns associated with establishing roots in early adulthood. Key organizational influences for competency-building teachers include the climate of community trust and societal expectations and the administrative environment and management style that they experience daily. Competency-building teachers need professional growth activities that enable them to pursue their individual growth needs in a supportive climate. This is a pivotal period in the career cycle, for those teachers successful in building their teaching competencies are likely to move into the enthusiastic and growing stage described in the next chapter. Alternatively, those who are unable to build appropriate competencies during this period are likely to move toward stages of frustration, stability/stagnancy, or early career exit. The nature and extent of administrative and supervisory support may play an important role in determining which direction the competency-building teacher moves.

CHAPTER SIX

Enthusiastic and Growing

PETER J. BURKE   JOHN H. McDONNELL

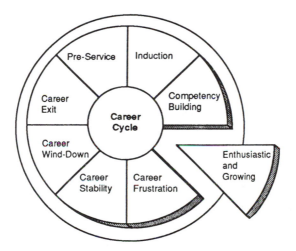

At this stage, teachers have reached a high level of competence in their job, but continue to progress as professionals. Enthusiastic and growing teachers love their jobs, look forward to going to school and to the interaction with their students, and are constantly seeking new ways to enrich their teaching. Key ingredients here are enthusiasm and high levels of job commitment and satisfaction. These teachers are often supportive and helpful in identifying appropriate staff development activities for their schools.

The enthusiastic and growing stage of the Teacher Career Cycle Model represents all the personal and professional traits associated with master teachers and the master teacher literature. If the induction stage is "reality shock," and the competency-building stage is "grabbing the handles of teaching," then the enthusiastic and growing stage can be described as a "getting on with it" phase of teaching. These teachers are described as competent and self-confident professionals. They seek improvement opportunities in a discriminating way and are providers of growth opportunities for their peers. The enthusiastic and growing stage is one where most administrators would prefer to find most of their staff members. It is the stage where all parents and students want their teachers to dwell.

The enthusiastic and growing stage is the goal for all teachers. Those in the induction stage are receiving help and support as outlined in Chapter 4 to move toward this stage. The competency-building teachers are planning development programs like those outlined in Chapter 5 to reach this stage. Teachers who are experiencing career frustration are described in Chapter 7, and career development for these teachers includes activities to create enthusiasm for them. The stable and stagnant teacher, discussed in Chapter 8, needs motivation to rekindle an enthusiastic spirit. Teachers winding down their careers, the topic of Chapter 9, are an important group for fostering maintained enthusiasm about teaching. The goal for teachers in the enthusiastic and growing stage is to remain there.

Views of the Enthusiastic Stage

Two recent theories of teacher career stages were used as reference points in Chapter 5. The first was Burden's (1982b) three-stage approach to teacher growth and development. Just as Burden's second stage of adjustment can be compared to the competency-building stage of the career cycle, so can his third and final stage of mastery be compared to the enthusiastic and growing stage of the teacher career cycle. The mastery stage, for Burden, comes after the fifth year of teaching. Teachers at this stage are fully functioning professionals who have all the skills necessary to plan, provide, and evaluate instruction.

The second theory mentioned in Chapter 4 (Feiman & Floden 1980), was a four-stage theory with the last stage being maturity. The mature teacher for these researchers is a fully developed professional similar to the mastery teacher in the Burden work. This concept of teacher career growth is also very similar to the enthusiastic and growing stage of the teacher career cycle.

These and other conceptualizations identify the last, or top, stage in a career to be a mature, master, fully functioning professional teacher. These are consistent with the stage of enthusiastic and growing. The Career Cycle Model, however, recognizes that, first, not all teachers reach this stage and, second, those who do reach it may move to another stage at any point in their career due to influences from the personal or organizational environment.

This chapter develops the influences from the two environmental spheres as they have an impact upon enthusiastic and growing teachers. Growth needs, incentives, and support systems for teachers at this stage are discussed. The two exemplars used in this chapter illustrate the influences' impacts through interview excerpts, as in past chapters. The next section introduces the two enthusiastic and growing teachers, "Louise" and "Mary."

Teacher Profiles

Louise

Louise is 52 years old, married with two children, both away from home. She has been teaching off and on for about thirty years, the past seventeen years in her current school. She teaches in a union high school district with one high school of between 1100 and 1200 students. The district is the largest school district in terms of geographical area in the state. This means that students come not only from suburban communities but also from rural and farming areas. It is an expanding high school north of a large industrial city. She teaches advanced placement American history, psychology, and sociology, and is Chair of the Social Studies Department.

Louise has two master's degrees, one in education and one in American history. Her undergraduate major was also history. She was elected to Phi Beta Kappa and graduated Magna Cum Laude. She is active in the local, state, and National Education Association. She also belongs to professional organizations such as the state and National Council of Social Studies and the Organization of American Historians.

The awards she has received attest to the fact that she is indeed an enthusiastic and growing teacher. She has received the statewide Master Teacher Award and the Teacher of the Year Award at her high school twice. She also received a special award created by the local education association in recognition of the fact that a number of important breakthroughs for the association had been done under her leadership. She represented the association for a long time. She received recognition by the school board for her work with the local education association. She has also been a Fulbright Scholar, a National Humanities Fellow, a Jefferson Foundation Fellow, a Madison Fellow, and has been awarded funds from the National Endowment for the Humanities several times.

Louise clearly has been in the enthusiastic and growing stage for a number of years. Her success has also been recognized by the administration. In effect, she has been promoted up the career ladder but allowed to stay in the classroom.

If our school were formally organized in a career ladder, I suppose my designation would probably be Lead Teacher, because I function in an advisory role in staff development in my school. Since I teach social studies methods class for the local college and place people at my high school, I suppose that would be the kind of description that would be given.

Louise accepted a leadership role early in her teaching career.

I really took leadership in the second year of my teaching with a West Coast teachers' association. My first year I was a beginning teacher and had no particular role different than that of other teachers; by the second year, however, I was very active in the local association and I became Chair of the faculty. So then my role as a teacher was quite different. I guess that is what has happened throughout all my teaching career. I have been positioned as an educational leader among teachers.

Like many other teachers, education was not her first professional choice.

I've always been very excited and exhilarated by teaching, but I did not originally intend to become a teacher. I did not train for such, but my husband and I were married in our senior year in college. I trained for the foreign service with my history major and at that time women were not allowed to enter foreign service if they were married, so I decided to try teaching even though I thought at the time that it would be very temporary. It turned out that I loved it, loved it so much that my husband entered teaching a few years later because he enjoyed what I was talking about so much.

As an enthusiastic and growing teacher, Louise is clear on what she likes and does not like about the profession.

It's the classroom that I enjoy the most. I really resent inroads into my classroom time. I am increasingly not satisfied with the role of department chair because that is viewed as an administrative role that drives a wedge between you and the rest of your department. They no longer look upon you totally as a colleague but more as the boss. I don't like the administrative details, the increasing amount of paperwork it involves, and there are so many aspects to my career that right at the moment, I'm sort of unhappy with that. If I had wanted to be an administrator I would have gone into administration. Another thing that bothers me about administration is that the teaching organization is trying to cope with the new role of department chairs and, increasingly, this state regards chairs as administrators. Then, the national has taken the position that you cannot be a member of the organization if you are in administration. After being so active in the education association, if I am then excluded from membership, that would be an unhappy situation. I would be tempted to just give up the chair. So it's the classroom that I feel so good about—dynamic relationships being with the kids; you know, both of us learning together. That's the part I like.

Mary

Mary is a 46-year-old married woman with one child. She went to a small liberal arts college in the Midwest and majored in elementary education. She has been teaching for eighteen years, eight years in her current position. The district in which she teaches is a middle-sized school district of between 6000 and 7000 students. It is an urban district with a mixture of ethnic groups as well as a significant population of poor and working poor. She teaches first grade in an elementary school with about 400 students enrolled. Mary belongs to her local, state, and national education organizations. She is secretary of the local unit.

Mary's current view of her teaching is one of both enthusiasm and still growing while at the same time recognizing that teaching is more difficult than it once was. Mary's seemed reticent compared to Louise, yet her meaning was quite clear in its conciseness.

I think teaching is just as dynamic as it was at the beginning. I am learning all of the time. I keep taking courses. Each class is different, so you have different ways. We have adopted a new reading series which is exciting to work with. It is harder to teach now. There are learning problems, problems of parents and problems of society in general; thus, teaching is harder than it ever was. It is less fun but certainly not less dynamic.

Mary also is quick to point out some problems with teaching and the incentives surrounding it.

Pay is too low. Prep time—there is not enough of it. I would like to see rising standards for teachers and better preparation of teachers. I would like to see improvements in the ability to write and speak proper English for the students. They want us to teach a lot but they don't give us any time to prepare for additional duties in teaching. Nonteaching activities take a lot of time.

Personal Environmental Influences

The personal environment of a teacher in the enthusiastic and growing stage of the career cycle includes a number of interactive yet mutually identifiable characteristics that influence the teacher's work. Family support structures, positive critical incidents, accumulated life experiences or life stage, unique individual dispositions, and avocational interests are all categories that have an impact upon the careers of enthusiastic teachers. Influence items in these categories may act singularly or in combination, and, for the teacher in the enthusiastic and growing stage, they provide positive, nurturing, and reinforcing support. They are influences that do not foster conflict with career-related responsibilities.

Enthusiastic teachers, for the most part, have a stable personal environment. They are able to draw strength from their personal lives to maintain their enthusiasm and to help design and implement improvement goals to continue growing. These teachers have passed through the competency-building component of their careers, and the "growing" part of this stage reflects their willingness to stay on top of innovations in the profession. Their growth is, in many ways, tied to creating new structures in the profession.

Family Influences

The influence of their families is a key component of the positive support for enthusiastic teachers. Families recognize the professional nature of their parents' or spouses' work, and family members support and encourage the teachers' continual attention to perfecting already very successful techniques in the practice of that profession.

The family financial condition for these enthusiastic teachers is most often stable and comfortable, so attention to security needs does not interfere with their work. The education of their children is just as important to enthusiastic teachers as is the education of students in their classrooms. These teachers have the stability to meet any special needs of family members without it interfering with their work.

Adult and Developmental Influences

Enthusiastic teachers are often expert at interpersonal relationships. They relate well to peers, administrators, students, parents, and the community at large. Good teachers translate ideas into action. They encourage their colleagues to improve, they convince their administrators to allow innovation, they challenge their students to perform at the maximum range of their ability, they make parents realize the importance of being partners in their children's education, and they generate support in the community for education through their dedication and enthusiasm.

These teachers are comfortable with the priorities they have set for their lives. They are in a secure stage of adult development and have the good fortune to be practicing, and practicing effectively, their chosen profession. They generate and share a positive feeling of community all around them and make the positive atmosphere and dedication contagious.

Positive Critical Influences

Many of the positive critical incidents in the lives of enthusiastic teachers revolve around their work. Colleagues and peers are invited to share in the teachers' success or in special events for family members. Awards and recognition for their work or selection to noneducative endeavors as representative of the profession are two examples of positive incidents that support their work. Completion of advanced degrees may also be a positive environmental influence for teachers in the enthusiastic and growing stage of their career cycle.

Their degree work will usually be along the lines of discovering or designing better ways of teaching. Coursework, papers, or theses will be selected or dedicated to this end. These teachers often continue their relationship with a college or university through courses, guest lecturing, supervising practicum students, or in a variety of other ways. Professors may move from the tutorial role to a role of colleagueship for these professionals. Enthusiastic teachers often collaborate with college professors on research and writing projects to improve the profession of teaching.

Cumulative Experiences and Avocational Interests

Cumulative experiences play an especially important role for enthusiastic teachers. In addition to their educational background that has prepared them for their work, their experience with children or youth usually extends beyond their classroom assignment. This experience might include co-curricular or extracurricular assignments, civic youth groups, volunteer work, coaching youth teams, scouting, church groups, or a variety of other possibilities. Their work outside of the school would include education-related experiences, such as religious education, and would take advantage of their training, experience, and skill in pedagogical techniques.

Enthusiastic teachers often seek work outside the school where they can use their skill or where they can experiment with new techniques that might be added to their classroom repertoire. Individualized approaches, small-group techniques, telecommunications, discovery learning, or other methods are examples of this experimentation. They may also work at vocational, technical, adult, or higher-education institutions for the same reasons. Their goal in this regard is to share their expertise and to continue to grow as a professional educator.

Individual Dispositions

The influence that enthusiastic teachers receive from their individual dispositions are stable, positive, and continuous. They are living their life goals and aspirations. Their personal value system reflects the importance of education, and their in-depth knowledge of the value of education moves them to become models of those values. A crucial component of the value system of enthusiastic teachers is the knowledge or realization that students have a variable ability to learn. They recognize learning problems and respect alternate or differential learning styles. They are able to adjust to the differences and communicate the value of education so that it is understandable to most of the variety of learners. The recognition and acceptance of these differences and the willingness to relate to the differences in learning styles of each child are invaluable individual dispositions for teachers in the enthusiastic and growing stage of the teacher career cycle.

Professional development is a central focus for teachers in this stage. The components of their personal environment listed above are one part, an informal part, of their professional development. The formal experiences that they choose, just like the formal college coursework, are selected to either hone existing skills or to develop new techniques that might be helpful in the classroom. These teachers have experienced educational fads or trends and are able to select wisely from the plethora of inservice education offerings that are available to all teachers. Their experience allows them to be selective and make the best use of the time and resources available for professional development. In addition, as will be expanded upon later in the section on growth needs, these enthusiastic teachers often become leaders or providers of development opportunities for other teachers.

Thus, we see enthusiastic and growing teachers experiencing positive support and influence from their personal environment. This sphere of influence includes family, cumulative experience, individual dispositions, interpersonal relationships, and volunteer or other avocational efforts. The following section substantiates these influences through our exemplars, Louise and Mary.

Impact of Personal Environmental Influences on Louise and Mary

Louise
Louise's personal environment seems to be quite supportive of her role as a teacher.

It has been very enjoyable to both my husband and myself. It's been a nice occupation to share with the family because it does mean that we have our vacations together with the children. Our children are still trying to get used to the idea that most people don't have full summers. Their parents did; so they think "When do I get those vacations?"

Although Louise is now in the "empty-nest" period, she clearly remembers how tough it was to be a teacher and a mother.

I am now in the empty-nest period. Our children are both away from home. This gives me more time. I have fewer household duties—fewer family obligations—and I have a lot more time and freedom to experiment—to do things I want to do. It's tough when your children are growing up, combining a full-time career with housewife, mother, etc. I am glad those years are behind me so it's nice to look back and say, "Well, I still love what I'm doing." I do a lot of workshops for teachers in the state and I enjoy that very much. The family is supportive. My husband is in a related job and fully understands what it entails. My children are very independent. It's great!

Personal hobbies are also important in keeping Louise enthusiastic and growing.

I love to read and I read constantly. I have a book always going and that is a great help. We've also done a lot of traveling. I think travel has greatly broadened us. We travel pretty much every year, both abroad and in the states. That has been very rewarding.

Personal crises in life have been a reality for Louise. "The crises in my life have centered around serious illnesses or death in the family, but that has not interfered with my teaching and my colleagues have been very supportive and have helped when needed."
Her family has clearly been important to her.

Relatives are a very important part of my life because I come from a very large family and we do a lot of keeping in touch. My mother has been here and is in very poor health; we keep in very close touch with our kids. Friends play an important part in my life. Many of our friends come from either related institutions, professional people in the neighborhood, and we have a number of very close friends among my faculty.

Finally, the positive influence in her personal life that brought her into teaching came during her high school days.

I guess the first and most basic event was going to college in the first place. When I was a high school student I had not even thought about going to college, and it was a high school counselor who talked me into it, got me the money to enable me to do it, and really turned my life around.

Mary

Mary's personal life also has been somewhat simplified by the empty-nest syndrome, but she maintains a variety of avocational interests.

I'm very busy, but I think that most of the time they are activities that I get involved in which enhance teaching rather than detract from it. In addition, I travel a lot and I read a lot. My child is now in college so I don't feel guilty staying after school late. She's not home alone now so that's nice. Family responsibilities I think inhibit a lot of teachers.

Organizational Environmental Influences

Teachers in the enthusiastic and growing stage of the teacher career cycle use the influence available from the organizational environment to maintain and further develop their status in the organization. There are a variety of components to the sphere of influence that makes up the organization. Demands are placed upon the school by students, by parents, by community members, and by society as a whole. Rules and regulations are created by the various levels of government from the federal legislature to the local school board. Professional codes of ethics, common expectations for classes of professional employees, organizational memberships, and other concerns all blend to create a structure that can either challenge or support a professional teacher as he/she goes about the assigned tasks of educating a student population.

Enthusiastic teachers take advantage of the support items available from their organizational environment and learn to live with or, more important, learn to change the influences that might thwart their career goals. Foremost in the support category for enthusiastic teachers are administrative structures, or management style of the school, along with professional organizations in education. In similar ways, teacher unions and school regulations can be key components or characteristics of support. In addition, the public support and societal expectations that exist at any given time influence the career of enthusiastic teachers.

Professional Organizations

Professional organizations play an influential role for teachers in the enthusiastic and growing stage of the teacher career cycle. These organizations, such as the International Reading Association, the National Council of Teachers of Mathematics, the National Council of the Social Studies, the National Council of Teachers of English, Phi Delta Kappa, Kappa Delta Pi, and many other state, regional, or national organizations, provide a variety of opportunities for all classroom teachers. These opportunities include leadership, colleagueship, service, support, recognition, development, and research.

Enthusiastic teachers enjoy the community or colleagueship of their peers in these several organizations. They are able to branch out beyond the confines of their home district and engage in meaningful dialogue with other professionals with similar assignments or responsibilities. In many cases they are able to seek and be selected for leadership opportunities in these organizations. The meetings and publications that come as part of the membership provide an arena for discussion of new techniques and ideas as well as a support network for teachers who wish to experiment with these new ideas. Enthusiastic teachers are frequently willing to try these innovative methods.

Enthusiastic teachers take advantage of the growth and development that come as benefits of professional organization membership. Journals, newsletters, seminars, and conventions at the state, regional, or national level all foster professional development. The narrow focus of these groups on one content area or one specialty allows teachers to concentrate where they feel comfortable or where they have expertise to share. These organizations are often the best way for teachers to stay current in the latest methods in the specialty field.

Management Style

Interpersonal relations was mentioned as an important characteristic from the personal environment of these enthusiastic teachers. The interpersonal relationship with the building principal is one component of this influence. It is crucial that teachers understand and be able to work with the management style of their building administrators. There must be an atmosphere of trust and respect, along with a philosophical agreement about the needs of the students. Teachers and administrators must be cognizant of one another's goals and support the successful realization of those goals. Communication is the crucial aspect in making this organizational influence a positive support.

Teachers most often communicate at a horizontal level in the hierarchy of education; that is, teachers talk to other teachers. Enthusiastic teachers take advantage of every opportunity to have meaningful vertical communication; that is, they rely on communication with the principal as a support mechanism. They do not fear sanctions from the principal—rather, they anticipate support for their ideas or plans. In the case where philosophical agreement has not been reached, or where common goals are not evident, the enthusiastic teacher keeps the lines of communication open and conducts the discourse in a professional way. It is through this communication that disagreements can be solved and new structures can be created for the betterment of all concerned.

Regulations

Teachers in the enthusiastic stage have learned to live with school regulations as a part of the organizational environment. In most cases they have tenure in their job and are not negatively affected by personnel policies. They also have an adequate amount of experience to have reasonable class assignments and space availability. In some cases, in fact, these enthusiastic teachers seek out or volunteer for the more difficult assignments, such as programs for potential dropouts or other at-risk student populations. Their experience and dedication can give rise to recommendations to improve upon existing regulations, thus becoming an influence upon, rather than being influenced by, this component.

Unions

Unions and union membership offer a variety of influence opportunities for teachers in the enthusiastic stage. These teachers may be called upon by their peers to take leadership roles in the union. They recognize the importance of the collective voice of teachers, and the needs identified by the union become a component of the enthusiastic teachers' set of goals. These teachers acknowledge the part the union has played in guaranteeing protection and security and in allowing a modicum of academic freedom in the classroom. This protection is essential when a dysfunctional relationship exists with the management of the school.

Public Trust and Societal Expectations

Public trust and societal expectations play a lesser role of influence for enthusiastic teachers. Since they have self-confidence and are comfortable with their goals, the sensationalism of the national press or vocal attacks of local special-interest groups do not create a major problem for them. On the contrary, these teachers, working either independently or in groups, can help turn public opinion or create public policy that reflects confidence in schools and teachers. Enthusiastic and growing teachers are the best spokespersons for the profession of education in the local, state, or national arena.

The environmental influences from the organization, then, include professional organizations, unions, administrative management style, regulations, public support, and societal expectations. These categories of influence, combined with the items from the teachers' personal environment, give rise to special growth needs for teachers. The quotes that follow from our exemplars, Louise and Mary, attest to the influences from the organizational environment. The examples also point out how these influences are viewed and used by teachers in the enthusiastic and growing facet of the career cycle.

Impact of Organizational Environmental Influences on Louise and Mary

Louise

The organizational environment has played an important role in Louise's life. The key role of professional organizations is apparent.

I have been very active in all of my professional organizations, so they have played a very important role in my life. I have been very active in the National Education Association and affiliates. I have basically filled every job locally and also have attended a number of national conferences. I have not been as active in social studies organizations, but they are playing an increasing role in my life right now and one of the reasons is because of the fewer family responsibilities. Another thing of particular importance was the summer National Endowment of the Humanities Institute and Fulbright experiences. Now I can do those because I don't have family that I have to worry about, and that has made for very enriching experiences. It has been terrific, really. Those have kept me very importantly revitalized for the past several years.

School boards also can play a positive role in keeping a teacher active. Louise realizes this.

I've been very fortunate since our school board has been very supportive, very strongly pro-teacher, even though they have not been pro-union. One of the delights in my life is that I was able to change that in our local community and it has been very fulfilling. To have helped turn the school board around and say that the association can be helpful and to have them now accept that as a very important part of the teachers' group and to support the organization has been important.

She also indicates that the support of administrators is an important aspect in her career stage. "I have had cordial relationships with all my administrators. I have respect for some more than others."

What does she feel is negative in her organizational environment? Interestingly enough, it concerns administration.

We are literally being buried with a tremendous amount of paperwork. I'm part of a committee right now at our school appointed by the principal and we are looking at the school from every angle, called More Effective Schools. He appointed people he felt were not afraid of speaking out, and we are quite a vocal group of people and we are all saying pretty forthrightly we are doing too much trivial paperwork. I think we are making it clear that people are going to be burned out very soon if they don't find a way to cut back. It interferes with our relationships, spending too much time on paperwork.

Louise finds the management style of administrators important in her professional life.

The management style is most effective when it is collegial and they look upon teachers as part of the team and work together as a team. Administrators in my experience have frequently played some games with teachers in that they pretend that you are really being involved and form all kinds of committees but you are really not empowered to carry out decisions. You make suggestions and the administration doesn't carry them out. It's really fruitless. Some administrators genuinely want to involve teachers but they don't know how to do it. It's a tough task because if you are really going to work as part of a team, making decisions, it means endless meetings and so your day becomes terribly long. I leave the house before 7:00 and many times don't get finished with meetings until 5:30.

As an enthusiastic and growing teacher, Louise feels that relationships with her colleagues play a significant role.

I've had really good relationships with my colleagues. I have tried to keep them pretty professional. If you are too close to some members of the department and not to others, that creates really difficult feelings, and so in general, when I am having some social event, I try to have them all invited even though there are some couples that I would basically rather not have come. I try to choose my closest friends from people who are not in my department. I have cordial relationships with those in my own department but not really close. It's an uneasy compromise that's tough.

The public's respect for teaching plays an important role in Louise's life. While not feeling demeaned by the public attitude, she states:

I feel frustrated by the public being unwilling to go to comparable salary, and the reason that's frustrating is because clearly the American public puts their money where their values are and even though they can say that teachers should be public servants, there is also that little bit of contempt for teachers because they make so little money. Teachers would be more valued if they made more money. Money is a very important symbol in our society and so we are asking for higher salaries. Besides the question of standard of living, I think, and very importantly, is what status are you going to have with the public and I think this is a continuing important issue. We consider teaching a profession but you don't really have the private office, secretarial help. These are some things that could really change the public perception of teachers, and in schools that have a great deal of money, both are done, and it makes a difference in the way teachers are viewed by the community.

Mary

Even though Mary is an enthusiastic and growing teacher, she finds some lack of support in the area of organizational environment. Some of these include societal problems. She is, once again, very brief and to the point in her comments. "The problems society has—drugs, alcohol abuse, and the family structure deteriorating—is what has hurt teachers the most. The lack of public concern and support."

She is more positive about some recent changes in administrative support.

Administration right now has somehow gotten the idea that they need to do a little more work for teacher inservice. They have actually had half-day meetings during the day and gotten substitute teachers for us. This is a step in the right direction because it makes the teacher feel important rather than having meetings after school when everyone is tired and worn out. I think the school district is really trying hard to keep up with research in different areas and keep pace with national trends.

Finally, the support in her own school is significant. "In my school there is a lot of collegiality—we are very supportive of each other. Our principal is also very supportive." She is quick to point out, however, that that is true in her particular school, not in all the schools in the district.

Professional Growth Needs

Growth "demands" is perhaps a better way to describe the professional growth component for teachers in the enthusiastic and growing stage of the career cycle than the usual connotation of "needs." These teachers have had their basic professional needs met. The demands on them to continue growing professionally are, for the most part, self-imposed. It is true that they continue to grow. However, the professional growth is more based on interest than on any deficiency in their professional repertoire.

Role options defined by Christensen, McDonnell, and Price (1988) can serve, once again, as an organizing vehicle for defining the professional growth characteristics of enthusiastic teachers. These role functions are teacher as learner, knowledge producer, coach, teacher educator, mentor, and leader. The key functions for teachers in the enthusiastic and growing stage are knowledge production, coaching, mentoring, teacher education, and leadership. Of these, leadership plays the most important role option for enthusiastic teachers.

Leadership

Leadership options for teachers in this stage include curriculum development, instructional strategies design, materials selection or creation, school climate, and professionalism. Leadership opportunities come from components in the organizational environment, such as the principal's management style, and are available to the extent that the teachers desire to participate. Their participation is driven by the influence from their personal environment; components such as their individual disposition help define the amount and direction of leadership activities these enthusiastic teachers might pursue.

Curriculum leadership is, first, helping to shape the curriculum for the school or district and, second, using the written curriculum to design implementation techniques in their own classroom. A well-written district curriculum will include a listing of the subjects' scope, sequence, materials, objectives, time allocations, and an evaluation technique.

Teachers in the enthusiastic and growing stage of the career cycle can provide leadership for the curriculum by chairing curriculum committees. Committee work should include an analysis of current activities in the subject and a listing of the topics, materials, objectives, and evaluation methods in current use. The enthusiastic teacher, in a leadership role, should conduct this self-study, along with other members of the committee, by surveying all teachers. Once the current operation is defined, these teachers should take the lead in determining what is missing from the curriculum. New topics and, therefore, new resources, objectives, and measurement techniques may need to be added. Student success in meeting the current expectations should be measured, and new evaluation tools should be designed if those in use are found to be lacking. Finally, the enthusiastic teacher can take the lead in seeing that the revised curriculum is implemented.

Knowledge Production

Curriculum implementation is the instruction that takes place in the classroom. Developing new instructional strategies is a second leadership responsibility of teachers in the enthusiastic and growing stage. Team teaching, direct instruction, differentiated staffing, and cooperative learning are a few of the instructional techniques that relate to different parts of any curricular area. Enthusiastic teachers should be knowledgeable of these different strategies and should take a leadership role in designing ways to integrate the methods into the classroom. These teachers could provide seminars for other teachers in the technique or they could serve as models for classroom implementation.

A third leadership responsibility for teachers in the enthusiastic stage is in the area of materials production. The chalkboard, text, paper, and pencil era of education is long past. Diverse educational materials play a central role in teaching these days. Enthusiastic teachers are often willing to test new materials, reference sources, technology, videos, telecommunications, computers, and other devices that have a place in helping to communicate curriculum objectives to students, but it takes time and effort from a dedicated professional to select, test, and evaluate these rich resources. The enthusiastic teacher is such a professional, and the evaluation or creation of instructional materials is another professional growth component of this teacher's role.

Climate

School climate refers to the efficient and effective operation of the educational environment. Students must feel comfortable, know the rules, be aware of the sanctions for non- or misbehavior, and see a consistent treatment from classroom to classroom. Enthusiastic teachers are leaders in school climate through their attention to order, their caring for students, and their ability to communicate with both staff and students. They help set the rules, see to their appropriate enforcement, and help colleagues be consistent in their interpretation and enforcement. The leadership from enthusiastic teachers includes an ability to sense concerns with climate and help prevent problems from growing by taking or recommending immediate and effective action to stem any trouble before it gets out of hand.

Professionalism

All the responsibilities just discussed can be combined to define the enthusiastic teacher's role in professionalism. Their curriculum and instructional leadership, materials development or evaluation, and attention to the school climate are all representations of professional leadership. Beyond the school or district, the enthusiastic teacher gives leadership to the profession through taking an active role in professional organizations. This component of the organizational environment defines another leadership responsibility. Working on committees, seeking offices, and attending conventions or seminars are all part of this responsibility and form yet another component of the enthusiastic teacher's professional growth program.

Teacher Preparation and Coaching

Mentoring and coaching are two components of teacher preparation that also help to define the enthusiastic teacher's professional growth program. One way to implement new instructional strategies is to form a coaching team of teachers. Two or more teachers, working together, study and plan for the implementation of a new technique and then observe one another in the use of the method and materials. The teachers then give feedback to each other for improvement. The enthusiastic teacher can be paired with a colleague who may be in a different stage, such as competency building, in order for the enthusiastic teacher to provide growth for a teacher who may need support.

This supportive coaching on the part of an enthusiastic teacher is much like the responsibility of mentoring. By serving as a mentor to one or more other teachers, the enthusiastic teacher helps find ways for the others to understand the curriculum and use appropriate instructional strategies to communicate the objectives to students. Mentoring beginning teachers, as was discussed in Chapter 4, is one part of this role. The responsibilities of mentoring that were outlined in the chapter on the induction stage carry through for the enthusiastic teacher's work with other professionals.

A third component of teacher preparation as a growth opportunity for teachers in the enthusiastic and growing stage of the career cycle is collaboration with a teacher preparation institution. Where time and geography allow, enthusiastic teachers are often called upon to team with university professors to teach classes. Some are appointed as clinical professors and given responsibility for classes or other work with pre-service students. (Much of this work was expanded upon in Chapter 3 concerning the preservice stage of the career cycle.)

Enthusiastic teachers often become the conduit for the growth needs of others rather than spending time with their own needs. They are the leaders and providers of inservice education for staff and serve as role models and mentors for preservice students. Professional growth is more a demand upon them than a solution to problems and concerns in their professional lives. These teachers are unique in their relation to the professional growth concept when compared to teachers at other stages, and they are unique in how they view incentives. Incentives for teachers in the enthusiastic and growing stage of the career cycle will be outlined following the discussion of growth needs, or growth demands, for Louise and Mary.

Career Growth Needs for Louise and Mary

Louise

As an enthusiastic and growing teacher oriented to teaching, Louise sees her subject area as well as her students as critical in the support of her teaching and as central to her growth needs. Interestingly enough, when asked about growth needs, Louise did not focus on external professional support sources such as peers and administration.

> I guess one of the things that has kept me very interested in what I am doing and constantly learning is that I really have had a lot of recognition and a lot of summer institutes—a lot of unusual opportunities to grow. I have gone back and forth between high school and college teaching—I enjoy both levels and I stay in the high school level more because I don't have a specialty. One of the very nice things about the high school level, you can teach very different classes. I can move between psychology and sociology and history. On a college level, I would not be able to do that and I love all three fields so I really have tremendous diversity.
>
> It's part of my ego that likes the fact that the kids are very much influenced by my teaching. By the time they get to high school, the idea of mentor becomes very important to the students. That's been a very meaningful relationship to me, this relationship with my students. They keep in contact with me. In the past several weeks I have received letters from people I knew at my high school fourteen years ago or so. I also received a call this week from a former student who is now teaching whom I had in class about ten years ago. I got a letter from a student I had in 1959—I had that student on the West Coast. He somehow found my address. All these years later—he's 45 years old and he's writing his high school teacher. That's terrific! That's the sort of perk you get that you don't get in any other job. You realize that you are important in their lives and they are very important in your life. Just like an extended family. When I first started teaching I was more oriented towards the subject than the students; now I would say that that is not the case. I am more oriented around the students now, but I still have a great love for the subject matter.

Certainly this combination of competency and love for the subject matter as well as orientation to the students' needs is a mark of an enthusiastic and growing teacher.

Other areas that would allow this relationship to grow even more are further identified by Louise as additional support needs.

> We do need secretarial help. This is very important, especially in my role as Department Chair. We need more space—we are running out of room and that is crippling some of my activities simply because you cannot really function if you don't have enough room for books, files, materials, etc. We are increasingly having to share rooms, and if you don't have your own room during prep period, it makes it very difficult for you to get your academic work done.

But it is not all academics with Louise. This lack of space is also a problem when it comes to working with students.

> There are too few places in the school to meet with students privately. Not in your room—prep period—and there is no private office to go to. It's very difficult to have student counseling. This is a terrific handicap. Many times public schools are not designed to maximize the human element. They are built around the whole notion that all a teacher is is one person in the classroom, and it's really much more than that. There are times when we are one-on-one with students or parents. In our school, for instance, there is no private place a teacher can go, and if you are going to try to make a confidential call, let's say you are dealing with a subject that is really dynamite, for example, you expect that child is a victim of sexual abuse and you are trying to get authority and there's no place to go to talk about sexual abuse—this creates problems. These are real basic needs to encourage relationships, and I don't think there's much attention paid to it at all.

Mary

Mary's growth needs in this stage of her career are fairly simple.

> I need to get a master's degree. I feel like I am always growing. I don't think a master's degree would make me a better teacher, but if I want to get a higher salary, I have to get a master's. I have been teaching courses all along that have helped enhance my teaching.

Mary also is very serious about her teaching, as one might expect from one in an enthusiastic and growing stage. "I spend a lot of time at school. I get there early and stay as late as needed. I take it very seriously. I believe that I am very organized. I like to be ready the night before."

Incentives for Enthusiastic and Growing Teachers

Teachers in the enthusiastic and growing stage of the career cycle identified incentives that can be summarized into four broad categories (McDonnell, Christensen & Price 1987): support, status, responsibility, and flexibility. Research on incentives that were important for all teachers generated several items that were identified by teachers who were judged to be in the enthusiastic stage. These specific items are outlined here in relation to each of the categories listed. Examples are given to serve as models for enthusiastic teachers' incentives.

Research and Writing

Enthusiastic and growing teachers see research in classroom operations and writing about their findings to be important components of their professional lives. They have confidence in their ability to study what they are doing in the classroom, to initiate improvements in their instruction and, therefore, in student learning. An example of this incentive might be a local college or university providing support for research through encouraging action research projects. Personnel from higher education could team with enthusiastic teachers to identify areas for improvement, design methods or materials to meet the need, implement the technique, study its effectiveness, and report on the findings. Support from the organizational environment to participate in action research projects would be important to the implementation of this incentive as well.

Advanced Study

Scholarships for advanced study were also identified by enthusiastic teachers as an incentive to their work. These teachers may be seeking an advanced or terminal degree in their field. Some school districts no longer pay for tuition or fees for teachers to take advanced study, arguing instead that the credit columns on many salary schedules are reward enough for the graduate credits. Enthusiastic teachers see this support, the support for credit, as an important incentive. They may have several directions of study they might like to pursue, and probably will pursue, so support from the school district would be an extra benefit. One way for the organizational environment to support this work is to select a goal from the district list of goals—say, the education of gifted and talented students. The district could then select one of their enthusiastic teachers to be educated in the techniques of gifted education and the district could pay for the credit and then gain from the new expertise of the teacher.

Status

Status items are seen as important incentives for teachers in the enthusiastic and growing stage. These items include status as a lead teacher or department coordinator, master teacher identification, professional organization awards, and student praise.

Praise

In a recent study (Burke et al. 1987), enthusiastic teachers chose student praise as the most important component of praise, ranking it above administrator or peer praise as an incentive. This incentive could be put into action through a student selected "teacher of the week" or "teacher of the month" program. Student newspapers could have a column on "my favorite teacher." These are two examples of how to implement a student praise incentive program for enthusiastic teachers.

Master Teacher

Receiving the status of master teacher was also seen as an incentive by enthusiastic teachers. Districts or schools should take care when considering this incentive. Attempts at implementing teacher career ladders with several steps leading to a master teacher designation have not always been well received by the teachers who are involved. Concerns have arisen about the requirements for the status, the selection procedure, and the rewards once selected. Some teachers do not want others to be labeled as "better than" their peers. They do, however, accept that some of their peers are "different than" they are.

The "different than" category leads into the third category for status incentives for enthusiastic teachers. These teachers, by and large, agree that selection as a unit leader, lead teacher, department chairperson, or other such role is a positive incentive for their work. Too often, however, this status is conferred based on seniority without sufficient thought given to merit or ability. It is also too often a status conferred for life. Districts or schools should consider a rotation, or election, schedule to fill these positions. Rotation would increase opportunities for teachers to experience leadership roles, and election would add peer recognition to the status as well.

Professional Organizations

Professional organization awards are the fourth category of status incentives for enthusiastic teachers. Professional organizations form a crucial environmental influence for teachers at this stage. These teachers would like to have their work either for the organization or in the classroom recognized by the organization or association. This incentive can be implemented through special recognition awards in specific categories of work such as "best journal article" or "most innovative teaching technique." Association leaders need to be aware of the importance of this incentive and take time to create opportunities for recognition through certificates or other commendations.

Flexible Time Schedules

Enthusiastic and growing teachers desire flexibility as an incentive (Burke et al. 1987). Examples include having a flexible work day, being eligible for paid sabbatical leave, being in control of instructional decisions, and having released time for professional activities. Teaching is the one profession in which practitioners are locked into a tight time schedule. It is not possible for a teacher to leave a classroom for an hour, much less a day or several days, without having a substitute sit in with the students. Budget restrictions and timing difficulties take much of the flexibility away from classroom teachers during the school day. Absences must be planned days or even weeks in advance. Because of this, teachers lose the spontaneity to respond to a demand or, more importantly, to take advantage of a growth opportunity if one should surface on short notice. Enthusiastic teachers see the need for such flexibility. One way to address this need is to group teachers in teams or provide aide support to cover classrooms when situations require that teachers should be elsewhere. Once again, support and flexibility from the organizational environment are important to accomplish this task.

The organizational environment is also very important in providing paid sabbatical leaves for teachers. Sabbaticals are a necessary and important benefit available to college and university professors. They are used to renew and develop new ideas, concepts, materials, or constructs for teaching. They are also used to design new courses to be taught. A sabbatical of a semester or a year is a costly proposition for elementary and secondary schools. The return on this investment in terms of improved programs, however, can be outstanding. School districts should consider budgeting for a series of sabbatical leaves that could be granted to teachers in order to pursue a specific task for the school. The money for this budget item could be reallocated from an administrative position where the administrative responsibilities, such as discipline and attendance, could be handled by a group of teachers or shared by other administrators. Several options for differentiating a teacher's career exist as an incentive for enthusiastic teachers (Jandura & Burke 1989).

Time is a very valuable commodity. Enthusiastic teachers identified time to carry out their professional responsibilities as another important incentive. Just as paid sabbaticals would give teachers time to renew or redirect their professional lives, time during the school day is important to teachers to prepare lessons, review materials, evaluate the effectiveness of their teaching, and design ways to change their instructional strategies in order to be even more effective. The organizational environment can help with finding time through reducing assignments when responsibilities are differentiated or adding staff to create teams or departments where sharing of responsibilities would create more time for professional responsibilities.

The final item under flexibility that is an incentive for enthusiastic teachers is being given control of instructional decisions. Teachers in the enthusiastic and growing stage of the career cycle are confident and capable professionals. They follow the directives set for them by the state or local authority because they are professionals, but they desire an opportunity to make change where they see change is necessary. For example, it may be a state requirement that elementary teachers have a health education unit every week. Enthusiastic teachers may wish to teach an extensive and in-depth health program over a nine-week time period and then use the next nine weeks for another topic, such as careers. They would like the flexibility and autonomy to make a change such as this, and they see the ability to make change, to control the instructional decisions, as a valid incentive. Respite from rules can come from the regulations, or the regulatory bodies, that are a part of the organizational environment. Teachers should work with legislators and inspectors to come to an agreement about modifications in instructional programs that enthusiastic teachers could be sanctioned to use.

Responsibility

Responsibility is the fourth category of incentives that is important to teachers in the enthusiastic and growing stage. Components of the responsibility category include extra duties or assignments, leadership opportunities, and influence in school decision making. These are all identified by enthusiastic teachers as incentives important to their professional lives.

Influence that leads to enthusiastic teachers identifying responsibility items begins in the personal environment. Family members must be supportive of the enthusiastic teacher taking on summer assignments or extended day responsibilities at the school. Teachers must have an individual disposition toward leadership and have the personal confidence to want to be part of the school decision-making authority.

These personal influences must be balanced by the organizational environment categories of management, regulations, and public trust. Managers must be willing to delegate responsibility to teachers who are able to take on the authority. The public should see the value of shared decision making and support its construct, and regulations must be revised or created to give teachers leadership opportunities, such as in curriculum or instruction as discussed above.

The responsibility category of incentives is perhaps the most important to the organization since it not only provides an incentive for enthusiastic teachers but it also guarantees positive and enthusiastic leadership for school programs. Teachers at this stage are ready and willing to take on special assignments. They have the skill and dedication to do a good job, so an incentive for the teachers becomes a necessary condition of leadership for the schools. Giving enthusiastic teachers the responsibility for leadership and other activities at the school is both good for the school and good for the teacher.

Teachers in the enthusiastic and growing stage of the career cycle, then, see incentives in status, support, flexibility, and responsibility. Any factor that helps them do a better job in the classroom or adds positively to their profession is seen as an incentive, as shown in the examples that follow.

Appropriate Incentives for Louise and Mary

Louise

As an enthusiastic and growing teacher, Louise has some strong feelings about appropriate incentives. Perhaps she already is foreshadowing her next stage, that of career wind-down, when she makes statements concerning salary.

> I believe that I am royally underpaid. It still hurts a little bit to realize that if I had stayed with my first career choice, as a buyer in a department store, that I never make any more than I would have made there in my second or third year. I have been in the teaching profession for thirty years and have no realistic expectation that I will ever make enough money. I do think teaching is of more value than being a buyer in a department store.

Administration is not an incentive for her. She enjoys being department chair and lead teacher and doing staff development as a workshop coordinator. Nevertheless, the salary inadequacies do bother her.

> If I were to do anything outside of the classroom at this point I would leave altogether. If I were to decide I needed a new challenge, I would go with some kind of organization which works with educational policies. For instance, the advanced placement program operating in the Midwest.

Even an enthusiastic and growing teacher can look elsewhere and be somewhat frustrated by the value given to teaching in this society.

Coursework and other kinds of workshops have been important to her. "I think one of the reasons I have been successful as a teacher is that I have loved it so much, because I really love learning and I've been able to keep doing it." But she is also discerning in educational opportunities.

> Some inservice I have liked and others have been a waste of time. It's hard to say how to avoid that. One of the things that I don't particularly like that I see happening in education is that people are so frustrated about how to plan inservice. They tend to simply hire outside people—the Madeline Hunter kind of thing. Everybody gets on the bandwagon and does the same thing and many times these people forget what's going on in the classroom. They've gotten so much onto the lecture circuit, but while they are entertaining and amusing, they are many times not really very helpful in the classroom.

Another type of educational experience that has been important to Louise are sabbaticals. "I have had one paid sabbatical and I enjoyed it very much. But I really wouldn't go again because I miss the classroom too much. At my age I have too few classroom days left so I wouldn't want to do that again."

The employment time of the teaching year was important to Louise when she had a family, as has been indicated earlier, but it is still important to her for other reasons.

> I don't want to spend a full year teaching because I really enjoy my summers. Going to other learning experiences is great and teaching is a rough job. All you have to do is take pictures of people in May and then in September. Full-year employment would be stressful. Teaching is a tough job.

The idea of team teaching collaboration appeals to Louise. "I've done some of that, but you have to have more prep time than usual. Much team teaching is simply trading off to optimize your time. Collaborative teaching can be exhilarating."

Another important incentive and support system for Louise is the peer group both in and out of the classroom.

> The peer group interaction is very important to my professional life. As I mentioned before, it is sort of a tricky part. One of the nice things that has happened in our school is that we have formed an exercise group. Aerobics. There are about eighteen of us. Men and women. We have a "Y" instructor and we do it right after school two days a week—it's been wonderful—it has really built relationships. Two years ago about six of us started walking together and we walk about three to five miles before we go home. So now we are alternating—we walk one night and do aerobics the next night. Teaching is tough—you get so tired. It snaps you back again before you go home. It gets the brain oxygenated. A terrific UP feeling. The problem is scheduling your meetings because we have so many of them. The principal happens to be one of the persons in the aerobic class so he tried to make sure we don't have meetings on that night.

Finally, as an enthusiastic and growing teacher Louise has several important insights into the problems of evaluation as an appropriate incentive.

> Evaluations are just terrible. As Department Chair I have to evaluate my department first and I try to do that in the most positive manner possible. But it's so threatening to teachers. They look upon it with a great deal of alarm. They feel threatened. If they are really doing a terrible job, the kids let everyone know. The kids see you everyday—they know what teachers are like. I think we ought to have more student input as to who is doing a good job. I don't think administrators really know how to do it. They don't

spend enough time doing it. It's very tough—the time for the meaningful observation is not there, and if we are going to do it we must put more money into it if it is going to be meaningful. What we really need is more teacher self-evaluation. Teach teachers how to do that. Teach other teachers how to be peer coaches and say, "Hey, come on into my room, see what you think about this, and I'll come to yours." Let the kids talk with you.

In sum, the use of incentives has been a successful strategy for Louise in working toward her goals as an enthusiastic and growing teacher. She points out that the school board and administration have been very supportive in her case—they are genuinely appreciative of the time spent.

Mary
As an enthusiastic and growing teacher, Mary has quite a few insights into appropriate incentives. She was more open in discussing this topic than any of the previous ones. Time and recognition are both important to her.

More time off would be very important so we could have more of those meetings once in a while where we bring people in to speak to us, and which allows us to get together with other teachers at the same grade level to exchange ideas. I also think recognition of people who are very good is important. We rarely get a pat on the back. I don't think the system knows what fine teachers they have, and I don't know how they can get around it without making other people jealous. I think they should somehow recognize good teaching.

She expands on this idea by suggesting that

When you do things in a class that are outstanding or successful, maybe the administration or principal could write a note. For example, there was an administrator one time who looked for your name in the paper and when he saw that name in the paper, he would send a copy of the article and a little note with it. That hasn't happened since.

She also shares the importance of principal support, both within and without observational settings.

When they come to evaluate and observe you, and I've always had positive observations, I think they are reluctant to point out a lot of things you do in front of other people, but my principal is very supportive and when any problem arises she is always on your side. A principal who supports you is one way of getting recognition, but somehow I think they need to do more.

She also provides an example of how not to recognize people. "We get birthday cards from the superintendent. It's funny, because my birthday is in April and I get the card in September and sometimes in October. That's not very personal."

Some of the new ideas such as merit pay and career ladders are not significant to her. "I think merit pay would be just too difficult to administer fairly."

However, classroom autonomy is important to her, and she feels satisfied here. "I have a lot of autonomy, but I'm not representative of everybody in the school district. For our principal and for me, I would say I have a lot of autonomy."

She is involved with the union and feels that the union can be very supportive and protective of teachers. She realizes its place in protecting teachers.

> We cannot get rid of bad teachers—the union can't get rid of them—it's up to the administration to do it. Before I got involved in the union I always thought they protected mediocrity, but I don't agree with that now; all they are protecting is proper procedure. I go to negotiations and I sit and listen to teachers' rights and I don't believe they protect teachers who are bad. They protect the right to due process.

Finally, she is supportive of team teaching and sabbaticals. "I think team teaching is great if you have people with whom you can work. I've done it before and it can work. It would be great to have a paid sabbatical. Now, you would have to take it in the summertime."

Support Systems for Enthusiastic and Growing Teachers

Enthusiastic and growing teachers frequently see collaborative work, professional associations, and district meetings as components of a support system for their own professional growth. The component of collaboration includes visitation of other classrooms within or outside the district and exchange teaching with teachers in different schools or grades or subjects. Professional associations have conventions or conferences that provide enthusiastic teachers a support mechanism. Meetings in their own district provide an opportunity for leadership, status, and responsibility that are important incentives for these teachers.

Opportunities for Collaboration

Enthusiastic teachers are continually searching for new methods or techniques that can be transported to their classrooms to improve instruction and student performance. They look forward to an opportunity to visit other classrooms looking for improvement items, or exchanging with other teachers to measure the effectiveness of established techniques on different populations. For example, a teacher from a suburban school might change places with a central city teacher to better understand the problems of urban students. Collaboration as a support system could also include action research with higher-education colleagues, as mentioned previously.

Professional Meetings

Teachers in the enthusiastic and growing stage see opportunities to attend professional meetings as a support system for their jobs. Resources spent to this end are well invested by school districts. While the sectional presentations and keynote speakers at the meetings are worthwhile, the contacts made with other professionals from other locations are invaluable. Teachers, like any other professionals, learn from each other. The informal conversations at professional meetings offer a wealth of information about issues, problems, and their resolution. Enthusiastic teachers also may become involved with the governance of the associations through leadership positions or committee memberships. This involvement gives status to the home school as well as to the teachers and, in addition, adds to the professional development of the entire staff through contact with the teacher/member.

District Meetings

This professional development for in-district teachers can come through a series of different system meetings in which the enthusiastic teacher may participate. School improvement councils, instructional improvement committees, curriculum subcommittees, staff development councils, and other special work groups all give enthusiastic teachers an avenue to share the expertise they have gained.

The key for management when considering these or other support systems for teachers in the enthusiastic and growing stage of the career cycle is to find ways to maintain the enthusiasm and to continue to challenge these teachers to stay on top of their profession. The reactions of Louise and Mary to the question of support systems give some direction to the discussion above.

Support Systems for Louise and Mary

Louise

Louise is still focused on teacher associations when it comes to support systems, undoubtedly because of her past leadership roles in them. "I still believe that teachers' associations have a major role to play, and that's just going to be ongoing. I think the subject matter of professional associations are very important."

She is less certain of some of the education reforms such as career ladders.

There's a real problem with having differentiated roles. So many times the teacher has to be out of the classroom, so you take your very best teachers and you make them the consultants or the lead teacher or the chair and you give them release time and then you've lost them in the classroom.

She favors more traditional approaches that support teachers in the classroom.

The kinds of proposals I like the most are those that say, "Hey, this teacher is a wonderful teacher. Let's pay him/her more, give them support systems like teacher aides, volunteer parents helping correct papers, one-on-one tutoring, and let them stay in the classroom. Let them do what they do best and don't try to give them release time." I really think that is very important.

But this enthusiastic and growing teacher comes back to the classroom for her major support.

I really think that writing is so terribly important. Doing an essay a week with over 100 students; that's tough and yet they need that. If we could get help in the reading of essays through teacher aides, it would be wonderful. One of the schools I visited while we were on a sabbatical had teacher aides come in and they went to the library and students came in every hour with their compositions and they worked with them one-on-one, helping them with their writing. We should have that operating in every school; it would really be terrific. I think that would be a great use you could make of people who want to retire early.

In sum, it is the classroom that is fulfilling to this enthusiastic and growing teacher. As she looks forward to career wind-down, her goal is the classroom, but support that would reduce paperwork is what she desires.

I would like to stay in the classroom full-time, but I have a lot of paperwork and I would like that to be done in some other way and I think as I get older and I become more tired, that's what I would do. I would spend my salary in hiring people to help with paperwork.

Louise evidently has been in the enthusiastic and growing stage from very early on in her teaching career, as evidenced by the variety of awards she has won at both state and national levels. What has been important to her throughout her career has been these awards and the support of colleagues and administration. She has enjoyed leadership positions, but ultimately the most rewarding incentive for her has been the relationships with her students, their appreciation of her by keeping in contact with her. Louise will undoubtedly maintain her enthusiastic and growing stage even during her wind-down period. It is clear that as she starts thinking about wind-down and exit, the oncoming of these events will be determined by the rewards she gets from her students.

Mary

Mary continued her openness in response to this area. In terms of strategies for improvement, Mary is primarily interested in additional courses and in-service.

> I continue to take courses that will make me a better teacher. Everything I have taken has been a very pragmatic approach and I've learned a lot. Inservice is great also. They have frequently had inservice here. The most recent one was terrific. I do think that having them after school when teachers are tired is wrong. They ought to get substitutes so teachers can take them during the day when we are fresh and receptive.

Mary is clearly an enthusiastic and growing teacher. It is also clear that whether she maintains this stage or slips into career frustration or stability and maintaining depends on the type of support she receives, and she is clear about what the nature of that support is. She sees the union as very important. "The union is prepared to support you in any way. If you have any trouble, the teachers' rights are there to help you."

She also sees administration as being supportive.

> The Director of Curriculum and Instruction is very supportive and some of the other people under the superintendent. I think they are stepped on and leaned upon by people who are over them, however. I think they work hard and their goals are worthy goals. I think they support us very much.

She is also clear about the potential for the school board.

> I don't think the school board is supportive except for one member, but a lot of the rest of them have no idea what is going on in the schools. I don't think they care. I just feel that they don't really listen to us. I think the school board is unaware of what the administration is doing. I think communication among all levels are not that good. I would like the school board to meet more directly with teachers as long as they will listen.

External forces also can be supportive or nonsupportive, as the case may be. For instance, "The local newspaper is very anti-education. They have very little to say that's good about the school system."

As to national reports and, again, the press, she feels:

> I just think they are extremely narrow and unaware of problems that teachers are facing today. When "The Nation at Risk" report came out, there are all of these problems that no one ever sees; only the teachers know the problems that we are dealing with. Kids come to kindergarten or first grade from a home where there is no order—conceived when their parents were on drugs—and thus, of course, they have learning disabilities. No wonder, with murder, rape, and mayhem at home. We get these kids and we are supposed to teach them. No one talks about teachers who get attacked by children or by parents. We have to put up with a lot and the public is not aware of it. I don't know if they care.

With these types of problems in the schools, it is clear to Mary that class size must be looked at.

> We have an assistant superintendent who firmly believes that class size makes no difference. Well, I'm a teacher and I say that it does. If you have thirty kids and half of them have special problems, how effective can you be? If these kids are getting into junior high and high school they need special treatment and it's not all our fault. There are a lot of other factors involved. That has to be addressed. I was at a Gifted and Talented Conference and one of the speakers there said that he had written legislation for Indiana that will result in grades K–3 no class being larger than seventeen and each teacher will have an aide who has had two years of training. Now that's getting at the root of the problem.

Mary's final series of comments indicates what can happen to an enthusiastic and growing teacher as frustration begins to set in.

> I don't know if I would like to be doing something else. There are times when I think that I just can't take it anymore because there are so many problems, but in the end I always go back to teaching. I realize that I am an effective teacher and I'm always learning—I'm trying—it is not easy and it is not as fun as it used to be. It's really hard work and especially in the elementary schools. Teachers feel this stress an awful lot. We had an additional 30 minutes tacked to our day and I could not believe how tired that made me. We don't have time to prepare during the day—to grade papers or whatever. I get there between quarter after seven every morning and stay until 4:30 or 5:00 or later and it's hard to get everything done.

There are some days when I don't have prep time at all—we are supposed to have an average of 30 minutes a day, but that's very little and when it comes to reading new units of study and gathering materials together to take to class—you have no help—you do it all yourself—so how can you really be creative? I have to force myself—I'm TIRED after school. Force myself to go to K-Mart to get things. I can see why a lot of people don't do it. They have children at home—pick up kids from babysitters, whatever, and you just have no time. It's hard—it's hard to be a creative and exciting teacher. You must be totally dedicated to spend lots of time and money. I've spent a lot of money for teaching materials. Hundreds of dollars every year of my own money. I like to do it, though; teaching is exciting and challenging, but at the same time is very wearing and stressful. Administration has to recognize it. I think they really don't know. They have not walked in our shoes and don't understand.

Mary has been an enthusiastic and growing teacher for some time, yet one can clearly see that, as she progresses in her comments, accumulated strains and stresses could create a change in her teaching stage. The future is unclear for Mary.

Summary

The enthusiastic and growing stage of the teacher career cycle is the period associated with "master" or "expert" teachers who are competent and self-confident professionals. These individuals are not only experiencing very positive periods in their own professional lives, but also tend to have a very positive influence on school climate and upon other teachers. Enthusiastic and growing teachers generally receive positive, nurturing influences from their own personal environments and frequently are able to work effectively with and have a positive influence upon their organizational environment. Their professional growth needs include opportunities for creative outlets and reinforcement of their leadership in a variety of areas, including curriculum, professional activities, teacher preparation, and mentoring. Administrative and supervisory strategies most appropriate for these individuals are those that reinforce and reward their enthusiasm and achievements and provide outlets for their leadership and creativity. This stage should be a target for teachers in all stages. The challenge for administrators and supervisors is to attempt to create a climate that maximizes the opportunity for teachers to enter and remain in the enthusiastic and growing stage.

CHAPTER SEVEN

Career Frustration

JAY R. PRICE

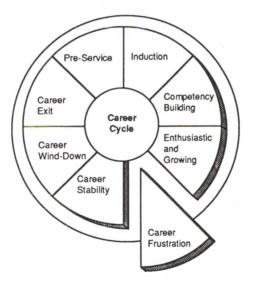

This period is characterized by frustration and disillusionment with teaching. Job satisfaction is waning and teachers begin to question why they are doing this work. Much of what is described as "teacher burnout" in the literature occurs in this stage.

This stage of the teacher career cycle is characterized by a number of attitudinal and personal characteristics of teachers that make it considerably different from the earlier growth stages. Although the period of frustration frequently occurs during a teacher's mid-career and mid-life, the seeds of frustration may be planted earlier when teachers find themselves torn between contradictions and conflicting demands. It is a time when the individual feels locked into a position and sees few possibilities for change available. This stage is a period when coping skills must be changed or new ones found to permit appropriate adjustment to challenges from the personal and organizational environments. For some this is a period of stress and subsequent burnout, while for others it is a time of withdrawal.

Individuals may react to frustration in different ways. It may cause them to reevaluate their reasons for teaching and may provide the impetus to exit. Frustration also may cause teachers to reexamine and then reaffirm their reasons for choosing teaching, leading them to reenergize themselves into an enthusiastic mode. Still others may move into the stable stage discussed in the next chapter. Whatever the emotions of this stage, however, teachers are seeking and reaching for help. This is a critical period in the lives of many teachers. Attention must be given to those environmental factors that may influence teachers' frustrations and to those that could help move them to a more positive and productive mode.

Views of Career Frustration

The label for this stage of the teacher career cycle has been based on the perspectives provided by a number of lines of research both on teaching and on work and occupations in general. This literature covers issues of incentives and rewards in teaching as well as theories about why people are satisfied with their work.

In this section of the chapter, three areas of research will be examined briefly to suggest sources, characteristics, and psychological and sociological perspectives on career frustration. The first section covers teachers' perspectives on work and their work lives, the second section deals with stress and burnout, and the third examines psychological and sociological perspectives of the origins of frustration.

Teaching as Work

In several large-scale surveys of members of various occupations, Lowther and colleagues (1981, 1985) have dealt with the concepts of job lock-in and job satisfaction. *Lock-in* defines a person's feelings of being trapped in a particular job because of lack of mobility caused by factors such as saturation of the market within a geographic region. This version of lock-in generally applies to horizontal mobility, but in teaching vertical mobility is a consideration as well since job mobility frequently means moving out of the classroom and into administration or counseling. Lowther, Gill, and Coppard (1981) found that experienced teachers more than other professionals or nonprofessionals indicated higher levels of feeling locked into their positions and were more likely to express feelings that they were occupying the same positions as when they came to work for their employers. At the same time, teachers reported high levels of work-related problems having to do with maintaining effort and energy, as well as immobility of jobs and not being able to change assignments. Although more teachers in Lowther's study were seemingly happier and more satisfied with their lives and work than other professionals, the largest proportion of teachers reported that they were less than happy and less than completely satisfied with their lives.

In a later study examining teachers' views of their work lives, career teachers were compared to individuals prepared to teach but who were not teaching. Lowther and others (1985) reported that career teachers felt more job lock-in and less opportunity for vertical advancement than did the nonteaching teacher graduates. To account for their length of service, the researchers suggested that career teachers might find intrinsic rewards in teaching that substitute for traditional extrinsic rewards like job mobility. However, this study also suggested that other forms of extrinsic reward and recognition are not characteristic or seemingly expected by the career teachers. These themes become very important and are the subject of the teacher discussions provided in later sections of this chapter.

While Lowther's work suggests the sources of the emotional content of the career frustration stage, survey research by Burke and colleagues (1987) provides a broader picture of factors that differentiate teachers at this stage. The first and most important way in which these teachers differ is in their enthusiasm for teaching. Teachers who identified themselves at this stage reported that each year it becomes increasingly difficult to be enthusiastic about teaching. They reported also that they were frustrated, that the academic climate in their schools was discouraging, and that their students did not respect them.

The second difference between this stage and the growth stages is that career-frustrated teachers report they are not happy with the day-to-day business of teaching. They indicate that they are not as comfortable with most of what they teach, provide fewer opportunities to meet with parents, enjoy their colleagues less, and do not work with student teachers as frequently.

A third difference noted at this stage relates to teachers' attitudes toward teaching and students. In addition to their lower levels of enthusiasm, these teachers report a desire to teach part-time in order to pursue other interests. They see lack of funding as problematic to teaching, as well as problems with their schools' academic climate. At the same time they are relatively less upset than growth-stage teachers by the lack of rapport with students and lack of administrative support for teachers. This difference suggests that at this stage, teachers are not overly concerned about constraints in teaching and have begun to question teaching effectiveness and their commitments to students' learning and well-being.

The fourth way in which career frustration teachers differ is in terms of their attitudes toward teaching as a profession. They tend to be not very optimistic about teaching, are not comfortable or secure as a result of experience, and tend not to enjoy the students as much or not at all.

In general, the picture of the career-frustrated teacher emerging from these studies is one of an individual who is withdrawing from teaching and from the school, in frustration and perhaps in anger. When this portrait is combined with the work previously cited on job lock-in, it seems appropriate to speculate on the kinds of changes to the environments and reward structures of schools that might lead to different kinds of outcomes in the career cycle. To examine the nature and impact of environments on individuals, the next section explores relevant literature on teacher burnout for its import in defining and describing the career frustration stage of the career cycle.

Burnout

This section focuses on the definition of *burnout* and its relation to stress. The term is widely used to cover everything from boredom to end-of-year exhaustion. If a discussion of burnout is to provide elaboration on career frustration as a stage, then the concept needs to be differentiated from the terms *tension, anxiety, identity crises,* or *fatigue*.

In early investigations, Freudenberger (1974) defined burnout as the characteristic of individuals who become inoperative due to excessive demands on energy, strength, or resources. Maslach (1982), in a rigorous review of the construct, cited some fifteen definitions of burnout but noted that there was general agreement that burnout was an internal phenomenon involving feelings, attitudes, motives, and expectations. As a negative experience for the individual, it includes distress, dysfunctions, and negative consequences and outcomes. Beyond this basic level of agreement, however, clinical conceptions of burnout have included irritability, loss of self esteem, withdrawal, and low morale. These concepts were formalized by Maslach and Jackson (1981) in an instrument designed to assess an individual's self-perceptions of burnout. For this assessment, burnout was defined as emotional exhaustion, depersonalization, a lack of a sense of personal accomplishment, and a detachment from the work role.

In addition to the preceding clinical and psychometric perspectives used to define burnout, sociology has added the conceptions of role theory. This perspective holds that individuals find meaning and satisfaction in the roles they fulfill until alienation occurs: Burnout is the consequence of this alienation. Schwab and Iwanicki (1982) found that role conflict and role ambiguity as perceived by teachers related to their feelings of emotional exhaustion and depersonalization, both components of a clinical definition of burnout. Lack of a sense of accomplishment, an additional component of burnout, was related to only role ambiguity and not to role conflict, however. These results suggest that the nature of the work of teaching is an important contributor to teacher burnout.

Additional evidence on burnout as a construct comes from Dworkin's (1987) large-scale study of burnout based also on the idea of role theory and alienation. Burnout in this study was defined as having four components, namely: (1) the feeling that work is meaningless—students will not solve their problems as a result of a teacher's efforts; (2) teachers' perception that they are powerless in the face of immovable bureaucracies; (3) confronted with few or no standards to guide them, teachers are often torn between system demands and student needs and wind up inevitably not being able to help enough, leading to a sense of normlessness; and (4) feelings of isolation. Faced with these frustrations, teachers withdraw from the professional ideals that first attracted them and begin to feel that no one cares about them or their work. They sense rejection from students and isolate themselves from their colleagues.

Stress

The link between stress and burnout is basically straightforward; stress is the origin of burnout (e.g., Dworkin 1987), and teaching is fraught with stress. The work on stress in teaching has attempted to identify and explain the sources of job-related stress. The definitions and models discussed here attempt to indicate how stress as a process occurs.

That stress exists in teaching is not at issue; rather, the issue is its prevalence. Research has not clarified how many teachers are victims of stress. Nevertheless, the consequences of stress are readily apparent in both the psychological and physiological symptoms that are prevalent among teachers.

Sources of stress (sometimes labeled issues, concerns, or problems) in the work place relate to the demands, conflicts, and ambiguities in the teaching role. This type of conflict, noted in the previous section, pertains to such ambiguities as how much control teachers have over the curriculum, their own actions, and their creativity versus the demands of a bureaucracy concerning uniformity and homogeneity in curriculum, methods, and response to requirements. Other demands of the work place concern relationships with students, colleagues, and administrators. Student-related stressors include management and disciplinary issues, class size, and supplies, all of which are related to the task of teaching. Administrative stressors include evaluation and assignment to classes, and colleague relations would include disputes and differences in points of view. It is the teaching task category, however, that has produced the most consistent pattern of linkage to the emotional exhaustion and depersonalization categories of burnout (e.g., Adams, Martray, & Alexander 1982).

The remainder of this chapter focuses on the career frustration stage of the career cycle and examines the impact of both personal and organizational influences. As in preceding chapters, incentives for this stage are discussed, along with needs of these teachers and the implications for support programs as well. The following section introduces the teachers who exemplify those in the career frustration stage.

Teacher Profiles

Eleanor

Eleanor is 41 years old and currently unmarried, with two children about to enter college. She has been teaching approximately twelve years, the last five in her current position as a high school special education/learning disabilities teacher. Her regional high school is located in a small community in the upper Midwest and serves a largely rural, small-town population. Eleanor has just received her master's degree in learning disabilities from a regional state university to which she has commuted during the past several years. She has received no special awards and reports that due to her schooling and life as a single parent, she belongs only to the teachers' union and the Association for Retarded Citizens, an outgrowth of her serving as foster parent to a third daughter with mental retardation.

Kathy

Kathy is 50 years old, currently unmarried, and has four children in their 20s, none living at home with her. She has taught for twenty-six years, with three years in her current position as a third-grade teacher. Her elementary school, located in a city of over 100,000 population in the upper Midwest, serves a culturally diverse population of students. She has acquired various collections of graduate credits but never finished her master's degree, due to changing states and graduate schools as she followed her former spouse's career moves around the country. Her memberships include the local teachers' association as well as the state reading and middle school associations. She is surprised that her work has not been recognized because of her service and leadership at the district level, especially in curriculum. Though she is proud of the accolades and appreciation she receives from parents and students at the end of the year, she wishes these were ongoing during the year when she needs the support.

Both teachers are at the level of frustration in their careers. They recognize and articulate a great deal of their unrest with teaching as being due to the situations they are in and trying to control. Each compares her present situation to a former stage in the teaching career, and Eleanor reports:

> Currently, I am very frustrated in the position that I hold. I always enjoyed working with the secondary age group. I had always found it exciting and looked forward to going back in the fall, but last year I took a real turn. I was frustrated the entire year. Even though I put in many hours, I felt a lot of effort was wasted even though I really tried. I thought maybe I wasn't trying the right way that I should be. I tried to get some support and didn't get any. I was pretty vocal about how I felt to those around me, and no one seemed to care or listen.

Kathy suggests a somewhat different and perhaps more self-contained stage of frustration. She says:

> I'm partly discouraged. I feel right now that what I'm doing is just holding on—just maintaining. In fact, it's real important to me that I not go back to the school I was just in. . . . I've been there three years and did not choose to go there. It was an assignment because of staff reduction in another school. The way I feel, it's not just the student population . . . what we're talking here is . . . support was totally lacking this year. I'm really down about teaching.

It is apparent from these teachers' descriptions of their stage that their views of their work are subject to the effects of their work environments. More details about these effects will be examined in a later section on organizational influences. However, it is important to note at this point that these teachers are not entirely negative about teaching and their work. When asked to point out the areas in teaching that she feels good about, Eleanor indicates that she

> . . . is able to get along with other staff members. I'm able to get along with the principal and the director of special education even though I'm not really happy with him. I'm able to work in the community successfully with employers, and I just feel good about myself even though my job is really bothering me.

Kathy also sees positive things about her work and says:

> I feel good about what I do with kids and how they react and about the many different types and styles of kids I've worked with who seem to get turned on and feel happy. I feel good about what I know. I think I've learned a lot, and that's the experience part of what you are, the professional, as well as the educational types of things I've done too.

These two experienced teachers have faced events in their personal lives that have had an impact on their teaching, and it is to the influences from the personal environment that this chapter now turns.

Personal Environmental Influences

Research on Personal Influences and Efficacy

Career stage research (Burke et al. 1987) has indicated that teachers at the career frustration stage characterize their personal lives differently from teachers at other career stages. With respect to personal needs and goals, these teachers report being influenced by a need for security and special needs of family members. Less important for these teachers are the drives to fulfill personal needs, goals, and life aspirations. At the same time, career-frustrated teachers differed from growth-stage teachers in terms of their need for acceptance and support. For these teachers, support from the principal, acceptance by the community, and the relationship of the union with the school board are highly important. Finally, career-frustrated teachers relate to external personal influences differently than do growth-stage teachers. They indicate that work outside the schools, religious activities, friendships, and family finances are important, while the support of professional organizations, research on effective teaching, and family expectations for their time are somewhat less important.

This research suggests that career-frustrated teachers feel significant influences on their work from their personal lives. At this particular time in their lives, they may be facing adjustments to children leaving home or crises with their own or their children's health. They may also have to think about further education for their children and the expense that that entails. Security, as well as monthly income, therefore assumes high priority.

While the preceding suggests influences from the personal side of teachers' lives, both personal characteristics and personality of teachers explain career frustration as well. These aspects begin to account for the role of environmental influences associated with career frustration. The personal constructs that seem so important to the career frustration stage have to do with personal and performance effectiveness and the notion that the individual is an effective human being. This sense of personal effectiveness applies not only to individuals' work but to their lives as well. According to social learning theory (Bandura 1982), this personal effectiveness is learned from interactions with others who provide feedback about performance and success. Success and praise create efficacy in individuals when they perform well and thus provide the incentive to do well in the future.

In teaching, this sense of effectiveness, or *efficacy* as it is called in the literature, translates to a commitment to expend effort to improve student learning and to help the organization. Guskey (1987) found that teachers whose students achieve at higher levels hold the beliefs that they are effective teachers and cause their students' learning, and that teachers' feelings about teaching and themselves as teachers are positively related to their sense of efficacy. Other research has indicated that teachers who feel responsible for and have control over their own destinies are less prone to burnout (Dworkin 1987), report less stress in their work environments (Halpin, Harris, & Halpin 1985), hold and practice more progressive perspectives in teaching (Kremer & Lifmann 1982; Kremer 1982), and practice more inductive rather than prescriptive approaches to classroom discipline.

What is critical about this relatively recent work on efficacy is that it suggests that career-frustrated teachers may be individuals characterized by higher levels of efficacy. They look for evidence of their effectiveness and how to become more effective and find little or no evidence that they are effective or appreciated. Finding little feedback to confirm their concepts of themselves as teachers, they withdraw, isolate themselves, and burn out.

Impact of Personal Environment on Eleanor and Kathy

Eleanor and Kathy both seem representative of the career-frustrated teacher with respect to the influence of family and friends. These significant people provide the support that these teachers need to validate and authenticate feelings about themselves as people and teachers. Eleanor points out that her daughters "are really understanding. They attend the same high school I teach in. I can talk to both of my daughters about what I do and they really know my feelings and are there to listen." She reports also that her peers who teach in special education are also an important source of support and understanding because they teach under similar circumstances.

Kathy reports that living alone has both positive and negative effects. It is positive in that the time she spends in school does not take away from time with family. On the other hand, she says that the negative part is that "when you go to school you have this basket and you keep needing to take things out of it to give to kids. And then you need somewhere to fill it up again in order to keep giving. That's a lot harder to do when you live alone."

In addition, Kathy reveals that peers, colleagues, and friends outside of school are important to her and a positive influence in their support. She notes that many friends "are extremely supportive and positive about the kinds of things I do even though they don't see me doing it. You know, they're saying how great I am as a teacher or how much I do or whatever."

Hobbies, recreation, and outside activities also provide an area of influence for these teachers that provided relief from the frustration of their work. For Eleanor, summer and winter sports are important activities, but her primary activity is walking. "Walking is really important to me. It gets me totally away from concentrating on teaching. It's just my time alone and I have beautiful places to walk. I live in the middle of the woods and I don't even see a car where I walk."

For Kathy, outdoor activities are important in addition to music and political activities.

> I've gotten fairly active in the state level of the union and I'm serving on legislative committees, which means I'm more involved in politics and the educational part of it. I'm meeting with other teachers who are working on this and it gives me a really good perspective on what's happening in education or in the state at least.

This stage, like other stages, is sometimes complicated by crises in teachers' personal lives that have an impact on the teacher and classroom teaching. The crisis may involve family members or the teacher herself. In Eleanor's situation, the crisis involved her foster daughter whom she had to return to her natural parents because she was unable to care for her. Because of her daughter's deteriorating health, she reports:

> There were days that I just could not teach for about two weeks; well, one week she was so sick that we thought she could die at any time. . . . I explained to my students, and even those that have a great deal of difficulty with their behavior were very understanding because they could tell how down I was.

What is apparent from these profiles of teachers at the frustration stage is they seemingly need and are looking for support and recognition. To the extent they are receiving it, it comes from outside of a school's usual channels of administration or promotion. The next section moves to the influence of the organization on this career stage and demonstrates the impact that the organization holds.

Organizational Environmental Influences

For teachers in career frustration, influences from the organizational environment play an extremely important role in their attitudes toward teaching. They also are critical in their implications for teachers' opinions about their professional development needs. Unlike those at earlier stages, these teachers have seemingly formed strong values and opinions about what is important to them in teaching and their work. As the initial profiles have suggested, these teachers often discuss their work and their current stage with an element of surprise, apology, and shock over what they are feeling. Though they are aware of the local, state, and national communities, for these teachers the school environment assumes top priority for its impact on their career stage and the ways they look at teaching.

School Regulations and Management Style

Much of the school effectiveness research indicates how critical the principal's actions are in determining school outcomes. So, too, is the principal's import in the relationship between school policies and teacher career stage. These findings were reinforced in the research of Burke and colleagues (1987) and Dworkin (1987). Dworkin noted that teacher burnout is partially allayed by principals' support. Specifically, this support is defined as principals trying to improve teachers' work and working conditions by setting and enforcing student discipline measures, permitting grievances to be aired, and supplying teachers with feedback on how they are doing. The principal in these actions presumably demonstrates to teachers that someone thinks that what they do is important and is appreciated. When teachers are involved in curriculum decisions and implementation of school policies, these principals' actions seem to buffer teachers from isolation and lack of power and, thereby, forestall burnout.

Rosenholtz (1985) has proposed a model of organizational conditions that elaborates the key role of principals in effective schools. This model indicates that principal certainty that school achievement can be raised mobilizes a sequence of rational planning around institutional goals for attaining higher school achievement. This sequence includes recruiting and socializing teachers to these goals; minimizing classroom distractions that interfere with goal attainment; monitoring performance and providing assistance in teaching; developing cohesiveness around teaching achievements; and including teachers in shared decision making, problem solving, and experimentation. The outcome of this sequence is an organizational climate that seemingly helps to block the emotional components that characterize burnout.

Rosenholtz (1987a) also has begun to detail the organizational conditions created by state reforms that permit or prevent personal efficacy to operate and maintain. The results of this study of the effects of Tennessee's minimal competency testing program for students and the career ladder program for teachers indicate that these reforms seemed to decrease teachers' feelings of efficacy because of the time needed to handle additional paperwork documenting testing and teaching. State competencies were often different from district competencies, and teachers perceived that their judgments about pupil needs were being supplanted by state authority, a threat to their professional autonomy.

The preceding discussion has suggested that teachers at the career frustration stage are greatly influenced by the schools in which they work, especially by principals and their management styles. Influences from the organization and the larger environment are next explored from the teachers' perspectives.

Organizational and Environmental Influences on Eleanor and Kathy

Both teachers report that the organizational environment plays a large part in how they feel about teaching and their work. The role of the local teacher union is viewed as very positive, though there may be negative aspects of unionization as well. Kathy says:

> Unions are both positive and negative. I say positive in that they make sure that so many little things are there for us, like planning time or sick days. On the other hand, because they are out there, they are protecting people that you know shouldn't be protected. And these are the teachers who are pulling the rest of us down with them. . . . I'm really glad there's a union; on the other hand there are things that I wish we could just be individuals on and work out in an agreeable fashion.

Eleanor's positive views on the union's effects are partly due to her experiences initiating a grievance procedure. She reports:

> I wanted to go to a conference and the other teacher also wanted to go to the same conference. The administration said no even though there was nothing in the master contract that said two teachers from the same unit couldn't go. They said there was nothing in the contract that said two could go so I filed a grievance . . . and we both got to go. Couldn't they see that it was for my own and my students' benefit? Everyone had lived with this policy for years and I was the first to file a grievance. I think this was the start of the way I now feel about teaching and my work.

Another positive influence on these teachers when available is the opportunity for professional development within the school district. Kathy notes that her school district

> really has good inservice programs offering a lot of workshops on professional topics. I think that we have more of these than other districts and that's good. They offer a day off and get a sub so that you can attend. I don't know how common that is, but it means a lot to me. The district also provides a visiting day so that you can go somewhere else to see what's happening there.

With respect to local, state, and national influences on their teaching, teachers at this stage may differ considerably. Kathy reports that with respect to public opinion she "does not feel it so much. It doesn't affect me. I don't know, I guess I don't listen to it."

On the other hand, Eleanor seems to think about local issues in education and to a lesser extent the impact of the state. For her:

> Locally, there are a lot of people who look at you as being overpaid; I feel that a lot in the community where I live with a lot of retirees and tourists, and taxes are high. I guess at the state level I sometimes wonder what the Department of Public Instruction is doing with all the requirements, and that bothers me.

Peer and colleague relations have been mentioned earlier as primary support for these teachers in their professional and personal activity. Feedback and help in their problems seem to be the positive information that these teachers seek. Eleanor reports:

> In the high school where I teach, we have another LD teacher plus a TMR and an ED teacher as well; all of us try really hard to work closely whenever there may be a problem. We all work alone and are good friends, see each other outside of school; and then I have a lot of relationships with other teachers also. I'm primarily a special-ed teacher but I really feel that I am on an equal level with most of the staff I work with.

As indicated earlier, the principal seemingly plays a key role in how teachers feel about themselves. As part of the organizational influences having an impact on teachers, principals provide the feedback from an authority about the teacher's teaching effectiveness and provides reinforcement for the quality of work being done. Both teachers at the frustration stage reflect the importance of this administrator in how they currently feel about teaching.

Kathy credits her current feelings to a new building administrator:

> What we're talking about here is administrators needing to support and talk to teachers. It was totally lacking this year . . . not even a hello, which would have been nice. Even though I'm secure with what I do in the classroom, I still need to hear from my supervisor that I'm doing all right.

Eleanor describes her situation in very different terms. Though the issues seem to involve support, unlike Kathy's need for feedback on her classroom, Eleanor's issue involves being consulted as a professional and having input on school decisions. She has not been consulted about the type of teacher they need to find to replace a colleague who has burned out and resigned. She says of her supervisor:

He does not listen to me . . . it's like talking to the wind. . . . I get real frustrated with that because I've worked enough with teacher aides in the past and I value their ideas. And you know, just because I happen to be a great teacher doesn't mean that someone working as my assistant doesn't have many fine thoughts and ideas.

Given the impact of the organizational environment on their work lives, this chapter now turns to the growth needs of career-frustrated teachers.

Professional Growth Needs

This section first examines the directions for growth suggested by teacher roles, as has been done in preceding chapters. It also includes a discussion of incentive preferences of teachers at this stage because many of the preferred incentives have to do with professional growth activities. The concluding section of the chapter turns to teacher commentary to illustrate the kinds of proposals suggested for personal and professional development.

Teacher as Learner

One form of teacher as learner has to do with teaching skills and demonstrable teaching effectiveness and relates to the concepts of efficacy discussed earlier. For example, Guskey's work (1989) reports the changes in the attitudes and perceptions of teachers who have worked with mastery learning. Teachers trained and then supported during implementation reported that they liked teaching more, felt more effective as teachers, and believed they could meet the challenge of various instructional problems. Some also described this experience as a rebirth of teaching excitement that years of failure and frustration in their classes had nearly extinguished.

What this work indicates is that frustration-stage teachers may benefit from training that reskills their teaching. This outcome seemingly relates to the efficacy construct described earlier; the outcomes of reskilling would be classrooms where student learning and attitude change are demonstrable. As Guskey (1989) indicates in his model of teacher change, it is knowledge of results about teaching effectiveness that provides the feedback responsible for teacher attitude change, not a commitment to or an involvement in program decision making.

Career stage research (Burke et al. 1987) has demonstrated that the incentive preferences of career-frustrated teachers differ from those of teachers at various other stages. For these teachers, promotion to administration, a pleasant physical environment, early retirement options, paid sabbatical leaves, released time for professional activities, and influence in school decision making were all viewed as appropriate incentives. Also appropriate were concrete incentives related to teaching performance such as recognition by organizations, aide support, support for research and writing, and advancement opportunity. Incentives also took the form of recognition and praise preferences and included verbal praise from supervisors, leadership opportunities, and flexible work days.

For these teachers, time, money, and professional activity—incentives preferred by teachers at other stages—are notably less significant. Instead, what seems preferred by these teachers are those incentives having to do with recognition of personal and professional effectiveness. In some instances these incentives can be viewed as rewards. It is tempting to believe that creating new leadership roles for teachers in the schools, then placing these teachers in these roles, would change their attitudes and perceptions of effectiveness. Preparation for these roles would fall under teacher-as-learner as well.

Professional Growth Needs of Eleanor and Kathy

With respect to our teachers' perceptions of their personal and professional growth needs, Eleanor and Kathy reveal self-perceptions that are both sensitive and representative of the career-frustrated teacher. At the same time, however, neither teacher indicates a need for new or different classroom skills, rather more simply the recognition that each possesses those skills.

Eleanor remarks that her needs are personal rather than professional:

> I need to be able to find some innovative ways to begin my year because I am really afraid of going through nine months feeling the way I did last year. I felt like I started to complain, I hear myself complaining, and I can't stop. I need to sit down and see what I can do and look over professionally what I can do and what I'm going to do. Personally I really feel good about myself but . . .

Kathy, on the other hand, looks for change as a way to meet her personal and professional growth needs. She says:

> At this point I think I really need a change, a break, or a reverse. I've toyed with the idea of taking a year off next year, a career exploration leave [an unfunded district program for teachers seeking alternatives], but I can't come up with enough money to live on. I need to get away from what I do—the routine.

Another alternative Kathy considers is a different job. Her description of the job she is considering contains a number of incentives that teachers at this stage say they prefer:

I've been talking with this book company and what the job is sounds real positive; you know, going to schools and talking, doing some workshops and displays. It's not really hard-sell so it's maintaining the customers and what they need. You get to travel and talk to adults; it's a flexible schedule and it sounds wonderful, but they want only a part-time person. I'd like to find out what a year away from teaching is like. Then I'd know whether I was ready to come back to the classroom because it was really meant for me to teach.

Kathy also indicates that new roles in teaching would be appropriate for her both in terms of the changes she is seeking and as incentives through recognition that they would provide. Kathy says that these new roles, like peer supervision, coaching, mentoring, and curiculum development and leadership especially tied to a career ladder, would be meaningful to her. These changes "would do it. They would be really big for me. And the reason is changing the routine and feeling valued outside of the classroom. It's feeling that I could give something to someone because it was valued and I had it."

As noted in the earlier section on burnout, one of the feelings associated with burnout is isolation. For Eleanor, workshops are a major incentive. While they provide her with information she finds generally useful, more important is the contact they provide with other special-education teachers. A very important part of this contact is the feedback they provide to her about her programs. "When I think I don't have many really big things going on in my classroom. I find that I really do compared to a lot of the secondary programs I hear about. So I feel really good about that when I talk to other teachers."

Another incentive that is focused on by these teachers concerns evaluation. For these teachers, evaluation in the form of constructive feedback would serve as an incentive because it seemingly would provide the kind of affirmation of their effectiveness that they are seeking. Kathy says:

I wish I had evaluation. I had principals that were required to do it every so often and I never thought it was a help to me. . . . I would like more detailed evaluations instead of "This is good, this is why you're good, this is what you're doing that makes you good." I would like to know what I could do to be better. Being an experienced teacher, I think I would like that.

Eleanor perceives that evaluations might function to give her feedback, but not in quite the same way that Kathy indicated.

At the end of the year I hadn't had my evaluation and I wanted it. They said they'd do it, not that I care that much whether anyone evaluates me, but I thought "Does anyone care? Does anyone care that we bang our heads against the wall?" And one day, the last day of school for my seniors, there it was.

What is apparent from these discussions of incentives and rewards is that these teachers are looking for rewards that demonstrate their competence, competence visible not primarily to others but rather competence felt by themselves that comes when someone recognizes them individually for their abilities and their work.

Given these growth needs in the personal and professional areas, it is time to consider the kinds of support structures and mechanisms that are appropriate for teachers at this stage.

Support Systems for Career-Frustrated Teachers

In discussing influences and incentives, the career-frustrated teachers indicated the need for support. This support was defined in terms of people to listen to their problems and frustrations and to share their ideas and experiences. The principal is a key person to provide this support in the form of involving teachers in decision making, giving oral and written feedback and praise for teaching, and participation in activities at the school, district, or community. Encouraging teachers to take a leadership role in new strategies and providing them with support for courses and workshops or released time for peer coaching or other activities would help bring these teachers back to a growth stage of the cycle. In addition, support must be provided to build teaching skills and competencies that are lacking. Deficiencies in performance may be important factors that lead to feeling of frustration.

As developed here, the major theme emerging from career frustration is, as the name implies, frustration over a lack of recognition. This frustration seems to derive from teaching effectiveness that goes unrecognized by administators or from teaching that teachers are hoping to improve but receive no guidance about.

For these teachers, a change in the organizational roles of the schools may be apropriate both as an incentive as well as a way to reward and recognize effectiveness. Kathy sums up the import of this organizational change for her when she says that of all possible school support mechanisms

> if I were to get something that really makes a difference, change in the organizational structure would do it for me . . . career ladders, differentiated staffing, team teaching. Administration is not for me, but I do have a lot to offer and a ladder, lattice, or differentiated staffing would provide the mechanism.

Summary

This chapter has discussed the characteristics of career-frustrated teachers and related these to the literature on teacher burnout and teacher efficacy. Though selected personal characteristics of teachers suggested origins of frustration, the nature of the teaching environment was considered as well. The portrait emerging of the career-frustrated teacher is one of an upset and somewhat angry individual who is frustrated at the lack of recognition rather than the lack of extrinsic reward. It seems possible also that frustration may evolve from lack of teaching effectiveness and failure to find the support that would improve teaching success. This chapter suggests that the career-frustrated teacher is suffering the beginnings of burnout but cares about students enough to find rewards in working with them. The career-frustrated teacher has not yet withdrawn from the job of teaching but is at high risk for doing so. The nature of the support from supervisors, principals, and peers may be crucial in determining if career-frustrated teachers enter furture periods of stagnancy or exit or, alternatively, have their enthusiasm rekindled and become enthusiastic, committed professionals.

CHAPTER EIGHT

Stability

JAY R. PRICE

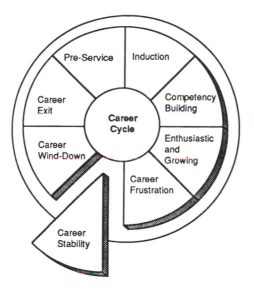

Stable teachers have plateaued in their careers. Some have become stagnant and have resigned themselves to putting in "a fair day's work for a fair day's pay." These teachers are doing what is expected of them, but little more. They may be doing an acceptable job, but are not committed to the pursuit of excellence and growth. These teachers are often going through the motions to fulfill their terms of contract. Others at this stable stage can be characterized as maintaining, with selective enthusiasm for teaching. They are doing a competent job, but lack enthusiasm and commitment to continued growth and pursuit of excellence. Teachers at this stable stage are in the process of disengaging from their commitment to teaching.

The period of stability in the career cycle often occurs during a teacher's mid-life and mid-career. It may be a time of consolidation and renewal, a time of stagnation, or a time of bitter resignation. It is a period of time in teachers' lives that may follow frustration or burnout or a time when some reassess their original motives for entering teaching and reaffirm their levels of satisfaction with teaching as an occupation. For some, it may be a time of coping and learning new mechanisms for managing to stay in teaching, putting in their time while waiting for retirement. Stability, contrary to its name, may be a particularly problematic time in teachers' lives paralleling the changes brought about by various life events. It is a time when individuals may no longer be tied to the immediate demands of a young family or their own youth but again a time to reflect on the meaning of work, its worth, and rewards. Teachers at this stage are no longer the neophytes described in preceding chapters but frequently are seasoned hands. As mature individuals, they generally are people who have been in one school for an extended period of time and have experienced the work of teaching. They have experienced also the effects of public policies and bureaucracies on teaching as well as the impact that negative waves of public opinion and the vagaries of politically motivated reform have on their feelings. They "know the ropes."

What is critical for teachers during this period of their lives and careers is the opportunity for renewal to occur that is experimental and novel in nature and under their own control. This sort of development implies that teachers will find themselves in a flexible environment with sufficient resources to experiment and to succeed as well as fail. At this point in their careers, teachers may move into patterns of maintenance, stagnation, or renewed growth. Environmental factors are crucial in determining which direction they will go.

Views of Stability

Several perspectives have been used in the literature on teacher stages to conceptualize teachers' work lives and the latter stages of development. One perspective is the work of Fuller (Fuller & Bown 1975), which identified clusters of concerns or issues that characterized the process of becoming a teacher. The so-called *impact stage* is the final stage where the individual pupil becomes the focus of the teacher's concerns about appropriateness of curriculum, social and emotional needs, and instructional methods. Not all teachers reach this stage, and many seemingly settle into comfortable routines.

Time also has been used as a framework for characterizing the changes that occur among teachers. Burden's (1982) *mature stage* occurred at five years and beyond in a teacher's work experience and described teachers who were secure and confident in their roles, were willing to try new methods, and were concerned about the welfare of their pupils.

Using a similar time perspective, Newman (see Newman, Burden, & Applegate 1980) found that, unlike those teachers in the Burden study, second-decade teachers reported increased dissatisfaction. They changed grade levels or subject areas to reenergize their outlook on teaching. Other research has generally paralleled the findings for this latter stage of a teaching career, especially with respect to attitude changes, morale, and need to recharge the commitments to teaching (Newman, Burden, & Applegate 1980; Unruh & Turner 1970; Gregorc 1973).

A third position from which to view stability in the teacher career cycle is from the perspective of cognitive/developmental theory. In very general terms this theory posits developmental differences among individuals with respect to complexity of thought and action in such areas as interpersonal relations and moral/ethical alternatives. At higher, more complex levels, individuals are more capable of flexible, adaptive behavior, taking full responsibility for their actions. At lower levels, individuals seemingly function according to convention and rules without much consideration of alternatives (Hunt 1975; Kohlberg 1968). With respect to teaching and stability, the higher-level teacher is most likely to be open to new experiences. This level teacher views all knowledge as in the process of becoming, yet never complete. At the same time the teacher can take on alternative perspectives and consider the student's point of view. Utilizing this theoretical perspective, Glassberg and Oja (1981, 1980) determined that teacher conceptual levels were changeable to higher level perspectives through the use of such strategies as role taking, reflection, and instructor support/ supervision. Though little supporting evidence is available, it is implicit in the application of such theories to teaching that teachers at the highest cognitive levels make the "best" classroom teachers.

More recently, Huberman (1989) reported in a study of phases in the teacher's professional life cycle that stability might take on several forms. A high proportion of teachers indicated a progression of phases leading to either positive or defensive focusing or disenchantment at this time of their careers. *Positive focusing* referred to teachers specializing in one area or set of tasks, focusing on one group of students, or following their own interests. *Defensive focusing,* on the other hand, referred to teachers who focused on their own interests but were traditionalists who disapproved of changes their schools had encountered; these teachers were seemingly looking to derive some form of satisfaction from their remaining years in teaching. Finally, *disenchantment* refers to an actual bitterness about teaching felt by teachers in this study. This feeling evolved from several sources, including reform efforts, paperwork, administration's failures, and students themselves.

Other data from this study indicate, as might be predicted from the life cycle literature, that these teachers decreased in their engagement and activity levels in teaching, becoming more passive, serene, confident, and self-accepting. The impact of teachers who fit this profile remains to be investigated.

The remainder of this chapter concentrates on the stability stage of the career cycle by examining the impact of both personal and organizational influences. Incentives for this stage are discussed, along with needs and implications for possible support programs. The following section introduces the teachers who exemplify the various types of stability.

Teacher Profiles

Chad, Jerry, and Adam

Chad

Chad is 41 years old, married with two children, and has been teaching high school social studies for sixteen years in a small midwestern city whose regional school district serves rural and suburban students from lower to middle income levels. The local state university holds a major educational and cultural influence in the life of the community and Chad received a master's degree from the institution. Chad has received the teacher of the year award from the university's history department. His professional memberships include local, state, and national affiliations with the NEA as well as local, state, and national professional subject area organizations. His outside interests include strong leadership of a local historical society.

Chad is at the level of stability in his life and his teaching career. He recognizes that teaching now is different from what teaching once was for him. Chad points out that after sixteen years of teaching:

> Teaching is still a ball. I enjoy doing the reading, the preparation and all that sort of stuff. In fact, this has been one of the most fun semesters we ever had in terms of the senior class just now graduating—their emotional maturity and being personable but maybe not being the brightest. I guess for my first twelve years, maybe less than that, I used to bring tons and tons of work home all the time. Paper correcting, tests, etc., and every weekend after about nine years I began to develop intense headaches. It got to the migraine level where I was physically sick. It would start on Friday night; Sunday night when I had to gear up again, it would go away. So I'd spend the whole weekend sick. After a while I chose not to take my work home—if it gets done at work, it gets done; if it doesn't, it doesn't. It always manages to get done, so I don't have a problem with it, but I just stopped bringing it home and my headaches went away.

As indicated earlier, this period of the mid-career teachers' life is a time of stability for some teachers, which means a fair day's work but nothing more. The teacher has settled into comfortable routines that meet the letter if not the spirit of the contract, and teaching has become just another job. Change is something that is not expected nor anticipated with any degree of excitement. Change also is viewed as unnecessary. At this stage the teacher has effectively divorced the actions of teaching from student outcomes, which are viewed as being beyond the teacher's impact except for certain kinds of students—those whose home environments are appropriate and supportive. Classroom excitement is gone. For teachers at this stage, teaching is attractive because it provides a secure income with benefits like time and medical care affording the opportunity to work outside of school. In many ways this stage validates a stereotype that public opinion holds of teachers—teaching is an easy job with great security, little responsibility, and summers off.

Jerry

Jerry is 45, married with three children, and has been teaching middle school mathematics for twenty years. His middle school is located in a small city in the Midwest, serves a regional population of rural and small-city students, and enrolls about 800 students. He received both baccalaureate and master's degrees at the local state university but has taken no coursework since earning his master's five years ago. He belongs to a state math teachers' association but is inactive. His major activity when he is not teaching is his real estate sales position. He had previously tried construction, creating his own small firm, but found that he could not manage both building and teaching at the same time. He subsequently studied for his broker's license and works as a part-time sales associate during the year but full-time during the summer months. Jerry clearly exemplifies the teacher who during mid-life views teaching as a stable job. He says about his career:

> Teaching is not anything like what they prepared me for during college or my master's program. It was basically a lot of theory that had little relevance to the school I was working in. I mean the instructors hadn't been in a classroom with middle school kids in years, if ever, and I was pretty much left on my own to figure out what to do. Math in middle schools is math, pretty general stuff with basic algebra thrown in for the more advanced kids, but it never really changes. . . . I was excited when I first started teaching and I still enjoy seeing kids learn, but it seems that fewer and fewer kids these days come to school ready to learn . . . and they don't care about the work that math requires for learning. Because of all the problems which I'm not equipped to handle, teaching isn't as much fun as it used to be.

Adam

Adam, on the other hand, exemplifies the stagnancy stage that some enthusiastic teachers may move into as a result of policies in the organizational environment. In this case the policy disrupted the teacher's sense of his own effectiveness. His recognition of stagnancy is shown by his remarks that he is recovering slowly from this stage. More details about this second stage are given in a later section on organizational influences.

> I think I've gone through two stages in my teaching career. The first one . . . I was ready to give my life to the cause. . . . So then I went into the second phase where it didn't matter what I did . . . so long as I got the teaching done during the allotted time. It's like I went through a separation from the job and now I'm reaffiliating myself . . . it's much healthier.

This career stage is subject also to influence from events occurring in teachers' lives outside of schools. Each of these teachers has faced events that have had an impact on the way they view their teaching careers. It is to the personal environment that this chapter now turns.

Personal Environmental Influences

Teachers who are at the stability stage of their careers are responsive to personal environmental influences in ways that make them similar to and, at the same time, dissimilar from the earlier-stage teachers. Their families play an important part in their lives and have an impact on their professional lives. These teachers have often experienced events and even crises that have played a part in their professional lives and the ways they view teaching. At this stage, too, hobbies and avocational interests may play an important part and influence their lives as teachers.

Family Influences

Teachers at this stage of their careers frequently have established families, and some still have young children. Many may be attempting to share the parenting tasks with a spouse who also works outside the home. This role demands more of the teacher's time to shuttle children from appointment to appointment or to provide at-home child care. Teachers at this stage often express the desire to experience quality time with their children, perhaps influenced by the conviction that problems they see in their own classrooms are due to lack of effective parenting. They are adjusting to the growth and accomplishments of their own children and begin to understand and apply the relevant ideas to their own classrooms. The family at this stage often provides the main source of support and interest and receives top priority in many teachers' lives.

Adult and Developmental Influences

Unlike earlier-stage teachers who have many personal goals and objectives in mind, teachers at this stage generally have reached a level of experience where their values, beliefs, and goals have become established. Many teachers want to be effective and recognized for their effectiveness. This does not necessarily mean that they wish to move into administrative or other leadership roles. Rather, they believe they are capable of positively influencing children, want to do more of it and be recognized for it, and want an environment that is supportive of their work. Consequently, as research (Burke et al. 1987) has demonstrated, teachers at this stage, more so than during earlier stages, are concerned more about organizational environmental matters than about personal influences, apart from the family issues described above. The impact of these will be described in a later section on organizational influences.

Some stable-level teachers may be experiencing aspects of mid-life crises (Sheehy 1976; Levinson et al. 1978). Individuals at this point of their lives frequently face personal crises related to their feelings of mortality. This is a time of reflection and evaluation of previous decisions made about career, family, and values. The introspection and questioning that occur during this adult life period sometimes result in settling into a stable, maintaining period. Some evolve from this experience renewed and recommitted to teaching, others use the reassessment as an opportunity to move on to new career options or opportunities, and still others stagnate for long periods of time.

Crises

For many teachers this period is a time of increasing physical problems and growing recognition of their own mortality. Coupled with possible changes in family relationships due to older children leaving home, teachers at this stage are coming to grips with decreased job mobility and increasing need for job security. At the same time they may be creating a new set of values that will be more compatible with the changes that are occurring in their organizational and professional environments. Though outwardly stable in terms of work, this mid-life period may be an unsettling and unsettled period in their personal and professional lives.

Cumulative Experiences and Avocational Interests

Hobbies and interests have a high level of influence for teachers at this stage. Even among those who are stagnant and seemingly unengaged by teaching, out-of-school activities are recognized as time that permits recuperation from the stress of daily activities. Some teachers pursue avocational interests as a way to seek personal need fulfillment they are not experiencing in their work. The esteem and personal satisfaction from outside activities may go a long way to compensate for their feelings of stagnancy on their jobs.

For other teachers, outside interests may be a source of added income that permits the extras a single family income alone could not provide. Real estate sales is a prime example of this aspect of avocations. For other teachers it is a way of demonstrating their competence away from schools.

In summary, the personal environmental influences of family and life stage seem to play a role in teachers' outlooks on teaching at stability. They are affected by health concerns, family and home pressures, and decreasing job mobility as well as hobbies and avocational interests. The following sections take examples from stability-stage teachers to elucidate their perspectives on influences and professional growth needs.

Impact of Personal Environmental Influences on Chad and Jerry

Chad

The extent to which a disciplinary interest extends to a hobby and community service interest is exemplified by Chad's leadership as president of a local historical society. Though his academic area is Asian history, it was virtually impossible for him to practice Asian history in his local teaching context, but he was able to use the training to dig into his own state's history. He is now teaching state history and pursuing local history as well because

> teaching history in a classroom doesn't let you pursue history in a hands-on sort of way because of the nature or type of people you're dealing with. You don't get a chance to do a lot of the nuts and bolts of doing history, the primary sources, buildings, what have you, whereas state and local history does provide this. So, I get the same satisfaction of doing history while at the same time dealing with teaching.

What is clear from Chad's remarks is that his dedication to doing history carries over to his classroom; it has even benefited other schools as well. With funding from a state humanities grant, he has packaged local artifacts in several display trunks together with a script for use among district elementary and middle school classes to promote awareness of local and state history.

Jerry

Jerry's business experience plays a part in his teaching in that it provides a way to make his subject matter, math, more relevant to his students. He reports:

I'll usually pull examples from real estate of how math applies in the real world. Sometimes, for like evaluating or estimating, I'll give them a problem about how to come up with appraising a property or other times I'll create some story problems so they'll figure out how to find out taxes on property. Some of the kids have gone on to figure out assessments and taxes on their parents' homes.

What comes through the interviews with these stability-stage teachers is their accommodation to teaching as a career and their varying degrees of success in accommodating. They are notable for the fact that, when they are presented with opportunities, they have taken them, seemingly believing in their own abilities to be in control and make things happen. From the professional development standpoint these people, at least those who are selectively enthusiastic, need little incentive to go after those things that interest them since doing so is part of their satisfaction in teaching. For those who are stagnant, though many have families and outside business interests, the issue of professional development raises serious questions about the obligations and boundaries of educational institutions to helping or managing their employees. Though only hinted at in the interviews, the suggestion exists that freedom to experiment and recognition for such may be a key to alleviating stagnancy.

Organizational Environmental Influences

For stable teachers, influences from the organizational environment are critical to their attitudes about their teaching and the occupation and may be crucial to their attitudes about their professional development needs. Many stability-stage teachers have firm values and have established long-term commitments that they are acting on and attempting to fulfill. It is the environment that plays the primary role in determining how well they can perform and accomplish their goals.

Public Trust

Stability-stage teachers seemingly have seen too little impact from national levels and are more concerned about public opinion at the local and state levels. At the local level, stability-stage teachers are concerned about support for comfortable levels of salary but are more emphatic about their concerns for improving the conditions under which they teach.

As an instrument of public opinion, the state also concerns these teachers because of its mandate powers regarding curriculum and time allocations. The interviews indicate that, for the most part, teachers see the state regulations as responding to public opinion but not meeting the real needs of their students.

A particular issue for these teachers concerning local opinion is parental trust—specifically, whether parents accept teachers' judgments about what is best for their children. While many teachers encourage parent involvement in their programs, some believe that parents want more control over what their children are doing in classes. This involvement is perceived as nonsupportive, stressful, and a vote of no-confidence in their teaching. It is an environmental influence that is especially aggravating when the parent seemingly supports the child instead of the authority of the teacher and the school.

School Regulations and Management Style

The major influences from the organizational environment come from the school's policies, regulations, administrative staff, and colleagues. Of these, career stage research has demonstrated that for teachers at this stage, principal's management style, philosophy, and to a lesser extent his/her support are critically important for teachers (Burke et al. 1987). One form of support for teachers comes with teaching assignments. Teachers at the middle and high school levels seemingly have achieved the seniority to determine within limits what and whom they will teach. To a lesser extent this seniority policy holds in elementary schools as well. In part, a principal who seeks and permits this assignment policy to operate will be positively reviewed by teachers at this stage. Furthermore, it is this policy that helps to promote the trust between administrators and their faculty.

As indicated by the teacher interviews, a second component promoting positive relationships between administration and teachers at this stage is policy decisions concerning the time and money to support teachers' experimentation and changes within the schools, especially regarding curriculum and student control policies. Administration receives praise when district policies ensure that substitutes and support dollars are available for attendance at conferences.

Principals also are praised if their management style is consultative, respecting and soliciting teachers' opinions in running certain aspects of the schools. For example, for many of the teachers at this stage, evaluation is a particularly aversive experience because it is based on rarely performed observations; therefore, it is not viewed as a necessarily valid or reliable process. Principals who respect the inadequacy of infrequent observations and yet somehow recognize teachers' worth will be viewed favorably because they are building and maintaining trust with faculty.

Professional Organizations and Unions

As indicated in the examples that follow, professional organizations play a different role for stable teachers depending upon whether the teacher is energized about teaching or falling into stagnation. These groups seem to play only a minor role in the lives of teachers who are stagnant. For the selectively enthusiastic secondary teacher, state or regional organizations devoted to subject matter areas receive much praise. At the elementary level, selectively enthusiastic teachers attribute much importance to local or state associations in reading, math, or science. The main reason that teachers at this stage seem to respect these groups is that they function in two ways. The first is that they provide a source of information about subject matter and new methods that is generally unavailable to these teachers in their local schools. Thus, these organizations function in much the same way coursework did when these teachers were working on graduate degrees, which most of them have completed.

A second way these organizations function is to provide a forum where teachers may share ideas and common interests. If their school settings do not provide this site or people who are interested, then the meetings of these organizations serve this purpose well. In all, these conferences help teachers feel that they are stimulated and not outdated but able still to learn and apply new information.

Interestingly, unlike those teachers who are selectively enthusiastic, stagnant teachers see little or no importance in, or influence from, these organizations. They have had little contact with them. Although they know that they exist, they show no indication that these avenues may be appropriate for them or an antidote to their decreasing interest in teaching.

Unions, for the most part, receive little attention from stable teachers other than their gratitude. These teachers are grateful for their union's help in providing a respectable wage, increased benefits and job security, as well as the union's increasing interest in working conditions. At the same time, however, many of these teachers express the opinion that unions are protecting teachers who deserve dismissal for ineffective teaching, but they also believe that the unions have little to do with the professional development of teachers.

For stagnant and stable teachers, union leadership is not a consideration, while for the selectively enthusiastic teacher, union leadership seems like a viable option. It may well be that stagnant teachers view most unions as avoiding any real change, but selectively enthusiastic teachers see participation in unions as an opportunity to create education as they would wish it to be. This change then is another opportunity to show their effectiveness as educators.

Organizational influences have included the important role of the principal and administration as well as colleagues and professional organizations. The examples below detail more specific instances of these support categories.

Impact of Influences from the Organizational Environment on Teachers

The organizational environment plays a major role in determining how stable teachers view teaching and their work in schools.

Chad notes the positive effects of the relationships in his department. "My department is generally very well read, very well prepared. We get into some really good discussions in our field on a whole broad spectrum of backgrounds and ideas. In terms of my department, there is lots of mutual support."

Adam expresses his appreciation of the principals whom he has taught under for their even-handed approach to evaluation.

> I've had three principals in the school I've been in since I started teaching and I got good evaluations from all of them . . . but I'm not sure that the first one really ever knew what I was doing. And now we've been Hunterized and I'm totally opposed to that. How can any single observation like that show what your teaching's like. . . . I just play the game on observation days.

What does not receive praise from these teachers is any regulation or policy that remains unexplained to the teachers or seems unjustifiable. Adam's experience of stagnation seemingly has been induced by a district policy of teacher transfer. Apparently, teachers are not consulted about transfers within the district's schools and are given no advance notice about the transfers until the last week of the school year. Though the union is negotiating the process of transfer, no solution has yet evolved. Adam, facing a second transfer, indicates that his second stage in teaching, the stagnation phase,

> came on when I found out I was transferred the first time. . . . I was doing things like computerizing science and other things at school; I was a workaholic for about fourteen years. And then for about the first year of my transfer I just went in from 8:00 to 4:00. . . . I thought I was a good teacher my first fourteen years, but then all of a sudden they tell you you're being moved; they don't tell you why. To me the process is not well thought through. You hear four or five different stories why you're being moved and you're wondering. You never get the right story. Anyway, I feel uncomfortable teaching.

Apart from the negative impact of administration's policy on teachers' feelings, these teachers also recognize the role of the state as it affects their teaching. Unlike the competency-building teacher, teachers at this stage are not necessarily convinced of the worth of increasing state regulation. Adam says:

> Increased teaching load and paper work I would say have a negative effect. For example, in elementary you teach reading, English, spelling, handwriting, science, social studies, health, math, the Drug and Alcohol Abuse Program, the Personal Safety Program, environmental education, computers, and we just keep adding and adding. Some of it's getting integrated into the regular curriculum, but I'm feeling increasing pressure toward the

total child, with the increasing curriculum load, and not being free to give more time to the total child, especially when the child is having personal problems and I'm trying to help them out.

State regulations and commensurate paper work are not the only source of pressures on these teachers. Having been in the occupation for several years, they have begun to reflect on changes they believe they have seen in society and the impact it has had on their classrooms. In large part these changes are tied to their perceptions of students and their parents. Chad indicates his perception that the public in general does not seem to have a high regard for teachers—

except that the public wants teachers to do everything, everything from teaching their kid to parenting, and everything in between. . . . I think that is in part why I'm getting less and less time to do whatever I'm in the classroom to do. If I wanted to be a guidance counselor I would have gone into guidance.

Adam reports a somewhat different version of a similar view of changes. He indicates that in the past several years, parents are more and more involved in their children's education, which he appreciates. However, he notes:

there are certain parents who will call you and question you no matter what you do. It could be your typing, poor quality of your dittoes, sometimes even censoring the materials I read to the class. There are so many parents who come in like they're going to run their own show.

The opportunity for leadership in schools is somewhat limited by the small number of leadership positions. Nevertheless, the union is one source of opportunity, and teachers at this stage are interested in this role. Chad, whose area is history, was asked to write a new constitution for the local union and subsequently, became very active. He reports:

The union has had a positive influence on my teaching, surprisingly enough. After writing the constitution, I moved up to building representative and eventually the president of the local. I had the distinct honor of being the president at the time we went on strike and my house was strike headquarters. . . . It did generate quite a bit of leadership potential in the sense that I had to act quickly and a lot of things were going on.

In contrast to those teachers who are selectively enthusiastic, teachers who are stagnant seemingly do not belong to educational organizations other than the union. Even with in the union, they do not see membership as an opportunity or chance to alter routines or see professional organizations as a way of influencing their perspectives. The professional growth needs and strategies for affecting professional growth of teachers at this stage of stability will be explored in the next section.

Professional Growth Needs

As in the preceding chapters' discussions of stage-related professional growth needs, this chapter follows the directions for growth suggested by teachers' roles. These roles, as indicated earlier, are a synthesis of teacher responsibilities suggested by discussions about career ladders, differentiated staffing, and master teacher plans. They include the teacher as learner, coach, teacher educator, mentor, and leader.

Teacher as Learner

The most notable aspect of stable/maintaining teachers' comments on their own development is their frequent reference to what they do for their own learning. Some of these teachers view themselves as life-long learners, and they are prime examples of the learner portrayed in the adult learning literature (e.g., Levine 1989). An important consideration for teachers in this learner role then is that, because of their narrow focus, they believe that they know the needs of their particular schools and therefore can provide direction for themselves and others in school improvement efforts. Some of these teachers may prefer traditional coursework when larger change efforts are undertaken such as at-risk or cooperative learning programs. Others may prefer reading or workshop attendance and working on their own, waiting to exchange ideas at a later time when they are comfortable with new ideas.

One preferred incentive among these teachers is having more available time for visiting, observing, and interacting with other teachers. This activity is consistent with the idea of teacher-as-learner in that the object of these visitations is to obtain new ideas and to view how others handle similar information and problems. Such visitation would also provide opportunity for learning by those who are visited because the purpose of the visitation is interaction as well.

A second perspective on teacher-as-learner is provided by opportunities for sabbaticals. These are ranked highly by teachers as important incentives, though infrequently used and not often available. Nevertheless, instituting sabbaticals for public school teachers would provide opportunity to reenergize teachers to explore new areas and update skills. Sabbaticals might also afford the opportunity for stagnant teachers to reenergize through periods of study and reflection on the problems of stagnancy or career reexploration.

Peer Supervision/Coaching/Mentoring

Some stability-stage teachers will serve as peer supervisors, coaches, or mentors for newer staff as well as more experienced staff. Experienced teachers have been serving these roles for years, as teachers new to the occupation have been inducted and socialized into the occupation. The point to be made here again, however, is that due to their experience, some of these teachers have a great deal to offer. If these roles are formalized and resources provided to make the roles possible, the traditional responsibilities that principals have assumed may be more consistently enacted by involving more people. This higher level of involvement may lead to greater school improvement.

While the preceding roles do not separately fit the traditional definition of needs, they are presented here as suggestions for ways that stable teachers may be able to meet a universal need—recognition. Research on teacher effectiveness and social learning theory (e.g., Rosenholtz 1989; Bandura 1977) is beginning to relate teachers' concepts of self-efficacy to positive student learning outcomes. In the most simple terms, we all like to view ourselves and have others view us as effective and capable human beings. Praise and recognition provide the feedback that tells us about our effectiveness. These new, formalized roles in schools would provide the opportunity for feedback and recognition for teachers.

The examples that follow have been selected to convey the kinds of incentives and professional growth needs expressed by teachers at the stability stage.

Career/Professional Growth Needs of the Teachers

A very traditional perspective expressed by one of the teachers illustrates what may be a typical perspective among teachers at this stage. Chad believes and states that

> I have to provide for my own professional growth needs. I see that that's my job, taking care of myself. . . . I have been able to move into situations where I can get help if I need help. And I am not afraid to ask when I had a class like I had last semester.

Many stable-stage teachers believe that professional needs are met by the individual and are not provided for by the schools. As functional as this position may be for the schools in terms of costs, it may very well be the reason for teacher failure in the schools. Unlike business and industry's expenditures for professional development, public schools have often relied on the individual teachers for both definition of needs and dollars for development.

A second aspect of stable teachers' growth needs contrasts sharply with the needs expressed by earlier-stage teachers. This aspect is teachers' lack of detail about particular areas in which they perceive weaknesses and therefore need help. As noted in other research (Huberman 1989), teaching for stable teachers may be something that they think they have mastered and therefore they need no further help in changing or improving. Instead, these teachers tend to define personal and professional growth needs in terms of data, novelty, ideas, and changes that are personally satisfying and pursued individually or in small, focused groups of colleagues. These needs come close to defining incentive preferences for teachers at this stage, and it is to these incentives that this chapter now turns.

Incentives for Stable Teachers

Research on incentives that are important to teachers in various phases of the career cycle (McDonnell, Christensen, & Price 1987, 1989) indicates that, for teachers at the phase of stability in their careers, incentives are both personal and organizational. In terms of the personal component, often cited incentives are retirement options and security, together with recognition like praise or appointment to new teaching roles. In organizational terms, stable teachers view input into school decision making as well as leadership opportunities as incentives, together with support for research and writing.

Chad indicates that development for him is pursuing those things that interest him. He says,

> In-services are a joke . . . I'm not real big on education workshops. They never seem to get at the kinds of things I need or want to know or learn. . . . I tend to go to content-oriented things. . . . The school district allows me to take classes when I feel like it and I have arrangements with the university to make my own classes when I want to pursue something and get credit for it.

These remarks reflect the desire for independent and novel activities and the reward received from being able to operate according to one's own designs and interests. These remarks also indicate a strong sense of effectiveness as teachers and people, a sensibility that should be given top priority in any program designed to promote teachers' professional growth. Chad's words indicate perhaps what is the most effective incentive and reward for these teachers which contributes to their sense of efficacy. "I guess the big thing, I guess just about everybody says it, is some sort of recognition for what you're doing. A pat on the back occasionally from, you know, outside or other sources, not just family or friends. Maybe a city-wide recognition day?"

Adam views incentives in much the same way. His words provide a fitting conclusion to the discussion of primary personal and professional needs and incentives of stable teachers: "Praise from professionals—administrators, parents, peers, students. It makes a difference. You seem to walk a little higher off the ground when you get it. Or I do. Don't you feel that?"

Support Systems for Stable Teachers

Teachers at the stable stage of their careers utilize a number of sources of support. These sources include peers, family and friends, district agencies and, less frequently, association-sponsored courses and workshops. Research on career stages (Burke et al. 1987; Collegial Research Consortium 1987) has indicated that, unlike teachers at earlier stages, stability-stage teachers tend not to favor university and college courses or workshops presented by university personnel. Presumably, these sources of support are too rigid, not timely enough, or too broad in scope to appeal to the narrower interests and needs of teachers at this stage. At the same time, stable teachers seemingly discount regularly scheduled staff meetings but generally accept classroom visitation and exchange as appropriate modes of professional development. The element of peer support may account for the preference of exchange programs as support systems.

District policies and procedures are commented upon by stable teachers with respect to change providing more positive support and support systems in their organizational environments. Stable teachers suggest that employee assistance programs, team teaching arrangements, and peer observation/evaluation opportunities might enhance the support system they believe is necessary. For the most part, however, structural systems such as merit pay plans or career ladders are viewed as basically incompatible with the idea of support, introducing too much opportunity for favoritism and polarization among colleagues.

Chad's remarks on the issue of support emphasize the idea of support from the community, including involvement and direct support from policy makers. He indicates that he

> never sees school board members in the building, ever. You'd think they'd come in once in a while . . . how in heaven's name do you get a sense of what's going on if you just listen to the superintendent all the time; however well motivated he may be, you still don't get a sense of what's going on. So there has to be some sort of organizational change, and the school board has to become more directly involved in at least observing what's going on.

A second approach to the idea of community involvement comes from Adam, who wishes that more opportunity for parental understanding of his school, its programs, and his classroom might develop. Adam realizes that parental roles are changing and that many parents are so busy that they may have little time to become involved with their child's education. However, he argues that

> you should never stop trying; whether it's effective or not, teachers shouldn't stop. . . . I sent home eighteen newsletters this year that I typed up and personalized letters to parents on what's going on in the classroom every other weekend. . . . I asked for and got some real opinions about some classroom projects.

Support for stable teachers comes from other sources in the work environment, and these provide both technical and emotional support as well. On the technical side, teachers note the influence of colleagues in either a one-to-one arrangement or in teams. On the emotional side, teachers remark about the worth of employee assistance programs in terms of health and wellness promotion or more severe cases of mental illness and addictions. If any generalization can be made about teachers' observations on support systems, it is that more projects need to be developed and available for more teachers.

With respect to teaming, Adam remarks that in his school,

> we work well as a unit and they're all such good teachers. I've always been proud of our unit in that we are really a happy group together. Socially, we're compatible and we've always had our problems, which are small. We've had a good relationship working with each other and everyone has pulled their own weight. At times I've wondered whether I was pulling my own, but I haven't worried about others pulling theirs.

A variation on the idea of peer and collegial support comes from Chad, who teaches in a history department at the secondary level. For Chad this support would come if evaluation were turned over to departments rather than maintained at the administrator level. Chad reasons that the departmental teacher "probably knows more about what anybody in the department is doing because anyone else is separated from the department. Occasionally, we do sit down and talk about problems on an informal basis—you know, how would you have done such and such, how do you handle this?"

With respect to the sort of support provided by employee assistance programs, Chad says that

> it is a good idea. If it is operating, I don't hear much about it; it's very low key but I think that that's a good idea. . . . We tried one wellness-day activity sponsored by the district, but it didn't last. One day of this sort of thing is going to make you healthy? It needs to be ongoing and longer term.

An interesting support idea comes from Adam; it contains within it one of the frequently voiced concerns that teachers have about assistance programs. Adam says:

> I think one of the things we need . . . is some sort of support group in place where people can set up their own rules, sit down, and talk about how they feel about what they are doing so they don't take it home and take it out on their spouses and themselves. We have an employees' assistance program but I don't think anyone wants to turn in their best friend with an alcohol or drug problem. We need to provide support to one another against abuses from higher up.

Summary

Teachers in the stability stage include those who have lost their enthusiasm and have settled into a pattern of delivering a "fair day's work for a fair day's pay." For others, stability may reflect a posture of maintaining, with a competent and steady commitment to teaching. Teachers who have arrived at this point in their careers have evolved from other stages. Some have accommodated their changing environment and made adjustments that allow them to feel comfortable and productive in their work settings. For others, no such accommodations have occurred. For this latter group, job plateauing or stagnation may represent a rejection of work and the work environment rather than an attempt to manage it.

Overall, the needs of teachers at the stability stage vary greatly. Professional development support systems must reflect this diversity and should encourage these teachers to move toward positive, growing stages of the career cycle.

CHAPTER NINE

Career Wind-Down

JOHN H. MCDONNELL   PETER J. BURKE

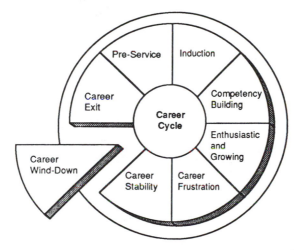

This is the stage when a teacher is preparing to leave the profession. For some, it may be a pleasant period in which they reflect on the many positive experiences they have had and look forward to a career change or retirement. For others, it may be a bitter period, one in which a teacher resents the forced job termination or, perhaps, cannot wait to leave an unrewarding job. A person may spend several years in this stage, or it may occur only during a matter of weeks or months.

The career wind-down stage of the teacher career cycle focuses on the last years of a teacher's experience in the classroom. It is a time of mixed emotions for most. While there is excitement about changing life's structure, there is also worry about the uncertainty that the future may hold. This stage can be compared to the latter stages of an adult's life when preparation for retirement is coupled with a retrospective review of one's life work.

Teachers in the wind-down stage, for the most part, have invested a number of years in the profession, although in some cases, teachers in this stage have only had a brief experience in teaching. Attitudes and influences at this stage vary according to the reasons behind the teacher's being there. Incentives and support systems are also variable based upon the same pressures. This stage can be described as "heading for home."

Teachers in the career wind-down stage of the career cycle may have moved into this stage through any one of the other stages. Although teachers in the induction stage are most often those with the least seniority, even they may be moved into the wind-down stage through a reduction-in-force due to shifting enrollment patterns and teacher density within their license category. Induction teachers may also realize that teaching is not meant for them and decide on their own to move into the wind-down stage. This move may come as the result of the influence of a mentor or because of limitations in the induction teacher's ability.

Competency-building teachers may move into career wind-down for the same reasons as induction teachers. In addition, these teachers may choose to develop their competence in areas other than classroom teaching. This might be in an area such as counseling, library service, administration, or higher education. Upon completion of the requisite preservice training for a pupil support or school administration position, or continued coursework in higher education, a competency-building teacher could wind down a teaching career at the end of an academic year in anticipation of an alternate assignment in another role in the education field.

Teachers in the enthusiastic and growing stage of the career cycle also may move into the wind-down stage of their teaching career by moving into another role in education. It is more likely, however, for these teachers to reach this stage following a long and successful career in teaching. Some enthusiastic teachers may be attracted out of the teaching profession by employment in the private sector because of the skills they exhibit in teaching. This movement would cause a sudden wind-down of their teaching careers.

Those teachers in the career frustration stage spend a good part of their time seeking alternatives to teaching. Wind-down for them begins as soon as alternate employment is found, if not before. Most often the career wind-down of frustrated teachers follows the same pattern as the time spent in the career frustration stage—mostly filled with negative feelings.

Finally, teachers in the stagnant aspect of the stable stage of the career cycle may move into career wind-down maintaining the same attitudes toward the profession they exhibited previously. These teachers may even regress in their effectiveness when they see a change coming and start planning for their exit. They may, however, become suddenly enlightened as they move into the exit stage and try to finish with one last burst of professional energy.

The wind-down stage, more than any other, is marked by unpredictability. As mentioned above, this can be either a positive or a negative or a neutral experience for teachers. This stage is a special challenge for those planning staff development activities because of the variability of influences, needs, and incentives. These factors, along with support systems for career wind-down teachers, are discussed in the sections that follow. The next section introduces the two career wind-down exemplars, "Brenda" and "Henry."

Teacher Profiles

Brenda

Brenda is a 62-year-old African-American female. She is widowed and has two grown children, both "out of the house and out of the city." One has followed in her mother's footsteps and is currently a teacher. Brenda has been teaching for twenty-seven years in a K–12 district in an industrial town in the upper Midwest. She is currently a first-grade teacher in a K–6 building with approximately 335 students. She serves as assistant principal in the building.

Brenda received her BA degree from a small liberal arts college in the upper Midwest where she majored in sociology. In the early 1960s she returned to complete elementary certification so she could become a teacher in her home community. She is a member of local, state, and national teachers' associations; at times she has taken an active role. She is a member of an education sorority and has been active in other organizations, especially those focusing on reading. During her career she has been honored as teacher of the year in her building and teacher of the month districtwide. She has long taught the basic skills of reading and math as well as social studies and science to her first-graders; more recently computers have become part of the curriculum. Reflecting the positive nature of her teaching experience, she indicates that it has been a very good assignment. The assistant principal assignment, which she has had for the past ten years, "has worked out for her. The children have respect for me. I really haven't had any problems" is Brenda's perception of her success in this role.

Brenda has entered career wind-down from the enthusiastic and growing career stage. Her statements focus on the importance of renewal and development: "Each year you begin brand new—you just keep growing and growing. I have reached the point now that I should stop and start something else."

Even in these waning days of her teaching career, Brenda is waiting an additional year to retire in order to help put in place a new reading program. Her concern is the children. "I wanted to see how the new reading program would go this year. I must say I had some apprehensions. In the end I hoped all the children could learn to read, and it was okay—it was fine."

Brenda, as a career wind-down teacher, looks back at her professional experience with pleasure. When asked how she feels about teaching, she replies, "Real good. Very good, as a matter of fact. I still feel positive . . . about teaching and that's one reason why I decided to retire while I still feel so positive." And what makes her feel good about her teaching?

> The children and the parents. Seeing the kids grow and down through the years you've had so many students come back and you feel good about them and about what they are doing and I have had some small part in their lives. That's good. Kids go to high school, college and then they come back to see you.

And, finally, Brenda is appreciative of her colleagues. They are important to her in this stage of her career. "It's being part of a team like the staff. You and your co-workers are always working toward the same goals. You feel you can have input there."

In the career wind-down stage of her profession, Brenda approaches career exit satisfied with her twenty-seven years as an elementary teacher.

Henry

Henry is a career wind-down teacher, but his situation is significantly different from Brenda's. While he has been an enthusiastic and growing teacher early in his career, he has entered the career frustration stage and is now in career wind-down as far as teaching is concerned at the middle school level. He is striving to exit into some other aspect of the profession.

Henry is 33, married, with no children. It is his second marriage. He has taught for ten years, four years in a K–6 building and the last six years as the teacher/coordinator for the gifted program working with seventh- and eighth-graders. Next year he has been reassigned as a sixth-grade teacher. He teaches in a small, rural community in the Midwest. The district consists of 440 K–8 students housed in one building. Henry is ready to move on.

Henry received his BA degree in anthropology with secondary certification from a small liberal arts college in the upper Midwest. He received a department award upon graduation. He continued there for his MAT in elementary education and first taught in the district where he interned, a major suburb of a large Midwest city, before moving to his current district. He has continued his education at a state university where he received his Master of Science in Educational Administration. He is currently in a doctoral program in the area of curriculum and supervision. During his teaching career he has been active in local, state, and national education associations. He has been active locally as co-chief negotiator and secretary. He is also a member of the state Council for the Gifted and Talented and served for two years as executive first vice-president.

Henry definitely sees his career in teaching as fitting into stages. He is now in career wind-down as a teacher looking to partake of other job opportunities in education. "I am looking to relocate to a different type of educational assignment, administrative or quasi-administrative position other than just teaching, a leadership role of a staff development, curriculum nature. Eventually I would like to work in teacher training, teaching methods classes, placement and supervision of student teachers."

Career frustration has led to this. "After ten years in the classroom, I think the frustration has been external rather than internal. There are some conditions and forces acting from outside, basically from my current administration, causing me to want to leave my current position."

But Henry remains excited about the profession. "I'm still personally excited about teaching. I have enjoyed teaching and would view an administrative position as a teaching role in terms of working with adults rather than students . . . in sharing your expertise and knowledge and wisdom with them, I would ultimately be affecting the children."

Henry has been an enthusiastic and growing teacher and has engaged in personal growth and development. Yet his situation has led to frustration and wind-down.

> I have continued to receive further training in education and have continued to grow personally and as a professional in terms of seeking a doctorate, an advanced degree in curriculum and supervision. I feel that I have not gotten an opportunity to apply all that I have learned in a practical way and that may be part of my own internal frustration. I think I make a difference with kids and I guess that has to be the bottom line with any teacher, that they make a difference with the people that they are there to do a job for. Not being able to make full use of my training and background, at least in my current position; not being able to act as a leader in the school district in staff development or curriculum development has led me to explore new horizons in my professional life.

Brenda and Henry, two teachers in the career wind-down stage, have very different histories. Brenda, an enthusiastic and growing teacher, is satisfied with her years in the profession and is poised for an exciting career exit to retirement. Henry has also had his taste of being enthusiastic and growing but has moved into career frustration and now wind-down. Yet he remains excited about the future as he endeavors to exit teaching but stay within the field of education.

Personal Environmental Influences

Teachers who are in the career wind-down stage of the teacher career cycle are influenced by family, hobbies, individual dispositions, life stages, and crises from their personal environment. The personal side of the influence realm may play a larger role for these teachers than the organizational component when one is preparing for retirement. Since they realize that their time in the classroom will soon be over, the pressures from the job lessen and the characteristics from their private lives come into a sharper focus. For those entering wind-down from career frustration, the organizational influence may dominate. Nevertheless, personal environmental considerations will still be important. These influences from the personal environment play a central role in teachers' action on the job and plans for after the job is over.

Family Influences

Family relationships take on a new meaning for wind-down teachers. They realize a need to define their own lives in relation to the lives of those around them. One aspect of this redefinition might be a positive preparation for life after retirement. Another component would be a negative concern about fitting into the continuing busy schedule of family members. The family influence also could be responsible for the teacher's being in this stage. Family members might have convinced the teacher to seek new employment and, if successful, put the teacher in the wind-down phase. This could be due to role expectations for the teacher by family members or because of financial considerations the family is facing.

Financial considerations due to a special need of a family member may be one example of this type of influence. A sick child or a child with a chemical dependency problem could drive a teacher from the profession with a need to make more money. Being able to support a large or extended family could create this circumstance as well. A variety of influences, both positive and negative, from members of the family are present for a teacher in the wind-down stage.

Avocational Interests

Hobbies or avocational interests can also play a key role in influencing a teacher in the wind-down stage. A teacher may decide to devote energies full-time to an outside interest, such as working for a church. A summer occupation could turn into a full-time possibility for a teacher, moving that teacher from the wind-down stage to career exit. A desire to travel extensively is often an influence on teachers in the wind-down phase, and a need to accomplish these plans before it is too late can drive the activities of a teacher in this stage.

Often career wind-down teachers are anxiously anticipating the opportunity to pursue a hobby, such as fishing or writing, on a full-time basis as well.

Avocational interests can be more than a force pulling a teacher out of the profession. An inspired teacher in the wind-down stage will use hobbies or future plans as a teaching tool. Components of an interest can become parts of lessons through direct instruction or example. Used as an example, hobbies can give real-life meaning to curriculum objectives. If the hobbies involve mental or physical exercise, the activities might be responsible for keeping the teacher fit while moving through the wind-down stage. Thus these influences from avocational interests also can be supporting or thwarting the career of a wind-down teacher.

Individual Dispositions

The individual disposition of a career wind-down teacher is a major influential factor. This period of time might be a critical turning point for the teacher's life goals and aspirations. It may be that the teacher has accomplished professional goals or has come to the realization that the professional goals set will never be attained. Either the accomplishment or the realization could influence the winding down of a career teacher.

Life priorities must be restructured by teachers in the wind-down stage. As mentioned above, family relationships might take on new meaning. A new job might become the focus during this time, and priorities for that new profession must be set. Teachers in the wind-down stage are in jeopardy of losing sight of their short-term instructional goals due to this restructuring. On the other hand, their priorities might lead them to another position in the profession and to their seeing the wind-down stage as a time to do the best job possible and "go out with a bang."

Another individual disposition that can influence teachers in this stage is a shift in their personal value system. It might be that something in their experience has caused a reevaluation of their attitude toward education, and they see the necessity of winding down their teaching due to this value shift. They may feel betrayed by the students, for whatever reason, and lose interest in the classroom. They may find themselves placed in a compromising situation by the administration and decide to wind down rather than compromise values. Changing circumstances, as well as changing values, can be responsible for teacher actions in the wind-down stage.

Adult and Developmental Influences

The life stage of the teacher in wind-down is another important influence. A life crisis might have occurred creating a wind-down circumstance. A life shift into a psychological framework that deemphasizes teaching may be occurring. Experience with students may no longer be as rewarding as it once was, perhaps due in combination to an adult life-stage shift and a demographic shift of students. Teachers may move into a time in their lives when work with adults is more rewarding than work with students, necessitating a wind-down of their teaching career. A shift based on this influence does not necessarily have to be out of the profession. As mentioned earlier, the wind-down teacher could be anticipating a change within the profession to a position such as counseling, administration, or higher education. It can mean, of course, a shift out of the profession of education as well.

Crises

Crises in teachers' lives probably play the most crucial role in considering teachers in the wind-down stage of the teacher career cycle. It could be a crisis, such as being laid off from teaching, that puts the teacher involuntarily in the wind-down stage. It could be a crisis in the family, as discussed previously, that creates this structure. It could also be a personal problem or illness that drives the teacher into the wind-down stage.

Impact of Personal Environmental Influences on Brenda and Henry

Brenda

Personal environmental influences have had an important effect on Brenda in her professional stages, then and now. Her love of children is paramount.

> When I finished college I was certified to do social work; I did do that work about two years and having a young family at the time, I decided that I didn't particularly want to continue in this field. It wasn't satisfying work . . . with adults . . . so, with two children and a husband I went into teaching. I have always liked children. I have watched my family grow up and now my grandchildren. . . . I just think they are neat little people. It keeps me abreast with what is going on in the world with young people, the toys they are playing with, what songs they like.

Outside activities also support Brenda's teaching. "Our church has a tutoring program that I have always kept up with. I've worked with the children, tutored them. I have been vacation Bible school director for a number of years. I teach nine months in public school and in the summer go to that."

At this point Brenda reminisces about the personal environment and its influence on her entry into the profession. It is only natural for a wind-down teacher headed for exit to do so. Her story takes place in the late 1950s, a time of a teacher shortage. Majority college graduates had no trouble finding substitute teaching jobs. Yet this was not true for Brenda. Prejudice was rampant in the country. This was certainly true in this small industrial town in the upper Midwest. Brenda describes the situation in her hometown.

> When I decided to go into teaching and leave social work I had a difficult time; as a matter of fact, I was unable to find work as a substitute teacher. I thought I would do sub teaching; however, I was turned down for that, I guess that's when I really decided I would see what courses I needed to have for certification. I had run into a great deal of prejudice all of my life growing up in this city and my children at that time were very young. I guess I just became determined that I was going to do this. At that time the superintendent said he couldn't hire me as a substitute teacher and I decided right then and there I would work towards being certified. When you find out that you are turned down because of the color of your skin, it makes you determined to succeed. I had grown up with this; it wasn't anything new. I guess I was thinking about my own children. We were living here and they were going to come up with the same discrimination; at that time the unrest was all over the country. I decided then I wanted to teach and I would prove to myself that I could teach. Before I was hired, we changed superintendents, so the person who denied me employment, we didn't have. He left the area.

The strength of her family backing has been and continues to be critical influence and support from her personal life.

> At the time I decided to enter teaching my mother had come; she was quite ill and she came from a large family. It was a struggle to raise eight kids, but my parents were very supportive and it was something I wanted to do. My mom was very proud of me and that was 1961, the same year I went back. She passed away that year. She knew I was going back to school. She died that fall, but I am sure she would have been very happy at the time to know that I did make it into teaching. It was kind of funny too as I think back. I went into teaching and when I finished I thought, MOM! I made it all the way through! And of course she wasn't here, but she would have been very happy to think we had been brought up in this city and we had encountered prejudice and overcome.

Twenty-seven years later Brenda evidences the dignity that comes from over-coming adversity, in her case, racial prejudice.

As a wind-down teacher, prejudicial treatment of students is to Brenda a negative aspect of teaching and affects her personal life as well.

> You meet all kinds of people in your teaching career, but there have been some people that were not very kind—but that was their problem, not

mine. There have been times that teachers would discuss children and they would stereotype them and to me that's a hard thing to handle. Most of the time I would leave the room or later I would think of what I would say. They weren't necessarily always black, but sometimes the children had problems. But that was about the most negative thing.

Finally, personal life crises have affected Brenda's professional situation. In each case she was supported in the crisis by her profession.

When I had been teaching about six years or so, there was a divorce from my first husband and I found myself with two children to raise and support. . . . I pushed that into the background, but that was definitely a hard time in my life, but I think that teaching and dealing with children is what got me through. Held me together. Losing my second husband after a short marriage of eight months, that was also negative. After he died is when I decided to stay in this city to teach. I think I have tried to take the negative things and make them become positive things.

Brenda's personal environment has had a major effect on her entering and remaining in the teaching profession. As a wind-down teacher soon to exit from her field of work, Brenda clearly is satisfied, indeed pleased, with her career and her ability to persevere as a black teacher often in a hostile environment. Henry's situation stands in interesting contrast to that of Brenda's.

Henry

As a career wind-down teacher, Henry is in a different situation from Brenda. Rather than exiting the profession for retirement after long and success-ful years of teaching, Henry is looking to make a mid-career change from the classroom to some other aspect of education, either administration or higher education. This change comes after some years of enthusiastic teaching but more recently after a considerable amount of career frustration.

Henry comes from a family of teachers who have provided him personal support throughout his career.

My spouse is an educator, also in the same building at this point. I also see my parents in a role of educators; Mom is a school secretary; my dad is a pastor, which is education of a different type. Both my mother- and father-in-law are educators and two of my sisters-in-law are pursuing education and plan to go into the field. So there's a lot of education in the family.

Crises in Henry's family life have caused important restructuring of career goals.

Participating in a doctoral program would not have happened if I had not gone through a divorce. If I had continued in the relationship at that time, I don't think I would have had the motivation to go back to school. The timing was fortuitous; the breakup of the relationship at that time—I was looking for other outlets, things to do, and one of the things that crossed my mind was to pursue a doctorate, so the timing worked out well.

Discontinuity in his personal life has created new career goals for Henry and a new arena for personal success. "A second marriage has been very positive to me personally. That has to affect my professional life. The success I have had so far in the doctoral program. The relationships I have built there with my colleagues and also with professors—very positive."

Relationships have been most supportive of Henry thus far in his professional career. These include past friends from his undergraduate experience, both peers and professors. Currently, both teaching faculty and parents of his students also undergird his professional activities.

The teaching faculty has always been like a family. They are very supportive. I've always had someone to turn to in times of need, to help me through a situation. It's not just a place to work. Nice to be in a place where they have the same ideals and same motivation as I.

Finally, hobbies help maintain balance between his personal and organizational environments during this wind-down period of transition.

I do read quite a bit, both professional literature and educational. But I also read escapist type books—science fiction, fantasy. They act as kind of a balance to the tense professional type. Antiquing, doing small odd jobs around the house are therapeutic to me. Off-hour things which bring some sanity to my life.

Personal concerns, influences from the personal environment, are main reasons for teachers leaving the profession—that is, for entering the wind-down stage. Disillusionment, death, divorce, illness, or financial concerns can all be reasons. They can all create an influence factor for wind-down teachers. These concerns do, in fact, play a major role for better or for worse. Influences from the organizational environment also exist, and they, too, can play either a positive or a negative role for wind-down teachers. The next section describes some of these influences.

Organizational Environmental Influences

Influence from the organizational environment for teachers in the wind-down stage of the career cycle can be synthesized into four categories. These are school regulations and administrator management style, public trust and societal expectations, professional organizations, and the union. Components of each of these categories play some role in influencing teachers who are in the wind-down stage of their careers. These organizational influences do not play as important a role for wind-down teachers as they do for, say, enthusiastic or frustrated teachers as described in Chapters 6 and 7. Since, by definition, these teachers will soon be leaving teaching, it is difficult for the organization to have an impact on the career status of wind-down teachers. There are, however, some things to keep in mind in several of the categories of the organizational environment.

School Regulations and Administrative Management Style

Two of the categories, school regulations and administrative management style, can be combined into one area of influence for wind-down teachers. In a negative way, these items may be the direct reason for the teacher's being in this stage. On one hand, the management and regulations may be too tight and rigid for a teacher who needs flexibility and freedom to explore alternate teaching and learning methods, such as tight control of students in the building for a teacher who wants students to pursue community-based learning. On the other hand, the structure may be too loose for a teacher who needs direction and control to provide patterned instruction. In either case, if the regulations and management style do not fit the teacher's needs, they become influences to move the teacher to wind down his or her career.

There should be a commitment on the part of the administration addressing the needs of these wind-down teachers. Principals should recognize the fact that the teacher may soon be leaving and adjust expectations accordingly. Principals should also work to help those who need more structure to function better through giving individual attention to wind-down teacher needs. This may mean a self-analysis by both teacher and administrator of professional values and styles and a discussion of means to accommodate both.

Administrators must work with teachers in the career wind-down stage to develop open two-way communication channels. It is important to learn what these teachers need to make their final experiences comfortable and meaningful. This must be done in an open atmosphere of trust and support. Class assignments or other school policies might be adjusted to create a comfort level. These adjustments might mean some involvement of the teacher union as well.

Unions

The union can play an important influence from the organizational environment for teachers in the wind-down stage. Representatives at the building level should be knowledgeable of who is in this phase of their careers, and these building representatives should also add to the supportive atmosphere for the teachers. One way is to establish a realistic relationship on the wind-down teacher's behalf with the administration and school board. This relationship could include varying specific personnel policies, say the length of the teacher's day, where it is appropriate.

Protection and security are two items frequently attributed to union influence. These items are of crucial importance to teachers in the career wind-down stage. They need to be secure in their ability to complete their assigned tasks, and they should have the protection of alternate assignments for short periods of time when they are unable to successfully complete those tasks first assigned. Part of the master agreement between the school district and union might speak to the needs of teachers in this stage.

Unions can also be an important vehicle for recognition of departing employees. Visible awards or other benefits could be designed to recognize the contribution of teachers who will be leaving the profession. This is another area of influence where school districts and unions could work together for wind-down teachers. It is essential not to allow the teachers who are leaving the profession to do so in isolation and despair. Too often a feeling of depression creates a dysfunctional circumstance for teachers in the wind-down stage, and this feeling can result in poor classroom performance. It is the job of all involved with these teachers to help guard against this occurring.

Public Trust and Societal Expectations

This feeling of despair can be created by two other influences from the organizational environment. These are public trust and societal expectations surrounding their jobs. Constant challenges by parents or community members can wear away any trust relationship that might have been in existence. Challenges on budget, instruction, or other components of the school program may be the influences that push a teacher to decide to leave the profession. Lack of confidence or lack of trust and support are negative influences that exist in many school communities. It is much better to look to the public for a positive influence to the work of the schools.

The public can offer this positive influence to career wind-down teachers in several ways. Recognition or rewards for a job well done is one way. Sharing in the goals or aspirations of the departing employees is another. The public, along with other elements of the organizational environment, might facilitate a positive teacher wind-down stage through promoting the teacher to another role in the profession such as counselor, librarian, or administrator. This promotion could include resources or improvement to allow the teacher to qualify for the new role.

Special-interest groups are another source of influence for wind-down teachers. Retirement groups that influence legislation supportive of teachers and other retirees are one example. Other community groups could also offer support through recognition or special projects. Wind-down teachers may even become spokespersons for these groups, such as an organization for the gifted and talented student, without fear or reprisal from the school. Being in the career wind-down stage may give teachers the confidence to speak their convictions through special-interest groups where they see school efforts falling short of an established goal.

Professional Organizations

Professional organizations are another influence category that can provide a platform for this type of discussion. In addition, teachers in this stage may be provided leadership opportunities by these organizations, and these teachers may see their involvement as a means to stay close to the profession upon their exit. These organizations may also add to the recognition component as an influence for career wind-down teachers.

Professional education organizations are often in need of volunteer time to carry out their responsibilities. Teachers in the wind-down stage might be selected as executive secretaries or business managers for organizations that are usually led by teachers in other stages, such as the enthusiastic and growing stage. Enthusiastic teachers are looking for a vehicle to help with a specific professional agenda. They may give a brief, but intensive, commitment to the organization to accomplish their goals. Wind-down teachers, on the other hand, are willing to commit to a longer-term relationship for the purpose of keeping the affairs of the association, such as meetings or newsletters, orderly. This stable and long-term commitment to a professional organization can be a positive influence for wind-down teachers.

Impact of Organizational Environmental Influences on Brenda and Henry

Brenda

Brenda's view from the position of career wind-down is mixed on the effect of the organizational environment on her career. Parents and staff members are currently supportive of her. They have been responsible for her going into new fields previously mentioned—computers and the new reading program. "They say she can do this and do that and I say okay, I'll try," explains Brenda.

She is less certain that teacher unions are always beneficial. Some sixteen years later, when asked about the role of the union, she focuses on the only teacher strike that has occurred in the district.

I did not take part in the strike. First, they wanted me to carry a picket sign in front of one of the schools, which I refused to do; it was something I didn't want to do. Nobody said anything to me. There were a lot of hard feelings after the strike for some of the teachers who crossed the picket line. As a matter of fact, I did not cross; I stayed home. I feel that the union has some positive things and then again, they are not 100% behind everything.

While ambivalent on the role of teacher associations for herself, she does consider herself a professional. She takes umbrage with regulations in the organizational environment that limit areas of control by teachers.

Sometimes teachers are not treated as professionals but more or less like students. When you can leave and when you can't. Myself, I was in school everyday at 7 o'clock or before. Ordinarily, I would stay there until 4 or after. I'm a morning person—just get more done in the morning. To me as a professional, you are not going to leave until you are ready to leave regardless of time regulations. I can't see why they have such a policy.

In her professional role, Brenda feels it is important that she acts as a spokesperson for district policies and in changing public attitudes and garnering public support.

From time to time the people in the community have wanted different things done concerning the school system and I've had to defend the position of the school. Magnet schools, desegregation program—most of the people who asked me about the deseg program were concerned that the children were going to be bused out of their neighborhoods; so after I told them it was a volunteer program, they were satisfied.

This career wind-down teacher speaks up for what is important. She still cares about education in her district.

Henry

The organizational environment is Henry's source for his intense desire to stay in education; it is also the reason why he is in the career wind-down stage, leaving classroom teaching. Henry's problems started early in his career. As a competency-building teacher rapidly becoming enthusiastic and growing, Henry was faced with a reduction-in-force in his first teaching assignment.

I spent four years in this district. After four years there was a districtwide RIF. A substantial number of teachers were cut because of financial reasons. It had nothing to do with your ability; it had to do with seniority. It was a blow to my ego, because given other circumstances I don't think I would have been chosen to be cut. That was 1981.

Even though Henry was reassigned by the end of the year, it was a bitter blow. He left the district for his current position.

Here he has found the local teachers' association to be "an extension of family"; his peers have been most supportive, and he has undertaken leadership roles in the organization.

> I've been active as an officer and a negotiator for the union. Again, it has been a sense of family in terms of the people there; it's not a union in the strict definition of the word—it's just another extension of the family. It wasn't until recently that we even had a contract in the district. By state legislation, teachers had the right to request the opportunity to bargain for a contract. We did exercise that option. I would say it has been a very positive experience for me.

This positive influence of his organizational environment stands in stark contrast to the influence of the management style of his current administrators. In his first teaching position Henry had been in a K–6 building. He found a supportive principal who encouraged him as he went through his early growth stages into the profession. And then came his move to a new district and a change to the middle-level children. His teaching continued to go well, but the arrival of a new administrator quickly changed the organizational environment that Henry had found so supportive of his career.

> My experience is that I have had few opportunities where I have felt a collegial-type relationship with an administrator. . . . There have been some schisms developed with the new administrator. She has been there for a year now. In part, that administration has intentionally tried to break up the situation of family and it's a unique one in education I think; most school districts don't operate that way. There's a lot of collegiality, a lot of cooperation, sharing, that I don't think happens elsewhere. I think administratively that is now viewed as a threat. I have developed some good relationships with teachers of other school districts. My experiences here basically have been negative. I think, because I seem to be a threat to authority and power because of my knowledge and expertise and experience . . . my training, my background . . . that administration has been very reluctant to share their power with me and with others. It certainly hasn't given me an opportunity to grow professionally or personally. In fact, it has been somewhat degrading in some respects and also negative in that I have not been able to reach my full potential.

From Henry's point of view the style of management utilized by his district administrator has resulted in an organizational environment nonsupportive of teacher collegiality and destructive of Henry's professional growth. This has resulted in a career shift, from enthusiastic and growing to career wind-down. Henry sums it up:

> I think the biggest negative influence I have had on my teaching throughout the ten years has been what I have perceived as poor administrators who are unwilling to share or unwilling to relinquish some of their authority and power to the people they work directly with. I think the biggest way a person can show power is to empower others, and I haven't run across that mentality in the public schools in terms of administrators.

Henry will soon exit teaching due to lack of administrative support in the school environment.

Just as the influences from the personal and organizational environments are selective, so, too, are the growth needs of teachers in the wind-down stage of the teacher career cycle. The next section identifies and discusses a few of the more prominent needs of teachers in this stage.

Professional Growth Needs of Career Wind-Down Teachers

The growth needs of teachers in the career wind-down stage of the teacher career cycle revolve around activities that allow these teachers to produce a return on the investment they have made in the profession. The single exception to this concept is for those teachers who are in this stage through pressures external to their own decision—that is, teachers who have been laid off or nonrenewed. Those teachers who are not returning because of economic or efficiency reasons have very short-term and direct needs, not unlike teachers in the induction stage.

Teacher as Learner

If the reason for a teacher's departure is nonrenewal because of in-efficiency or ineffectiveness, the growth needs include those things that could be categorized as teacher-as-learner (Christensen, McDonnell, & Price 1988). There are specific needs such as discipline, classroom management, or in-structional strategies. Those in administrative positions must make a concerted effort to work directly with these teachers to ensure maintenance of learning in the classroom. Proper techniques for management or successful instructional procedures must be stressed. Coaching or peer tutoring from a teacher in the enthusiastic stage is another strategy to provide for the needs of these teachers. Monitoring of pupil progress is important to ensure no undue loss of learning.

If a teacher is in the wind-down stage due to a necessary reduction-in-force, the growth needs may not be as severe, but they may be short-term as well. The growth needs of a teacher facing lay-off could include the need to maintain an appropriate level of professionalism, to keep the lines of communication open regarding pupil performance, or to ensure that a positive classroom climate exists throughout the wind-down period. Too often there is neglect of the basic educational needs of students when any teacher faces the end of an assignment at a school and is unsure of returning. The key for the administration is to monitor the teacher's classroom on a continuous basis to measure if support is necessary to satisfy any need that appears suddenly.

Teachers who choose to be in the wind-down stage have growth needs in four categories. These needs reflect the overall desire on the part of most of these teachers to share the expertise they have developed with others in the profession—to give a return on the investment they have made to the profession. The categories of growth needs for these wind-down teachers include knowledge production, teacher preparation, mentoring, and leadership (Christensen, McDonnell, & Price 1988).

Knowledge Production

The category of knowledge production includes a synthesis of teachers' experiences and a sharing of those experiences through several methods. This sharing might be through writing curriculum, explaining successful instructional techniques, identifying goals for the school for the future, analyzing new materials or textbooks, or producing a handbook for students or faculty.

These teachers would need time and support services, such as secretarial support, to carry out this production. If basic needs are met, these teachers could produce individualized curricular materials that would be geared to the special needs of the students in the school. They could design teaching units based on the new curriculum that have proven successful to them in the past. These units could be specific and meaningful to the needs of the school. They could draw upon a wealth of experience to design handbooks for students, teachers, and even parents that would help maintain a positive school climate. It is important to take advantage of the wealth of knowledge available from these departing employees before they are gone for good.

Teacher Preparation and Coaching

The area of teacher preparation is also a growth need for wind-down teachers, and again they are the providers if the opportunity is given to them.

Within the building or district these teachers could work with inexperienced teachers, say in the induction or competency-building stage, to help them hone their skills. The wind-down teachers could act as peer tutors or coaches to those who will carry on the education of students after the experienced teachers depart. Outside of the district these teachers could work with teacher preparation institutions by team teaching courses for preservice students. Clinical professorships for experienced teachers are an excellent way to infuse solid practical techniques with current educational theory in college classrooms. These teachers offer a valuable resource to teacher preparation institutions, and their involvement could fulfill one part of the teachers' need to share the expertise they have developed throughout their careers.

Leadership

Leadership is the final category of growth needs for these teachers. This category also reflects the teachers' need to share the expertise they have developed in their teaching careers. These leadership opportunities can be school-based, through unions, or through professional organizations. Chairing a curriculum committee or a school improvement council are examples of school-based leadership that might satisfy this need. Union positions in governance areas, such as negotiations or professional rights and responsibilities, could also satisfy this need. Leadership positions in professional organizations, like executive secretary or newsletter editor, are a third technique to satisfy a growth need for leadership positions.

Career Growth Needs for Brenda and Henry

Brenda

As Brenda winds down her career for retirement, her growth needs are limited and focused.

> I've been more inclined to look for things that have to do with retirement—things and seminars having to do with teachers planning to retire and my future. I have found those quite helpful. At the district level last year they had quite a bit which dealt with your health and I found those interesting, too. I think the district could have done more. You know, you are retiring; you don't know too much; you are kind of groping in the dark.

This is an easy growth need area to overlook. Yet isn't a teacher who has provided years of service to the children of a district entitled to have these key areas of her wind-down stage met? Far too often the teachers at the end of their careers are not deemed to have growth needs that are important for a district to meet through appropriate staff development.

Henry

Henry's growth needs in the wind-down stage are quite different than Brenda's. They are probably critical to whether he will stay in education or leave the profession altogether. Henry states his needs clearly.

> I have spent ten years in the classroom. I have what I think are a sufficient number of experiences to share with colleagues. A position of leadership and being able to impart these experiences to other teachers would give me an opportunity to grow professionally and personally. Just some type of an outlet, whether it be in an administration position or a quasi-administration position—an opportunity to do a lot with staff development, curriculum development, at the district level or a number of school systems.

In Henry's current district it seems unlikely that his growth needs will be met.

> In my current position I have received very little. In terms of my education I am beyond where anyone else in my district is, so there's no sensitivity or empathy with where I am at. Few people have beyond their bachelor's degree where I am now and have not chosen to pursue education beyond that. There really hasn't been any district incentive to do so in terms of tuition or what have you.

Henry has taken steps to change his organizational environment and has entered a doctoral program at a large Midwestern state university. He has broadened his colleague base to include researchers in higher education. Rather than leaving the profession altogether, he is working to get into a situation that will more fully meet his growth needs. And he is finding this support. "The support of the professors and mentors in the program has been their encouragement to work on areas of mutual interests of the dissertation. Working with outside researchers—that type of support has been there."

While the change in organizational environment is helping Henry during this wind-down period, facets of his personal environment are also working in concert.

> I guess I just have to say to be successful professionally you have to be happy and successful personally. I've gotten to the point now where I've developed a very good relationship with someone who also is a teacher and can empathize with me—same type of problems—same daily types of occurrences that happen in the school setting.

With positive factors in both environments, Henry seems well supported during the wind-down stage of his career.

In summary, the growth needs of many career wind-down teachers are more as leaders than as participants. These teachers often have the need to lead in knowledge production, in teacher preparation, and in other aspects of the profession. This need to lead comes from a personal influence to share as much as possible the skills and knowledge they have gained during their tenure in teaching. The incentives that are important to attract the involvement of career wind-down teachers in these activities are, for the most part, extrinsic. These incentives are the topic of the next section.

Incentives for Career Wind-down Teachers

Incentives for teachers in the career wind-down stage of the teacher career cycle fall into four basic categories. These are tangible incentives, recognition, promotion, and incentives dealing with support items (McDonnell et al. 1987).

Tangible Incentives

Tangible incentives are key because these teachers are, in fact, leaving the profession. Thus, items that have an impact on their security beyond their time in the classroom play an important role. The first tangible incentive deals with the time they are spending in the classroom. These teachers see a pleasant work environment as an important incentive. They would like their final days in the classroom to be as comfortable and, optimally, as productive as possible. Positive working conditions during their denouement in the profession will engender positive feelings about leaving.

Other tangible items include good insurance benefits and options for early retirement. These incentives are a recognition of the needs that exist beyond the active days in the profession. Retirement benefits and insurance options will help to satisfy the basic security needs of these teachers and give them a comfortable feeling about finishing the tasks at hand, knowing that their future needs will be at least partially cared for by the profession.

Recognition

Incentives in the recognition category include conferring master teacher status, work as a mentor teacher, student praise, leadership in professional organizations, and influence in school decision making. Master teacher recognition is seen as a reward for the years of positive dedication to a school or to the profession. This is a titular designation, much like a chaired professorship, that gives a psychological boost to the teacher who is winding down his or her career.

Mentoring, as discussed in Chapter 4, is both a recognition of expertise and an assignment in the area of teacher preparation. Wind-down teachers might be selected or appointed as mentors because of recognized skill or ability and then assigned to help younger staff members learn the ropes of the profession. This assignment helps fulfill the need mentioned earlier to share their skill with the profession before departing.

It is interesting that wind-down teachers see student praise, more than praise from peers or administrators, as an incentive to their job. They have gone through or beyond the need for positive feedback from principals or other teachers and are cognizant of the fact that the true value of their worth is measured by the student. Praise from students is the final measure by which their professional investment shows dividends.

Much was said about the importance of professional organizations to these teachers as an influence from the organizational environment and as a satisfaction vehicle for growth needs. Professional organizations, once again, are identified as an incentive in the recognition category by wind-down teachers. Citations, awards, or other honors can be coupled with the opportunities for leadership by these organizations to recognize and revere the work of these teachers.

Influence in the decision making of the school is another recognition incentive. This involvement also was described in relation to the influence of the organization and the growth needs of these teachers. Membership or leadership on school or district committees, consultation on important school-related matters, and assignment to specific school-related tasks all provide an avenue to implement this incentive. Wind-down teachers have the constant need to be involved and to help direct school activities into the future. Their advice should be solicited and weighed as decisions are made.

Promotion

The category of promotion as an incentive for wind-down teachers is, perhaps, more applicable to those moving to another role in the profession. Items in this category that have been identified as incentives for wind-down teachers (McDonnell et al. 1987) include promotion to administrative positions, opportunities for professional advancement, and the general category of leadership opportunities. Those who are winding down their teaching career to take on another assignment see a positive incentive in promotion from within a district or school. They see this as recognition of their value, and they view this promotion as a positive incentive during their time in a wind-down stage.

Support

The support category of incentives for career wind-down teachers is directly related to their final period in the classroom. Items such as aide support, a flexible work day, and released time for professional activities all fall into this category. Just like the need for a positive work environment mentioned in the tangible incentive category, aide support or a flexible day would help these teachers to have the best experience possible while winding down their careers.

Released time for professional activities relates to the knowledge production or leadership growth needs mentioned earlier. Career wind-down teachers see released time as an incentive to pursue one or more culminating activities for the profession. These activities might be producing curriculum or working for a professional association or any other involvement that would leave them with the feeling that they have left a mark on the profession.

Appropriate Incentives for Brenda and Henry

Brenda

An important incentive for Brenda is clearly early retirement. She is taking advantage of a new law in her state. "Money is important especially when you are thinking about retirement," she states. Career advancement has not been a significant incentive for her. The assistant principal position was as far as she wanted to go.

Working with other teachers is important to Brenda. Inservice, when conducted by other teachers, is beneficial. "When we had teachers from another school district, that was excellent. These teachers were actually doing it," says Brenda. Sharing classes has also been a positive experience for her. She explains:

> I did do some of that with a first-grade teacher. We would alternate. One year I would teach all of the science to her class as well as mine, and she would do the social studies. Each year we would alternate. That was great. We then could do a much better job.

Finally, intangible incentives still have importance for Brenda. "A lot of times teachers' morale is low. No one tells you that you are doing a good job but if you do something wrong, you hear about it and it's just like kids and positive reinforcement. We would get feedback from each other."

Concerning the parents and former students, as she moves toward career exit Brenda finds that the visits from former students, the notes, and praise from parents are pay-offs that make it all worthwhile.

Henry

Henry's future as he moves through career wind-down is quite different from Brenda's. Yet intangible rewards are important incentives for him as they have been for Brenda. He says:

> I think the base incentive for me would be recognition from either peers or from others in education. Recognition that what I am doing is right—desired—needed. I've experienced some of that to a small degree among students and parents, but to have that type of respect from leaders and from people beyond the walls of the classroom would be great.

And how about praise from administration? "I'd LOVE some! Are there any administrators out there that give praise?"

Tangible rewards, such as salaries and benefits, are not always the key incentive to teachers. In fact, Henry points out:

> Money never has been a REAL incentive; in fact, I have taken a few pay cuts to take different positions. I take the cut in pay because of the opportunity. I took a cut in pay to be a teacher of the gifted and although the pay was less, the title and experience I have had was worth it.

Henry would find various types of professional development activities important incentives for him in this stage of his teaching career. These include the following:

> Courses—I fully intend to continue taking classes beyond my doctorate just because I enjoy taking classes.
>
> Workshops—They run from good to bad. Some have energized me, have been very practical in what I can use in the classroom. Others haven't been worth attending. It depends on the nature of the presentation.
>
> Conventions—They are helpful if you have the opportunity to attend. To get away from the classroom for two or three days is an incentive in itself and to rub elbows with your colleagues is a side benefit.
>
> Sabbaticals—I would love to be able to take a sabbatical to write my dissertation, but such an opportunity does not exist.

These incentives have been critical in Henry's professional life. If the organization had provided such incentives, an enthusiastic and growing teacher might have been kept at that career stage and stayed in teaching. Without such support, Henry is now winding down his career as a classroom teacher frustrated in his organization environment.

Henry sees the availability of professional aspects of teaching as important incentives. Autonomy has been important here. And it has generally been available to him in the classroom. "I generally have had autonomy in terms of what I have taught and how I have structured my classroom. That's been an incentive to me personally. I work much better under less control than more control."

Such autonomy in the school building would be an incentive also. But that is not in evidence in Henry's environment. He states: "I think for me that would be very appropriate but it hasn't been made evident. Shared decision making for example. Even on simple matters, such as selection of textbooks, those opportunities have not been made available."

Henry goes on to generalize about the professional empowerment of teachers.

> Teachers should be empowered, and they probably have been but really haven't known that they were. A lot of what happens when they shut their doors of the classroom, they are in full control with very little type of monitoring or evaluation of activities. What I think has to happen, though, those activities have to be tied into the overall plan or scheme of things in the school system as a whole so that whether it be student achievement or individual attainment of knowledge or whatever, there is some way to tie into that type of empowerment.

But for Henry this is too late. Teacher empowerment would not now be enough incentive to stay in the classroom. He is in wind-down and his goals are clear. He states, "I would like a position of leadership outside the classroom."

Teachers in the wind-down stage of the career cycle, therefore, see incentives in recognition, promotion, support, and basic tangible items. Once again, the right incentive is directly dependent upon the needs of the individual. The needs, in turn, are directly dependent upon the reasons for leaving, and these reasons may be tied very closely to influence from either the personal or the organizational environment. It is important to recognize the influences that exist, to identify the needs that may be present, and then to design incentives appropriate to make the wind-down stage a successful and satisfying experience.

Teachers in the wind-down stage also have unique support systems, which are the topic of the following section.

Support Systems for Career Wind-down Teachers

Participation Factors

Support systems that are important for wind-down teachers include university affiliations, district workshops, professional writing, and committee or professional association memberships. While these systems are similar to those found important to teachers in other stages, the unique factor for career wind-down teachers is how they view their participation.

The participation in university courses is no longer as a student. The university is a support system, however, in the use of the wind-down teacher's expertise. Team teaching, acting as a mentor or cooperating teacher, or being given recognition—as a distinguished alumnus, for example, all offer support to teachers in this career stage. It is the visible use of their expertise that becomes important.

District workshops that are support systems for these teachers are, for the most part, those that deal with plans for their job transition. Retirement planning or other such seminars become important to these teachers. In addition, workshops are important if these teachers are given leadership responsibility to share information with their peers or with others.

Leadership potential on committees or in professional organizations offers another support system. Much has been said earlier in this chapter about the importance of having an arena to share expertise. Committees or associations become this arena and play an important role in the success of the teacher's wind-down phase.

The opportunity to participate in professional writing exercises is another key support system for wind-down teachers. Writing curricula, handbooks, instructional manuals, or revising existing documents are all recognitions of the value of a departing employee.

Support Systems for Brenda and Henry

Brenda

Brenda's comments on support systems epitomize the importance of colleges or universities at both ends of a teacher's career cycle. She looks back and remembers how important her return to college had been to meet her own timeline and to enter the teaching profession, overcoming some of the racial prejudice she found in her local community in the late 1950s. And now she is returning to the college level as a cooperating teacher to pass along the craft of professional teaching. She recalls a recent example of her work.

> I guess I liked them basically because they were young and they had ideas, although there were several times that I knew some of their ideas were not good, but I did not like to tell them no, don't do that. Last year one student teacher came in with all the change, nickels, dimes, and pennies. (We have a lesson on counting money when we use paper money). She had it all allotted out, which was fine if she wanted to do it that way. I didn't tell her though, no, I didn't think that was good. At the end of the period she said, "I'll never do that again. The kids played with it, they wanted to keep it." Unless they are going to fall on their face, I just cooperate with them.

As a career wind-down teacher preparing for exit into retirement, Brenda is turning to the regeneration of the profession by providing support to teachers in their first foray as the classroom teacher during their student teaching experience. Brenda clearly has a feeling of efficacy—of having made a difference. She has overcome racial prejudice and bigotry and earned a place of respect in her community. She has become a positive role model for all children, but especially the black children growing up in a different world from hers. She moves to career exit with a sense of dignity and worth.

Henry

Henry's focus on support groups is quite different from Brenda's and much more academic. In wind-down he sees himself exiting teaching but staying within education. Either as an administrator or in higher education (teacher preparation), Henry is interested in support systems for teachers that will meet their professional needs and keep them in an enthusiastic and growing stage of their career—a support system that is not currently available in his organizational environment.

One aspect from the organizational environment that Henry sees as a potentially important support is evaluation.

> I think teacher evaluations could be used not in the granting or denial of tenure but rather . . . as a tool for personal growth in the classroom. Like the clinical supervision type of model in which goals are mutually set, specifics are viewed in the classroom, and conference time afterward in which you discuss what happened and how you can improve upon it. To use teacher evaluations not to get rid of or to promote staff but rather to use that as a tool for individual professional growth.

Directly tied to evaluation from Henry's perspective is staff development. But staff development often is not organized in a manner that is helpful to teachers. In his career stage Henry has specific suggestions on how staff development can be made more effective.

> I think staff development has to be tailored to individual needs of a teacher. It's silly to have elementary and high school teachers sit down and listen to the speaker speak on one topic and expect everyone to come away charged up because of what they have heard. It's really a waste of time. Perhaps having teachers break down into grade-level or interest-level groups that would cut across their teaching-level assignments and having them structure staff development to their needs would be a better method of providing staff development. Finding people who may even come from within their own ranks to provide in-house inservice on what things work for them makes more sense than the way inservice is now so frequently provided.

In this manner, staff development would be provided based on career stages and individual needs of teachers.

Finally, Henry objects to the tendency of some people to use a business analogy when talking about schooling and teacher support systems. He feels that this analogy is misused to make specific points about schools and does not include the ways in which teachers are supported.

One thing that really disturbs me greatly, it really makes me ill, is the tendency to equate business or corporate language to schools and school systems. For example, boards of education are very willing and ready to talk about school as a business but they don't apply that to each and every aspect of education. They make it more of a financial or personnel type of issue rather than a global analogy and I think that's erroneous. If they are going to use it at all, it should be applied at all levels. In the corporate world, people are paid for advanced training. If they are required to obtain certain skills for their position, their education is paid for and they are given released time from work to do so. That doesn't happen in education. I know very few teachers that drive a school system car, I know very few teachers who have an hour lunch, so the analogy really breaks down when it comes to organizational support of teachers.

Henry has moved through the various growth stages of the career teacher. Due to a variety of situations in his organizational environment he is now in a wind-down phase endeavoring to exit K–12 teaching and the classroom. His goal is to stay within the broad realm of education, however.

Ultimately, I have set a goal to be able to work with preservice teachers somewhere—at college or university level. Working with student teachers is a way of giving back to other people what I have been given by significant others along the way. Ultimately this impacts on students indirectly. Whether that happens in five or ten years, . . . time will tell.

Summary

The career wind-down stage occurs when a teacher is preparing to leave the profession. For some it is a time for positive reflection on accomplishments, relationships, and impact on the lives of others as one prepares for retirement or career change. For others it may be a bitter period, with reflections focusing on unsuccessful experiences, frustration, or involuntary job termination. Factors from personal and organizational environments often influence the way in which the career wind-down teacher views the career that is being left. Appropriate development programs may include assistance in making the transition from teaching into a new career or into retirement and may also include strategies for providing recognition and leadership opportunities for those who are preparing to leave teaching. While the career wind-down stage is generally viewed as a precursor to career exit, for some teachers it may be the lead-in for a fresh preservice or induction phase for a new position or role within schools or for a career option outside of education.

CHAPTER TEN

Career Exit

JOHN H. MCDONNELL   PETER J. BURKE

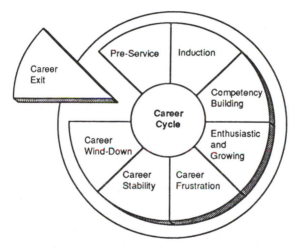

The exiting stage of a teacher's career is the period of time after the teacher leaves the job, but includes circumstances other than simply retirement after many years of service. It could be a period of unemployment after involuntary or elective job termination or a temporary career exit for child rearing. It could also be a time of alternative career exploration or of moving to a nonteaching position in education such as administration.

The career-exit stage of the career cycle focuses on the life of teachers once they have exited teaching. This stage may come at a variety of points in the career timeline and may occur in a variety of different circumstances. A traditional way of viewing this stage is voluntary retirement after years of service. Others leave after shorter periods of teaching for reasons of child rearing or to pursue alternative career options outside of teaching. Still others exit teaching in order to move into alternative career options within education, such as administration, supervision, counseling, or school psychology. In addition, still others leave teaching involuntarily, either because of reductions in staffing due to enrollment declines or because of unsatisfactory evaluations from administrators and supervisors. The environment surrounding career exit may be positive or negative, depending on the circumstances leading to the decision to leave.

Many teachers who are in the exit stage have moved through what the literature on adult development terms a "crisis" stage in their personal life (Sheehy 1976) or, if not a crisis, have at least moved through some sort of mid-life "transition" (Krupp 1981). One study of case histories of teachers identified two stressful transitional periods (Newman et al. 1980), which culminated at the tenth and twentieth years of teaching. At around the tenth year, teachers assess their career situation and decide whether to remain in the profession. At about year twenty they examine their careers and determine whether to exit or engage in professional renewal. Career exit may be the choice at either of these periods.

Teachers may arrive at the career-exit stage from any one of the other stages. A preservice student may realize through one of several required field-based assignments that teaching is not the right choice for a profession. This individual may exit the career before it even begins.

Induction experiences may cause an honest self-appraisal and result in a career exit as well. Teachers in the induction stage also are the most at risk for lay-off, and a reduction-in-force may be the reason for a movement from induction to career exit.

Competency-building teachers may also suffer from reduction-in-force exits. Demographic trends in enrollments or course selection could cause an unplanned or unwanted career exit for a teacher who is in the growth period of his/her career. These teachers may also self-select out of the profession. Their movement to the exit stage may come out of a realization that their needs are too great, or the distance necessary to travel to meet the needs is insurmountable. They, too, may exit the profession.

Enthusiastic and growing teachers may exit to another career or to another role in education. They may exhibit skills that are valued by outside employers, like communication or organization, and they can be lured out of teaching. They may have a need to have a greater impact on the profession and move to administration or to a teacher preparation role in higher education. The profession's biggest loss is the career exit of enthusiastic and growing teachers.

Teachers who are frustrated or burned out with their job are the most likely to move into the career-exit stage. If they are not doing their job, they should be forced out or encouraged to self-select out of teaching. The constant struggle of administration is to move teachers out of a career frustration mode either into a more productive role or into the career exit stage.

Career stability teachers, for the most part, move into the exit stage through retirement or planned resignation. They, too, may move to administrative positions or pupil support roles for a change of pace. It is possible, however, that these teachers will exit after having the same year's experience twenty or more times over.

Teachers in career wind-down will, by definition, move into the exit stage. They are cognizant of their next move and are, for the most part, looking forward to it.

Once in the career-exit stage, regardless of how the teachers moved through the cycle to arrive, there are few influences from either the organizational or the personal environment that create change for these teachers. They have departed. Yet often the impact of a teacher's career influences one's reaction to a new career. In the following sections, the lives of career-exited teachers will be chronicled concerning activities engaged in and how they are influenced by the past experiences of a teaching career. Reflections on a life career of teaching are highlighted by the retired teacher.

Teacher Profiles

Donna

Donna is 48, married, with two children away from home. She taught elementary children for six years in a mid-sized city in a Midwest farm state. She was active in a teachers' union at the time. She is also active in a professional women educators' association. She is currently the director of a regional teachers' organization in a state in the upper Midwest.

Donna was actively involved in the union during her classroom teaching career. Her reaction to what she viewed as "capricious actions" by administrators gradually led her to career exit into full-time union work.

> When I was a teacher, I was actively involved in the union. I became involved in the union because of what I saw were real arbitrary, capricious actions by building administrators as well as district administrators. I had some friends in the union and we felt that the only way we could fight back was to be part of a stronger union, so I became a local president with about 1300 members. I was a member of the negotiating team, and I found at some point that I was doing almost as much union work as teaching work.

My role as a union president provided 20 days a year by contract to do union business. I was married, I had two children, and I was spending almost every night to midnight doing union business. I wanted to get even for some of the terrible things I had seen happen. Then at some point I realized I could be as effective doing my union business as a full-time staff person as I could being a teacher. If I had any disillusionment with my teaching, it was as a result of arbitrary, capricious actions that I saw by the administrators. My work with the children was a delight up until the very end, but I was taken out of teaching in order to do union work.

Clearly, Donna's organizational environment in the form of her administration's leadership style resulted in her exiting teaching although staying in the field of education. This career change affected her personal life; she divorced just about the time a new bargaining law went into effect. The challenges of being a single parent working actively in a new career were demanding.

In my first years of this job they had the new bargaining law. About that time I was divorced. My children lived with me and I was working 7 days a week—12, 15, 18 hours a day. It was probably the most exhausting period of my life. I worked Thanksgiving Day—worked Christmas Eve—worked during Christmas vacation—terribly exhausting. It was especially difficult on my children, who have told me more than once how they really resented being left alone. But as a single parent, I didn't have an option. It was exciting; we were caught up in the cause of the union movement, bargaining for the first time in the state.

Donna certainly felt an excitement about her job that she did not evidence when discussing her six years in teaching.

Her work as union staff took her four years later to a neighboring state where she became a regional director working with seven local unions, a significant decrease from her former load of thirty-seven. During that time she seemed to have moved from an enthusiastic and growing stage to one of career frustration. "I felt very uncomfortable, but the newness of the job at first just kept me going. The bargaining laws were all new; it was very lonely. Our office was very isolated, and I had little contact with peers."

During the first few years, the lack of support from the parent organization took its toll. After eleven years on the job, Donna is showing signs of entering the career frustration stage and is again considering career exit. She has significant growth needs, which will be explored later in this chapter.

Peter

Peter is 40 years old, married, with two children—one in elementary school and one in preschool. He taught for thirteen years in a small suburban community in the upper Midwest. During this time he belonged to a local, state, and national teachers' association. He left teaching to work for an insurance company, where he serves as an insurance adjuster for crop damage.

Peter became interested in teaching while he was in high school due to an influential math teacher. He went to a state university where he majored in elementary education and then took advantage of a federally funded program to finish his master's degree in reading. He taught for five years in an elementary school, then for eight in a middle school and as a reading specialist. He describes his experiences over time as follows:

> I enjoyed teaching sixth grade because I like that particular age group. They were anxious to learn. I enjoyed the reading specialist work because of the fact that you could deal with remedial programs and development programs and work with the accelerated kids. That was interesting. I then did seventh and eighth grade. After doing that for eight years I started to get in a rut as far as where I was going, and I was just looking for something else.

He took the new job as a result of ongoing summer employment with the firm.

He cites several spillover skills from teaching that he utilizes in his current employment.

> Organization is important. Part of the job is training agents. I don't feel terribly frightened or intimidated getting in front of a group of people to present. It is just like being in a classroom situation. In teaching, with people, you are interacting, and on my current job that is the biggest part.

Peter looks back fondly on his teaching career.

> I had some very positive experiences. The camaraderie at the school where I taught was exceptional. I used to have a lot of flexibility. Looking back, it was a good staff to work with. When you get into a specialist role, you have people looking at you like you are not a classroom teacher. But I did get a lot of support. I tried not to force myself upon others. The person that was there before tried to do that. People tended to resent the programs as such. I tried to give them as much support as I could. I'll do what I can for you but I'm not going to tell you what you do in your classroom.
>
> I found that the wrong approach is telling others what to do. I think you do better if you can suggest that perhaps they can implement it into their classroom in some way.

This strategy for working with others certainly will support him in the business world.

Peter finds his new control over time refreshing, as well as the autonomy of being in control.

I like the flexibility. I'm my own boss. When the claims come in, if I want to work 12 hours that given day, if I want to do two claims, I can do that. When the work is there we work—long hours—but I like the flexibility in the fact that if I want to take 2 hours off in the middle of the day to go someplace I can do that, whereas as a teacher you are expected to be there from 8:00 to 4:00 every day.

The "summer time off" as a teacher was more ethereal than his time flexibility now. Then the summers were time for work to supplement his teacher's salary.

Gladys

Gladys is 79 years old, a widow, with three grown children and eight grandchildren. She taught English for 32 years, 26 of those in a high school in a small upper Midwest city. Gladys did take a leave from teaching for several years when her children were young. She received her B.A. degree from a small liberal arts college in the same city. She was a member of a local, state, and national teachers' association as well as a professional organization for teachers of English.

Although exited from her teaching career, she continues to be active in both paid and volunteer activities. She describes her job and indicates how the opportunity arose after years of being in the community.

I have a job at the local bank simply because one of my students was an officer there. He wanted to have a seniors' program and he knew that I would know the people because I've been in the city for almost fifty years now. I just had to write a description of what I do. The big thing is that I like working with people, and I know the senior citizens—a lot of them—because I had their kids in school.

She remembers her teaching career fondly. Throughout her interviews she had difficulty recalling negatives. When asked if there are any negative points about teaching that she can reflect back on, she replied:

Not really. There were some times when things were a little rougher than others. I think you have to learn to go with the flow. I got along well with the kids. I liked them. I let them know at the very beginning that I hoped they were going to like English and I was sure it would not be their favorite. I am a rotten mathematician, and I don't mind telling people that because I do something else. I only asked that they do the best they could, and, as a result, I never really had any problems. I never sent a kid to the office in 32 years. That's pretty good. I don't suppose that it would be such a good record these days since the students are so different. I went to school when teachers were really thought well of—almost revered, respected. If I called up a parent and said, "Hey, where is he?," his father and mother got on him and as a result we became friends after a while.

Gladys has been in education many years and readily points out changes that have occurred. Being a respected teacher, supported by parents, was then and is now a formula for a teacher's career that continues in an enthusiastic and growing stage. After 32 years she exited with fond memories of teaching and the enthusiasm to work and find other supportive activities, which will be documented elsewhere.

Personal Environmental Influences

Four categories of influence seem to be particularly important in the personal environment of career-exit teachers: life stage, family, individual dispositions, and avocational outlets. While influences from other categories do exist, these areas seem to be the major influences on the teacher career cycle at the exit stage.

Life-Stage Influences

Background information on teacher life stage, or adult life stage, was described in Chapter 1. Frequently, mid-life or later-life crises occur. In addition, there are transitional periods that may occur at certain chronological ages or following specific time periods of experience. These crises or periods of transition are influences from the personal environment that may be responsible for the teacher being in the career-exit stage.

A high school teacher, for example, may spend the first five or ten years in teaching being able to communicate with and understand the needs of adolescent students. This teacher might experience a transition that develops a distance between his/her own and the students' personal styles. The realization of this growing separateness may be the influence to push the teacher into the career-exit stage. In other words, a teacher may mature beyond the second or third generation of students, find it difficult to understand or develop rapport with these new and different students, and quit teaching.

Another example of a mid-life crisis that might be responsible for a career exit is sudden emotional shock. A divorce or the death of a loved one could force a teacher to take a careful, introspective look at him or herself and then to establish new life goals. These new goals may not include remaining in teaching and may result in a career exit.

Family Influences

Financial needs of the family are also an important influence from the personal environment of career-exit teachers. While intrinsic rewards are important, they do not put food on the table. Thus, as families grow and as needs and demands for more fiscal resources increase, the influence to leave the profession increases. This family financial need may first be met through moonlighting a second job in the evening, on weekends, or during summers. Often the promise of better conditions, more flexibility, and, most important, more money convinces teachers that their part-time job could be a very rewarding full-time occupation. Once again, they exit the career.

Individual Dispositions

Another personal influence for teachers who are in the career-exit stage is their own individual disposition. Their life goals may have changed and priorities may have been restructured, resulting in teaching being given a lower priority rating. Interpersonal relationships with colleagues, peers, or administrators may have soured or may never have ripened. Without a true feeling of community between and among co-workers, it is difficult to remain in the job. The teachers' personal value systems may be stronger, or weaker, than those of peers. This, too, can create an isolation and become an influence to leave the profession.

Avocational Outlets

The attraction of more time to pursue avocational outlets is an additional influence from the personal environment that may be important to the career-exit teacher. Early retirement to travel, pursue outdoor activities, write or spend time with civic, social, or religious organizations may be an exit impetus. Making a full-time occupation out of a part-time hobby, like art or music or home remodeling, could be another draw. The personal environment has influenced the career-exit stage of our three subjects in several different ways.

Impact of Personal Environment on Donna, Peter, and Gladys

Donna

Our introduction to Donna shows us a former teacher now actively engaged in staff activities for a teachers' organization. It may not be surprising that the growing forces that led her to career exit came primarily from the organizational environment and led her into an increasingly militant stance regarding teacher rights and protection. These elements from the organizational environment will be discussed in a later section.

Peter

On the other hand, Peter's withdrawal from teaching and entry into the business world was motivated partially from elements in his personal environment. The first element was money. In his 30s with two children, Peter found it necessary to take summer employment that evolved into a full-time job that enabled him to meet more fully the perceived needs of his family.

Two other elements of a personal nature cemented his decision: He found himself in the stage of career stability and at an age where career exit and change would become increasingly difficult.

> I really felt I was in a rut. It becomes very repetitious—even when the kids change—you try to change programs to meet kids' needs—but basically it was the same thing. I reflected on my age. I knew the longer I stayed in education, the harder it would be if I ever did want to get out. Once you get to be 45 years old, you can't go out into the job market. So I thought the age was right, timing was right. I had the advantage of knowing the job since I had been doing it for nine summers. I found out that it was much less stressful, much more flexible. It was actually a bonus as far as what I thought it would be. So I guess those were the key things—stagnation, money, age. I didn't think that I wanted to teach until I was 65.

Gladys

Gladys's personal environment has had a major influence on her career in teaching. Her family environment, her college experiences, and her status as a first-generation American were powerful stimulants for her pursuing a life in teaching. She remembers:

> I always knew that teaching was what I wanted to do. When I was a little kid, I liked teaching the dolls and kids in the neighborhood. But really I like working with people, and when I was at college, it was a real revelation to me because I'm a first-generation American. My father and mother were born in Czechoslovakia so I've had a very healthy regard for education. My father let me pick where I wanted to go to school. My favorite high school history teacher was a graduate of the first class that graduated women. So when I started college I planned to come to a small liberal arts college for two years, and then to a major private Midwestern university because they had a very fine school of speech. But I was so satisfied that I never left.

Gladys's college experience intertwined with her personality to prepare her to accept the ebb and flow of her organizational environment.

> In college I learned what I thought I needed here and I was willing to go with the flow. I think it's part of your personality. You make it or you don't. I never complained bitterly when administrators or people did things that I didn't agree with because I realized that they had a different view than I did. I don't think you should be a complainer—especially a teacher. I think it reflects on the kids. I really liked going to school every day.

Gladys' decision to exit teaching was simple—she reached 65 at a time prior to the passing of legislation allowing people to work based on their ability to do the job, not age. In Gladys's case an earlier change in federal legislation would have allowed an enthusiastic and growing teacher to maintain her career to the benefit of many of her students.

Any of these personal environmental influences mentioned above could work independently or in combination with others to create an impact on the career-exit teacher. Organizational influences also play a role in a teacher's decision to exit. Effects of the organization may still play a role in their lives. There may be specific influences that either push them to exit or continue to be important to them. These organizational influences are the topic of the next section.

Organizational Environmental Influences

The influences on career exit teachers from the organizational environment may work to keep the teachers in an exit posture or to attract them back to the profession in either the same or an alternate capacity. The influences responsible for the teacher's exit may also keep the teacher away. A valuable employee who has left the profession might be invited back by shifting organizational influences to make reentry more attractive. This reentry could be as a teacher, or it could be in another capacity that emphasizes the teacher's skills and abilities.

Categories of influence from the organizational environment that make a difference for the career-exit teacher include the union, public and societal attitudes, management style, and school regulations. Just as there are several reasons for a teacher's exit, so, too, are there varying attitudes about the influences from these several categories. The influence of one or another of the categories, such as public attitudes, may be quite different for a happily re-tired teacher than they are for one who has been dismissed for the use of contro-versial teaching techniques. For this reason it is difficult to generalize about organizational influences on career exit teachers. The discussion that follows divides the influences of each category into positive and negative components, and the case studies of teachers substantiate how these influences have an impact on teachers in the career exit stage of the career cycle.

Teachers' Union

The teachers' union, by and large, is a positive influence on teachers who have voluntarily left the profession. They often see the collegiality engendered by the united teaching profession as positive, and they are grateful for the protection and security afforded to them by union membership. Many career-exit teachers have been formally recognized for their work by the union, and the union could be a vehicle for continuing involvement following their exit. This involvement could range from accepting a staff position with the union, to being responsible for seminars on benefits, to helping individual union members improve in the face of termination or inefficiency, to participating in retired teachers' peer support systems.

Union influence might be viewed as negative by those who felt unprotected or by those who disagreed with the positions taken on issues by the majority of the membership. Teachers who have been dismissed might feel that the union was not strong enough on acting in their behalf. Because of this feeling the teacher might be reluctant to reenter the profession or might side with the administration or school board on a given issue and see the pressure brought to bear by the union on the issue as negative.

Public Opinion

Career-exit teachers become part of the public voice that influences education. This contribution by former teachers can be very positive, or it can take on an extremely pejorative connotation. Those who were satisfied and happy with their teaching experiences will speak positively about the profession. They will become citizen members of education councils or committees. Their experience in the profession provides a persuasive voice for change and improvement in local schools, school districts, or state and national initiatives in education. Career-exit teachers might take leadership roles in PTAs or PTOs in building renovation or referenda committees or in special interest groups that lobby for school effectiveness issues. Again, their experience is a valuable tool to argue for positive change.

Career-exit teachers who were disgruntled with their experience can, and often do, offer a negative voice to public or societal opinion about the schools. In this vein their experience is used to thwart positive action in the schools. Taxpayers' alliances, back-to-basics groups, critical councils, or other special-interest groups are continually looking for and using former teachers' voices to support their means and goals. This influence often works against the initiatives of the local school or against the policy plans of a district or of the state. In this case the influence of former teachers is a force for the status quo, or, unfortunately, a regressive force in the profession.

Management Style

Some teachers leave teaching because of an autocratic principal or superintendent. Recent research on effective schools has pointed out the value of shared decision making and the need for teacher input into this decision making, resulting in a renewed interest in a more democratic style of leadership. This change in management style might influence good teachers who left because of a feeling of powerlessness to reenter the profession. Changes in school rules, such as allowing job sharing or differentiated assignments, could also attract career-exit teachers back to the classroom and, therefore, be an important influence from the organizational environment.

Impact of Organizational Environment on Donna, Peter, and Gladys

Donna

Organizational influences have played an important role in the careers of our three teachers. This is especially true in Donna's case. Anti-union actions by administrators were key factors in her decision to become actively involved in the union movement and to eventually exit teaching for a staff position in a union. She states:

> My principal was terribly insecure. He could not stand having me, as president-elect with automatic succession to the presidency, in his building. I was leaving before 4:00 p.m. to go to the administration building to work with the superintendent of schools on something. The principal called to see if I was really going there, and it just got worse and worse. Finally, at Christmas time, I thought it would be better for the both of us if I would teach in another building. Today that would have been grounds for prohibitive practice, but this was in the '70s. The strong union folks taught in other buildings. Sometimes the principals would have open violations of teachers' rights. The contract said 8:00 to 4:00. They had no qualms about making teachers sit in on a meeting until 5:00 and we were like sheep; we did not protest much until some of us got some gumption.

Her experience in the teaching profession has important influences on her current professional responsibilities.

I don't think you can be a unit director unless you have a basic understanding of what teachers go through. Organization is critical. Teachers have to be organized—stick to it, are bound to a daily schedule. Teachers have to get to work on time. Unit workers ought to be prompt with meeting appointments. Punctuality. Thoroughness. Teachers teach until kids learn. Directors have to work on something until it gets resolved. Follow-through. As a teacher, if you say you are going to do a certain thing a certain way, you'd better do it or you will be in deep trouble. Organizational-type skills were learned from teaching. But you have to have a knowledge of what a teacher goes through on a day-to-day basis.

Other aspects of her teaching experience have been dysfunctional to her new role. Based on her evaluation and her self-perception, she was a good teacher; this sometimes leads to conflicts.

This job wants you to be on the lookout for things that are not right in the school system. You look for the negatives. The thing that I am finding out lately is I'm sometimes less than patient with teachers who aren't also good. I can't understand why teachers are not in school on time. There's very little excuse for that. I can't understand why they don't have lesson plans. Sometimes I'm afraid I hold teachers to a very high standard and that causes conflict. Yes, I have to defend all whether they are good or bad. Sometimes I have to say to them, "You really screwed up." That's not easy.

Peter

Peter exited teaching for private employment in business partially due to finding himself in the career stability stage. He is clear as to how aspects in the organizational environment might have influenced him not to exit teaching. Opportunities for sabbaticals and enhanced teacher mobility might have made a difference.

I was toying around with the idea of a sabbatical to get out for a year and then decide whether I would stay or exit. That did not happen, but I think if that program had been available I would have opted to do that. Another thing I would like to see is a bit more mobility. If you are certified K–12, as I was, give that person some mobility so that you are not teaching all seventh-graders. I talked to a lot of classroom teachers and they teach five hours and one hour a day study hall, five hours in a row. I don't see how you can help but get yourself in a rut. Even though those classes are all different, you still will be going over the same material. Why wouldn't you want to give that person a change? Possibly just even moving a grade. If you're teaching seventh grade, move to ninth, or whatever, as long as the teacher is qualified.

Upon further probing by the interviewer, Peter describes intuitively the career stage theory and indicates the beneficial effect of organizational change that would allow for more teacher mobility.

> There were a lot of people in the same rut. There were a lot of people who, if a job opened that they wanted to take, would have left teaching. Then there were people who really liked what they were doing and wanted to teach until they were 65 or so. Then you had people who were just putting in their time—waiting—hoping something would open up. That does not mean that those people who were just putting in their time weren't dedicated. I think if you go into any school district you will find people in all those categories. Some people are just putting in their time and that's all and then you've got the people who put in their time but also are prepared and do a good job. But I did hear comments from quite a few people that they were really getting burned out. I would have liked to explore elementary teaching, and I also would have liked to explore high school. But I was stuck. I didn't have that option. I didn't have that mobility. If I would have been able to do that, I might have stayed.

Additional organizational support systems could have made a difference.

For Peter, the relational aspect of the organizational environment was positive but was not influential enough to keep him in the profession.

> It gets back to the staff that I worked with. It was a very close knit group—no back stabbing. Administratively I never had a problem. I worked for the same administrator all through the years that I taught. I didn't step on his toes and he never stepped on mine. I did what was expected and didn't ask for things that I knew couldn't happen. In general, the group of teachers and administration that I worked with had a pretty good working relationship. We didn't have a lot of problems.

Gladys

The influence of the organizational environment on Gladys was mixed. The personal traits she identified earlier plus her college experiences did help her to be more accepting of the negatives than others in our case studies. A case in point was a teachers' strike.

> We had a strike. I guess I'm of the old school; I didn't believe in withholding services from the students. On the other hand, I felt that there were areas that needed looking into, such as too many kids in classrooms.

Thirty-three or more kids in an English class is too many because in my classes they wrote at least once a week and they got papers back the next week. I want to tell you I didn't get to sleep early too many nights, particularly when I was doing all the school drama productions. I struck and my children just thought, "Mother out striking!" However, I thought it was for a point. I don't like the idea. I think kids ought to be in school, but I think if that's the only way you can let people know how you feel then maybe you have to do it.

Looking back some eighteen years after the strike, Gladys feels the union was a positive organizational support. She cites an example:

I think we needed the union. One Sunday afternoon, I was ironing children's clothes and the football coach came to the door. We were having a problem with the coach, who was being leaned upon by a school board member. The coach was the kind that said you follow the rules or you don't play and this kid did not follow the rules. So the coach said, "You don't play." The board member was anxious to get rid of him. So we all decided that that was not fair. Our whole faculty supported the coach. I feel that we wanted to help each other. We felt that it wasn't right for a man to be maligned for doing what he said he would do. I thought of that many years later when we had the strike. I don't really believe in strikes. But there comes a time when it is necessary. We have never had another one. You have to realize what the situation is and, if you are in a school system that is doing things you disapprove of, you either have to speak up or get out.

Like Donna, Gladys was part of the transition to growing teacher militancy that occurred in the 1960s and 1970s. Donna was a new teacher and chose to become a union worker. Gladys had been in the classroom far too long to readily accept the new organization influence of the union, but accept it she did. Her commitment to teaching and her feelings of teacher efficacy led her to work together with other teachers in the union to obtain some degree of teacher empowerment.

One other element of the organizational environment is important to Gladys in her retirement. The collegiality developed during her teaching years remains as an important support for her now. She describes her "annual soiree."

In our department we always had a dozen or more teachers. On Sunday I am having our annual soiree, called this by my friends. It started out two or three years ago. I served dinner the Sunday before school closed for Christmas. I started with the English department and then as people left to go on to other things or some left this clime, I added a few other people on the faculty—a couple of musicians and the teachers in foreign languages.

Well, we are meeting and cooking next on Sunday. We still stick together after all of these years. I still exchange Christmas cards with at least a dozen old faculty members. We go to the class reunions. We have a fine old time.

The career-exit stage is the one facet of the teacher career cycle that has the teacher as an outsider looking into the profession. While influences do exist from both the personal and organizational environment, these categories of influence are viewed in a completely different light by teachers on the outside. Their views as former teachers may strengthen attitudes, or their new outlook might change formerly held opinions. These changes could have a positive influence on the profession, or they could be designed to have a negative impact. Growth needs for teachers in the career-exit stage are also unique due to their position outside of the classroom. These growth needs are the topic of the next section.

Growth Needs of Career-Exit Teachers

The concept of growth needs for career-exit teachers is most important to those who leave the classroom for another position in education. Even though they are no longer teaching, it is essential that they stay current with trends in classroom instruction in their new roles as counselors, librarians, administrators, or higher-education or professional association employees. In addition to the renewal on classroom work, these educators have growth needs for their new work as well. Professional development opportunities that combine both of these possibilities are the best method of meeting the growth needs of career-exit teachers.

Growth Needs and Role Options

Using the Christensen, McDonnell, and Price (1988) Career Lattice Model, three role options provide a description of growth needs for career-exit teachers: knowledge production, teacher preparation, and leadership. Responsibilities under these role options for career-exit teachers depend on the exact nature of their roles outside of the classroom. The following six role functions provide outlets for the growth needs of career-exit teachers: curriculum, instructional materials, classroom management, school climate, communication, and professionalism.

If the teacher has left the classroom for a position in higher education or in a professional association, the knowledge production option is most likely in the area of teacher preparation or professionalism. These exit teachers will be working with professional staff members in all of the other stages of the career cycle. Their job becomes one of communication between segments of the profession with a responsibility to maintain or increase the professionalism of those remaining in the classroom. Career-exit teachers may become an external resource for the professional development of inservice teachers. They may even become a provider of career growth opportunities.

Professional organizations often provide a continuous variety of seminars, workshops, conferences, or conventions for their membership. Those who plan and present the workshops are very often teachers, or former teachers, in the career-exit category. The growth need for these exit teachers, then, is to stay current with the needs of those in the classroom so that programs can be designed and delivered to meet those needs.

Those teachers who leave for a role in higher teacher education also have a role as a provider of staff development programs. They have an additional role, however, of determining the content and thrust of the programs. They are responsible for designing and carrying out the research that defines program improvement efforts. This is the key knowledge production responsibility. Beyond this research is the responsibility of communicating the findings to increase the professionalism of teaching. Growth needs for these career-exit teachers center around support systems for doing the research and communicating the findings.

Teachers who exit their classroom careers for support roles—counselors or librarians—have both growth needs of their own and collaborative needs with other teachers. Their own individual needs center on their new role in the profession. Seminars, workshops, and courses designed to improve their skills in their new jobs are of primary importance. Often their roles support classroom work as well. In this instance their needs include learning techniques to support classroom activities in their schools. Teachers may have exited their careers for positions in line or staff administration. The primary role option for these former teachers is often that of leadership. Responsibilities such as classroom management, curriculum writing, instructional materials, evaluation, or school climate improvement become their major tasks. Growth needs include mastery of techniques to provide leadership to classroom teachers in these several areas.

Growth Needs of Donna, Peter, and Gladys

The growth needs described by Donna, Peter, and Gladys reflect the universal nature of the need for continued learning and growth for any individual in any field.

Donna
Donna's growth needs are evident. After eleven years in her job, Donna feels that she is probably in a new stage of her career. "I've been through all the phases. Now I'm going through that of career stability." She describes her feelings:

I don't know if burnout is the right word. I'm not working near my potential because I'm 48. I don't know if I'm looking to exit—looking to maybe getting a better handle on what I'm doing because the enthusiasm isn't there anymore. I work with individual teachers who get themselves into scrapes and/or are incompetent. It's getting increasingly difficult to be patient with teachers who have caused trouble at their end. I think I'm going to seek out some peer help. Our national organization has a couple of workshops which are called "Survive and Thrive"—week-long layups which people go through so that they don't get stagnant and they want to continue, and that's where I am in my job.

During this phase Donna is once more considering career exit; her former career clearly has some attraction.

I know that what is going on in a teacher's life today is probably very different from what it was when I left. I know wistfully that it would be kind of fun to go back to the classroom. But I do have lots of doubts about it. So I question myself—what if I quit my job, could I teach again? I don't know if anyone would hire me. I'm a union person. I mean, I've burned a lot of bridges. It would take a very secure person to have a regional director in their school. I would have to be certified again. And then I think at 48, do I want to do that? Teachers have homework and preparation, but being at the job from 8:00 to 4:00 is really attractive. I worked until late last night, and I'm not going to get home until late tonight. So teaching still remains attractive.

Donna's confusion is evident, as are her growth needs.
Donna's focus on life-long learning has changed since she was a classroom teacher. Her teaching instilled in her this growth need.

One thing that I did as a teacher—I always took classes and I was working on my master's degree when I left. That instilled a real sense that to be successful you have got to be up in your field—but as a unit director I am not doing it. I feel I'm really lacking. I'm probably keeping up in my field, but I am not taking classes and courses like I should, such as a computer course. Growth and development—I'm not doing it and I'm using all sorts of excuses for not doing it. Wouldn't you know that there would be a final or paper due the same time I would have a mediation or an arbitration and there would be a conflict; therefore, I would let my work come ahead of my classes. So my class would go to pot and I wouldn't get the A that I am determined to get. I feel I'm really lacking in that area.

Interestingly enough, many of the growth needs of teachers that are often ignored by school districts are also being ignored by teacher unions regarding their own staff, at least as perceived by Donna.

Peter

Peter's growth needs in his current job are similar to those he faced as a classroom teacher—more guided experience, more coursework.

> The job that I currently have is an experience-based position. You look at certain crops, you have to be able to identify which stage the crop is in. They're constantly changing so we basically take a look at all the crops grown in the state. There's a world of knowledge out there that I feel that I don't have, but the guy that's leaving has been here 35 years. He has an unbelievable amount of knowledge. It's a learning job. It is a form of education in this field. I would hope that I would constantly be learning. I'm hoping to take some insurance courses and get a better background. I didn't really have an insurance background, so right now as I look at the job I need a few more courses.

Gladys

Gladys focuses on the role of teacher-as-learner. This is still a need for her, as it was when she was in the classroom. Her life-long love of reading was instilled by family and nurtured by her college experience.

> College instills this need for life-long learning. We were readers in our family and my brother and sisters still read. My children are readers. I think it's because I read. I read to them and I still do. My usual time to read is from 5:00 to 7:00 in the morning. It's a habit. I wake up and I'm reading the *New Yorker*. I'm a little behind now, but I do think that being in college and being required to do a fair amount of reading gets you into the habit of teaching you English. You have to keep up with the literature. I do think that teachers have to be readers. They ought to read the educational material. I don't see how you can be any kind of teacher without reading. You need to keep up with the new trends.

Gladys has clearly learned how to meet her growth needs throughout her teaching career. Habits of a lifetime stand her in good stead during her exit years.

The growth needs of career-exit teachers are either external to the classroom or are defined by their role as a provider of staff development activities. Incentives also may vary according to the new role taken by the former teacher. Incentives for career exit teachers are the topic of the next section.

Incentives for Career-Exit Teachers

One way to look at incentives in the career-exit stage of the teacher career cycle is to consider those incentives that might attract good former teachers back into the classroom. These might include leadership opportunities, paid sabbatical leaves, support for research and writing, job security, or opportunities for advancement.

Leadership Opportunities

Leadership opportunities (or lack thereof) may have been the response to growth needs and the reason for leaving the classroom in the first place. Once on the outside, a former teacher might see more opportunity for leadership activities that could be coupled with classroom teaching. This fresh point of view could give rise to a reentry incentive that would make a position such as team leader or department chair a satisfactory solution to the teacher's unmet leadership growth need.

Leaves

Teachers in career exit may have come to realize that the time away from the classroom was necessary to renew or redirect their professional lives. A short time out of the classroom could be valuable for this renewal, resulting in a firmer dedication to teaching upon reentry. Another category of career-exit teachers who experience this renewal might be those who chose to leave for child rearing or other family responsibilities. Paid sabbatical leaves are an important incentive for those teachers who see a need and recognize value in a specific amount of time away from the classroom for the purpose of renewal. A regular schedule of time away could make reentry more palatable to these career-exit teachers.

Research and Writing

Support for research and writing has been cited before as an important incentive for teachers in other stages. Those who leave the classroom, but not the profession, might see this support as an incentive to return. Action research was described in Chapter 5. Career-exit teachers, particularly those in higher education or administrative positions, could make classroom reentry through involvement in action research projects. Support for this type of research is an incentive for these people to get back into the classroom in a cooperative or collegial way. The result of this type of reentry should be an increased effectiveness of the classroom teacher.

Advancement

Similar to the need for leadership opportunities, the incentive for professional advancement weighs heavily with career-exit teachers. There have been many attempts to design a structure where the basically flat profession of teaching has advancement opportunities. A few leadership possibilities—such as department chair or unit leader—do exist. The profession has been testing career ladders and differentiated staffing to provide more opportunities. To date, these attempts have not given the broad-based possibilities for professional advancement that were designed to be part of the programs. In order to attract career exit teachers back into the classroom, the profession needs a firm and attractive professional advancement scheme.

Benefits and Security

A final incentive for career-exit teachers is in the area of benefits and security. The teacher may have left for alternative employment. The new experience may not be as promising as was thought, and the security and benefits of teaching might become very attractive to the teacher on the outside. Attractive retirement benefits are also incentives for teachers of retirement age. Financial security, adequate insurance benefits, and appropriate counseling for retirement planning are crucial.

In the following section our case study teachers discuss incentives they see as appropriate to them in their new roles and reflect back on incentives that were important to them while they were teaching. It is apparent that a variety of incentives are appropriate for people in roles outside of teaching as well.

Incentives for Donna, Peter, and Gladys

Donna

In Donna's position as a union unit director, appropriate incentives are similar to those valued by teachers. In fact, in Donna's organizational environment, few incentives seem to be available. In her words:

> The only real motivation in this job today, other than that paycheck, is self-motivation. I get very little support from the system. It's self pride— pride in your work that keeps you going. I think school districts did and are trying to do a decent job of motivating teachers.

Donna also sees evaluation as a positive incentive and refers back to her teaching days and its meaning for her at that stage in her career.

I haven't been evaluated for two years, in open violation of my contract. My contract specifies it should be done yearly.

Teachers get a lot more feedback. The evaluation process for the most part was very positive feedback, as was individual contact with parents. Parents were very grateful for the kinds of work the teachers would give recognition because of a program you had initiated. [In her current position] the members thank you here because of the receipt of dues and expect your work service in return for their dues. So they don't feel really obligated unless it is an extraordinary case.

Donna interprets evaluation broadly. It is clear that it was much more plentiful to her as a teacher than as a unit director.

Sabbaticals also have incentive appeal for Donna. Yet both her personal and organizational environments worked against her in utilizing one.

I have a son who is a sophomore in college. I can't afford to quit. He's going to be there two, probably three, more years. I sometimes wish I could have a leave of absence. It wouldn't even have to be a sabbatical. In this work I don't think six months is practical; you would have to take a year. They couldn't get anybody in for six months; there's no such thing as a substitute for directors. I think it would be GREAT! No strings attached. If you wanted to resign at the end you would just resign. If you want to clean out your desk and go, fine. A sabbatical, on the other hand, carries connotations that you would have to come back. You would come back refreshed.

For Donna a sabbatical would be an important incentive, but it is not available to her any more readily than it was when she was a classroom teacher.

Donna feels that financial incentives are important to her since her exit from the classroom. She realizes how different this is compared to many classroom teachers for whom she currently works. She remembers:

I started out a long time ago. The wages were low, but I never went into teaching with the thought of how much money I would be making. When I was in college, I never gave it a thought. I didn't have a vague notion of what teachers were being paid. In the late '50s it was akin to being a minister or a nurse. You weren't in it for the money; you were in it for the love of working with children. No one was fighting for my rights or for money in those days. You just knew that teachers accepted probably a lower standard of living than others. You lived comfortably and well, you dressed well, but you wouldn't go on big trips, etc. I think we were really quite content then.

The awareness of the teachers has changed because of the union. Teachers have a better understanding of their work. I think people really do say, well I'm doing the same work as so and so, but I'm only going to start at $19,000 and the engineers are going to start at $30,000. I'd like to think I'm wrong. I'd like to think that kids in college don't give thought to what they are going to get paid, but I don't think they are in the profession very long if they feel that way. When we get to them they want the highest possible salary. They want to compete socially and socio-economically with other people.

Donna's union position wins out over her former teaching role when it comes to financial incentives. But the intrinsic incentive associated with the professional teacher still remains. "Other than financial incentives, my own self-satisfaction is critical—to see a job well done. I don't get many thank you's or many rewards in my job. Personal satisfaction probably keeps me going."

Peter
The intrinsic motivation that maintains Donna in her new role is similar to Peter's response when asked what incentives are important to him in his new role in business.

I think the personal satisfaction of going out and doing a claim. Probably 96 or 97% of the time you don't have a lot of problems. I feel very good about the fact that someone gets a fair adjustment and then I feel that I've done a good job. It's basically self-motivating type thinking. Strive to do a good job every time you go out there. It doesn't make any difference whether there are 7 acres of corn or 7,000. One gets a check for $100, the other for $100,000. That shouldn't enter into it. It's just that when you leave there, you know that you did the best job that you could.

Peter clearly understands that this type of incentive was also important to him in his teaching days.

Getting back to remedial kids, you get a very good feeling when you can instruct them and definitely see that you have helped them. There is a lot of personal satisfaction in that. I still have parents write to me and say thank you very much for what you have done for Johnny. That means a lot. Every time you deal with people, whether you are teaching people who are young, or in the job that I have now, if you can't sit down and talk and explain and get your points across, then you will have problems. Being able to do that is very beneficial.

While a person may exit the teaching profession, intrinsic incentives from the personal environment that undergird the profession may still remain as strong incentives in a new work role.

Gladys

In her retirement, Gladys clearly remembers a variety of incentives that were important to her as a teacher, such as summer courses and conferences.

I liked going to the university to pick up extra credits. I also liked going to the seminars that we frequently had, particularly when the English curriculum was changing radically. We got away from teaching only classics and spread out a little bit. We went to a lot of conferences and took a lot of seminars and courses.

Autonomy in the classroom was an important incentive for her, yet as she looks back, she sees it as mixed in its effects on learning. When asked if she and her colleagues had enough classroom autonomy, she replied:

I think I did. Some teachers make a mistake in making a kid think that he is exactly on your level and so is everyone else—"We're all just chums and buddies together." I think there's a difference in letting a student know that you want him to do well and you will do all you can to help him from feeling you are going to be buddies. There should be a difference I think. He should feel you are there to teach him something he doesn't know. If he knows as much or more than you do, what is he doing there? Our school was really very liberal. They let us be as autocratic as we wanted to be. We had some people who really ran it like a marine camp but that's not my style. I think you have to teach according to your style. I was a mother and I knew that kids have good days and bad days, that there are some things you do better than others, and you have just to kind of meld it all together. I don't approve of their saying this is the way your class is going to be.

Like so many teachers, Gladys did not find salary to be an important incentive in her career. Yet the security incentive found in teaching is underlined by her comments on her retirement income.

When I started to teach in a small town in the upper Midwest my salary for the whole year was $1,350. In those days I lived with a family, a local dentist whose sister was in college with me. Her father was president of the school board, so guess how I got there to teach. It was 1930; things weren't doing so well. But I think teachers are now finally beginning to get closer to what they deserve.

I never earned more than $10,000 working 20 hours a day, but I did it because I wanted to. Now teachers start at $16,000 or $17,000 and I think you can go up to $30,000 or more now. When I was here, if you were making $12,000 or $13,000, you were lucky. I happened to leave the year salaries began to escalate. My teacher's retirement is better than that of people who retired two or three years before me. Teachers' retirement has done very well. My check is almost double what it was. But I don't think teachers have ever been overpaid. You don't really teach for the money.

Incentives for career-exit teachers, then, are both extrinsic and intrinsic. They deal with leadership, advancement, recognition, rewards, benefits, and self-satisfaction. The importance of intrinsic incentives to the teacher is well documented and is clearly evident in these three career-exit teachers, both as teachers and in their new careers. The financial incentives are underplayed; the security factor of retirement is important.

Support Systems for Career-Exit Teachers

Those career-exit teachers who have left the education profession utilize support systems that are external to the school. Unless they are anticipating a planned reentry into the classroom, there are not many education-related devices that serve to support any reconsideration of teaching.

Support for Reentry

Those who have moved into another role in the profession, however, or those who do plan to reenter at some future point in time do have specific support systems. The community, family, professional organizations, and continued school-based contact all work to support the reentry of a career-exit teacher.

Community involvement may shed a different light on the profession. A teacher may leave feeling unappreciated by the community, only to find out as a member of the community that there is great support and admiration for the teaching staff. Too often this support is from a nonvocal majority whose voice may have been lost in the din of special-interest groups. A realization of community trust is a key support for the career-exit teacher.

Support from the family works in much the same way. If a person has left teaching, only to find out that she or he really misses it, a supportive family— parents, spouses, or children—is a crucial support system to allow that person a chance to reenter. Family discussion of the pro's and con's of the job, the individual's motivation and future goals, and other considerations are an essential component of this support system.

Professional organizations were discussed in light of their importance to the lives of career-exit teachers, in the organizational environment influences and in the incentives sections of this chapter. These organizations or associations are an important source of support both for the reasons listed and for many other diverse reasons that could only be described on an individual basis. The awards, leadership opportunities, personal and professional development, and peer interaction that these groups provide are key sources of support for career-exit teachers if they continue to participate. These organizations can become a continuing link to the realities of the classroom.

Support Systems for Donna, Peter, and Gladys

Donna
As a classroom teacher, Donna learned strategies of survival that serve as a support mechanism for her role as a regional director of a teachers' union.

> You learn to play a game. You have principals to satisfy, curriculum supervisors to satisfy. You learn certain survival techniques, certain games that you play to keep principals off your back, to keep curriculum supervisors happy when they come to check your room. You really do learn survival skills—some ways to pacify people and to get along. If you learn those skills you are going to do okay on this job where you probably are more on your own than in a classroom situation. We are by ourselves in this office. I went to work last Friday in another unit office. They had four professional staff people there and a number of secretaries. I found it disconcerting to have that many people around when I'm used to working by myself. Those survival skills—the way you play the game—have really made it easier in this new work.

Donna recognizes the strengths and weaknesses of support systems when she was a teacher. The lack of union support is foremost in her comments, certainly an important reason for her move to union activity in her career exit and employment as a teacher union regional director.

> I don't know that my union provided me much support. We weren't even a union then. We didn't have a contract. I didn't teach under collective bargaining until the last two or three years of teaching. We had teachers' conventions, and we really took them seriously. You attended sessions that helped you in the classroom. I think they had other good services.

While union activities and advocacy often bring her into conflict with principals and school districts, Donna recognizes the support they can provide.

> I had good principals—even the one that drove me into the work that I'm in now. He was good in helping me through the problems with parents or curriculum. I think the district that I was in gave me freedom to try new

things in the classroom. For instance, teaching economics to elementary students. They encouraged me to try and let me have the time off during the school year to follow up on the work. We had a lot of enrichment. I don't think any needs of my classroom went unmet. The school district worked on a cooperative basis to help one another so the end result would be the product of the kids getting the best education.

Yet Donna feels that the future will see additional support needs for teachers that districts must meet.

I think districts are going to have to be more actively involved in employee assistance programs. We have teachers out there who are having problems—families, emotional, financial. I think there must be support groups. It's more than just saying call these people up if they are in trouble. They are going to have to encourage more wellness in situations. People are suffering from burnout which affects their physical and emotional lives. Districts will have more human resource people.

Peter

Other skills learned in the classroom continue to be of value to Peter and supportive in his new occupation.

In the insurance business, I go to meetings where people try to present something and they don't do a very good job. I think that the experience of getting in front of people—of being prepared—in all of those things "teacher qualifications" are being applied. You are selling a point, trying to get them to understand something. In teaching, you are also trying to sell a point.

Finally, Peter focuses on two types of support that were missing from his teaching career.

The ability to be a little bit flexible in getting some movement within positions would be very beneficial. There comes a time everybody reaches—the burnout point. I think that one way they could possibly keep people enthused about teaching is to get them new challenges, not to give the same thing over and over again. The other thing I would like to see would be the sabbatical. Even if it's just taking a year to get away and not do anything.

Perhaps if flexibility of assignments and sabbaticals had been part of the support system in Peter's district he might not have entered career exit.

Gladys

Strategies that supported Gladys during her teaching years are ones that she now uses to support her in her many and varied retirement activities. The tie-ins are many, and her enthusiasm in relating them to the interviewer is clear.

I think letting people know that you are interested in what they are doing and wanting to help them make their lives productive is the key. I did it with the kids by letting them know that. I kept a folder for every kid in my classes, put every single paper in there. I said, "I'm going to look at these every week and if you are making the same mistake three times you are getting the axe. You are going to have to write." The same is true now in my position as consultant to senior citizens in a local bank. People come in there because I'm willing to listen, and I don't make them feel they are stupid. A woman came in the other day and asked, "Gladys, do you think $5,000 is too much to keep in your checking account?" And I said, "How many checks do you write?" She said, "I probably write seven or eight checks. Oh, that's too much, isn't it?" And I said, "It all depends on what you want to do with it." I think the strategy is to let people know that you are interested in them and you want them to succeed and if you have a real dullard, that's hard.

Gladys makes her point by recalling a study done by researchers from a major regional research university.

Some years ago the university sent out a survey to our school and they said, "We'd like to know what your students think of some of your teachers. You got anybody who will do it?" And so they came around to me. I said yes. They administered the questions about how do you get along with the teacher, what do you think of the course, etc. They did it all during my classes, and, when all the papers came in, their service compiled the answers. The one I liked the best was, "She wants us to do good." I think that's the crux. If a kid in school thinks that, as a teacher, you want him to succeed. You're not saying, "We did this last week; don't you remember?" I think you need to let people know that you care about them.

That's why I believe in volunteering. This morning I was at The House, which is a Christian self-help group, and I was a volunteer receptionist. I had a man who came in and said he heard about The House. He didn't have a job; he was working at a local industry and was laid off. He came in with a denim lightweight jacket—no gloves. I said, "Aren't your hands cold?" He said, "I don't have any gloves." He needed everything. I said, "This is the place where everything is free. Go and see what you can get." He said that he had been living on peanut butter, so before he left we gave him emergency food. I also volunteer for the Senior Nutrition Program. This is for older folks to get a decent meal and have people to talk to. You would be surprised how many people come just for the fellowship. You have to have that, and a good teacher is somebody who utilizes things like that.

Gladys clearly likes people. Her strategies of letting people know of her interest in them and working to help them make their life productive is a support strategy that serves her as well in her retirement as it did during her many years of teaching.

Summary

Teachers at the career-exit stage include those who are retiring after many years of service, as well as those leaving after relatively short terms due to circumstances such as child rearing, exploration of career options inside and outside of education, and involuntary job termination. Factors from personal and organizational environments may have had a great impact on the decision to leave teaching. Appropriate support systems include providing benefits and security for retired teachers, as well as counseling to assist in the transition into retirement. For retiring "master teachers," opportunities for part-time employment provide continued professional outlets to the individual and enable school systems to utilize their expertise and experience. School systems might also want to explore incentives to encourage successful former teachers to return to the classroom. Finally, among career-exit teachers are those who have made the transition to other roles within education (for example, as principals, supervisors, or counselors). This group continues to play a key role in assisting with the growth and development of teachers at various stages of the career cycle.

In this chapter, three reasons for career exit were the subject of the case studies—movement to another position within education, movement to a position outside of education, and retirement. Other possibilities exist—dismissal due to reduction-in-force, dismissal for cause, and family responsibilities. Whatever the case, the skills and knowledge pertinent to teaching can well be significant in a person's new status. The dynamic ebb and flow among components of the model is well illustrated in this career stage.

In the following chapter, the entire Career Cycle Model is integrated and summarized, and implications for teachers' professional development are explored.

CHAPTER ELEVEN

Summary and Synthesis of Career Cycle Model

RALPH FESSLER   JUDITH C. CHRISTENSEN

In the previous nine chapters, stages of the teacher career cycle were identified and illustrated through the use of case studies. As one reflects on the specific stages put forth in this model, there may be a tendency to view them in a linear fashion. There is a level of surface logic to this approach, for it seems reasonable to assume a progression from preservice through induction, competency building, enthusiasm and growth, frustration, stability, wind-down, and exit. Indeed, this lock-step sequence may accurately describe the careers of some teachers. For most, however, it is too static an explanation. They are more likely to experience an ebb and flow, moving in and out of stages in response to both personal and organizational environmental influences. The following section summarizes the model presented in this book and, by revisiting some of the case studies cited earlier, provides illustrations of the dynamic nature of the career cycle. Finally, the last section of the chapter describes how the Career Cycle Model can be used as a proactive staff development and research tool.

Summary and Synthesis of the Career Cycle Model: Moving Toward the Professionalization of Teaching

The preceding chapters stress the need to look at individual needs when planning professional development options with teachers. Variety is necessary in role options, incentives, and learning structures. The traditional inservice education paradigms will not work in the professionalization process. Professional development must be seen in a broader perspective than the old deficiency model for teacher improvement. The differences between professional and staff development are succinctly outlined by Duke (1990) in the following summary:

Professional development:
- Is designed for individuals
- Fosters the cultivation of uniqueness and virtuosity
- Is guided by the individual's judgment
- Leads to increased personal understanding and awareness

Staff development:
- Is designed for groups
- Encourages collective growth in a common direction
- Focuses on similarities
- Is guided by school and district goals
- Leads to enhanced repertoire of skills/concepts (p. 72)

This section will review and highlight some of the individual needs and characteristics of teachers at various stages of their careers. Influences on teachers from the personal and organizational environments will be outlined, as well as appropriate incentives and support systems. The interactive nature of the career cycle and implications for professional development will be explored through examples of teachers introduced in earlier chapters.

The figures in this chapter provide a summary of key characteristics of each career stage and influences from the personal and the organizational environments, as well as potential growth needs, incentives, and support systems for each stage. Although the examples are general and certainly not all-inclusive, they serve to illustrate the possibility of moving in or out of each stage at any point in one's career and the support appropriate to meet individual needs.

Preservice stage teachers (see Figure 11-1) can be any age from late adolescence through mature adulthood—neophytes with no experience in the world of work or career changers with a vast amount of experience. They could also be experienced teachers getting additional education so they can take on new roles in the educational field. Each person brings a special set of talents, needs, and expectations. In Chapter 3, Sarah represented the more traditional preservice teacher—a 21-year-old who was student teaching while living with her parents. She was very different from Karen, a 40-year-old who was coming into teaching after several jobs in the business world. As students they were different in their attitudes toward courses. Sarah disliked theoretical courses, while Karen could not get enough. Student teaching was a satisfying experience for Sarah but frustrating for Karen.

Personal support systems also varied. Sarah's parents were close by and provided financial and psychological support. She was also planning her wedding and found support from her boyfriend. Karen's family lived in another state; she found support from friends, other students, and faculty.

The organizational structure for preservice teachers includes both the college/university and the K–12 schools. They have pressures and rewards from both areas and are constantly trying to balance their loyalty to each. Sarah found

---

FIGURE 11-1 • *Summary of Preservice Stage*

<u>Stage</u> - Preservice

<u>Definition/Description</u>

* Period of preparation for specific role
* Can be initial preparation or continuing education for new role

<u>Major Characteristics</u>

* Either a full- or part-time student in a higher education institution
* Continuing education students often working full-time in education
  while taking courses

<u>Influences from the Personal Environment</u>

* Family may be supportive psychologically and financially during
  initial preparation phase
* Returning students may have responsibility for family and finances

<u>Influences from the Organizational Environment</u>

* Higher education institutions are a primary organizational influence
  in initial preparation phase
* K-12 schools become influential as field work begins
* Returning students may be encouraged by their organization
  financially or psychologically

<u>Growth Needs</u>

* Opportunities to learn and apply new theories and practices
* Opportunities to explore new learning with experienced individuals
* Time to reflect on practice and feedback

<u>Incentives</u>

* Financial assistance
* Good prospects for jobs
* Higher salaries
* Recognition for doing something worthwhile for society

<u>Support Systems</u>
* Friends, families
* Professors
* Professionals in K-12 schools
* Professional organizations

---

more of her support coming from the K–12 setting, while Karen realized more support from her college. The need for cooperation among institutions is extremely important for the students caught in the middle.

Opportunities to try out new teaching strategies, receive constructive criticism, talk to experienced teachers, and get hands-on experience supported the growth of both Sarah and Karen. As they looked to the future, job prospects, repayment of loans, and recognition of teaching as a worth-while profession were concerns of both. Although Karen and Sarah are both in the preservice stage of their careers, there are great differences in their lives. These differences make it imperative that they are treated differently as they enter the teaching profession so they can both grow and mature in a way that will make maximum use of their talents.

Recent reform efforts in teacher education have focused a great deal of attention on the induction stage (see Figure 11-2). In an effort to retain teachers in the profession and make the transition to the job easier, induction programs have been developed for new teachers. It is important to recognize that experienced teachers also need induction programs as they move to new schools, different grade levels, or different positions within the same system.

FIGURE 11-2 • *Summary of Induction Stage*

Stage - Induction

Definition/Description

    * Period when teacher is being socialized into the system

Major Characteristics

    * Striving for acceptance by students, peers, administrators, parents
    * Seeking a comfort level in dealing with day-to-day issues
    * Some disillusionment when reality conflicts with ideals

Influences from the Personal Environment

    * Possible adjustment to new community, on one's own for first time; making new friends
    * Life revolves around school and school-related activities
    * For returning adult students, family support is essential

Influences from the Organizational Environment

    * School rules and regulations need to be explained clearly
    * Realistic expectations and job assignments
    * Principal and colleague support

Growth Needs

    * Learning the "language of practice"
    * Need individualized help on specific problems
    * Practical ideas and networking to discuss ideas

Incentives

    * Security items such as loan forgiveness, insurance benefits, job protection
    * Positive feedback, opportunities to learn in and out of school

Support Systems

    * An individualized induction program to meet needs of a 22- or 42-year-old beginner
    * Friends and other beginning teachers

Mark and Lee, who were introduced in Chapter 4, are examples of both types of teachers. Mark is new to teaching and experiencing the concerns of wanting to do the very best for all students yet feeling frustrated by the paperwork and governmental regulations for special education. Pressures from his personal environment stem from a move to a new community, providing for his family, and feeling some guilt about his wife giving up her education to care for a baby. However, his wife is supportive when he comes home from work, and she hopes one day to become a teacher as well. Mark has also become involved in some work-related community organizations that help him get to know people.

Unlike Mark, Lee has been a teacher for seventeen years. She changed jobs to get away from a position that was causing her great frustration. She has been thrust into an entirely new role that she finds challenging and time-consuming but rewarding. Her family has noticed that she does not come home miserable every day and is energetic and enthusiastic and spending much more time on her work. The autonomy and leadership in her new position are the two organizational influences in Lee's new position that she values most. Lee is ready to learn again to make her better prepared for her new role. She is challenged and proud of the part she plays in the services provided for her students.

While Mark is learning the system and the "language of practice," Lee is at another level of the induction stage. They need support of very different types as they assume their new roles and enter the competency-building stage.

The competency-building stage (see Figure 11-3) can be a "home" for teachers throughout their careers. Generally it is thought of as the first few years in a position when one is building a repertoire of teaching skills and learning how the formal and informal structure of the organization works. It is often a time of trying out new techniques and materials and finding a comfortable teaching style.

In Chapter 5, Greg was described as a teacher in the competency-building stage. He was in his second year of teaching and feeling much more relaxed and confident than in his first year. He felt he developed a closer, more positive relationship with students and feels better about his expectations for them.

Because Greg is single, he devotes a considerable amount of time to his job and to coaching as an extracurricular activity. His hobby of soccer has become part of his job as he coaches both boys' and girls' soccer teams. Greg's friends also play a significant role in his personal environment, and he devotes considerable time to being with them.

Within the organizational structure, Greg finds considerable support from his colleagues. As an untenured faculty member, he is acutely aware of accountability issues. He feels that many of the new regulations impinge on a teacher's autonomy and is trying to reconcile these seemingly conflicting issues. Teaching within his area of specialty would be an incentive for Greg. He wants to continue his education to add to his major academic area and increase his knowledge base for teaching.

Other incentives for Greg are positive feedback from his colleagues and

---

FIGURE 11-3 • *Summary of Competency—Building Stage*

Stage - Competency Building

Definition/Description

    * Period of striving to improve teaching skills

Major Characteristics

    * Teacher seeks out new materials and instructional strategies
    * Receptive to new ideas and willingly attends workshops and courses
    * Visits other classes
    * Job is seen as challenging

Influences from the Personal Environment

    * Marriages and starting families may cause conflict for teacher at
      this stage
    * Family support extremely important
    * Adjustment to "reality" of classroom may cause doubt

Influences from the Organizational Environment

    * Public expectations and support of teachers at local, state and
      national level is important
    * Personnel policies, tenure decisions, support of supervisor are
      extremely important

Growth Need

    * Collaboration with experienced staff to work on curriculum units or
      new teaching strategies
    * Hands-on, practical experiences

Incentives

    * Good working conditions - materials and supplies available
    * Opportunities for classroom visits
    * Course or workshop attendance
    * Extra curricular activities to earn extra money
    * Options for summer work

Support Systems

    * Peer coaching
    * Supervisor feedback and support
    * Mentors

---

department chair, more opportunities to work with colleagues in his department, and continuing opportunities for coaching.

    Greg represents one population of teachers in the competency-building stage. His characteristics are typical of many beginning teachers, but there are many more scenarios of people who move in and out of this stage a number of times in their careers. Their profiles may differ, but many of their needs will be similar.

    In Chapter 6, Mary was introduced as a teacher who fit into the enthusiastic and growing stage (see Figure 11-4). She has taught for eighteen years and views teaching as a dynamic activity that has had increasing challenges over the years. She sees herself as learning all the time through courses, travel, reading, curriculum committees, and outside organizations. Mary's personal life is simplified now that her child is in college. She says now she does not have to feel guilty about staying late after school and leaving her daughter home alone.

Mary feels the greatest pressures on her come from society at large. Drugs,

---

FIGURE 11-4 • *Summary of Enthusiastic and Growing Stage*

<u>Stage</u> - Enthusiastic and Growing

<u>Definition/Description</u>

* Phase at which teacher has reached a high level of competence and continues to progress as a professional with vigor and enthusiasm

<u>Major Characteristics</u>

* Teachers love their jobs and are eager to go to work each day
* Enjoy interactions with students and are constantly seeking new ways to enrich teaching
* High level of job satisfaction and commitment

<u>Influences from the Personal Environment</u>

* Generally stable personal environment
* Supportive family structure
* Wide variety of personal life experiences
* Life goals fit with job requirements

<u>Influences from the Organizational Environment</u>

* Tend to accommodate influences that might interfere with their teaching
* Professional organizations provide opportunities for learning and leadership
* Need trusting, supportive relationship with supervisor

<u>Growth Need</u>

* Generally self-imposed growth needs
* Role options for leadership in school or district are important outlets

<u>Incentives</u>

* Support for advanced study; sabbatical leaves
* Status of master teacher or mentor or team leader
* Praise from organizations, students, parents, etc.
* Flexible use of time

<u>Support Systems</u>

* Opportunities for collaboration and leadership
* Professional meetings - presenting information
* Time for research and reading
* Reinforcement, encouragement, and increased autonomy

deteriorating family structures, child abuse, and neglect all make her job more difficult. She gets support from her principal and peers and feels the district is doing more for teachers in support of inservice education offerings. She wants to complete her master's degree for salary benefits and to continue learning. Other incentives to Mary's teaching include classroom autonomy, praise from her principal, and recognition from others for successes in and out of the classroom. Mary and others in this stage see paid sabbatical leaves as an excellent incentive. They also see some type of differentiated staffing or role options as appropriate outlets for their leadership needs.

As with other stages of the Career Cycle Model, the frustration stage (see Figure 11-5) is not necessarily related to age or length of time in teaching. Many teachers jokingly will say they experience this stage about three or four times a year! It might be a stage that teachers never experience in their career or one that they will enter and, optimally, will be helped out of soon. Kathy was introduced in Chapter 7 as a teacher in this stage of her career. Her negative experiences came from her organizational environment. She had been forced to transfer schools twice due to staffing reductions even though she had been teaching in the district eight years. Her second move was to a school that was part of the district's desegregation plan and had many difficult student issues. She found support from the principal and district inservice plans and depended a great deal on friends outside of the school setting. She also found that her hobbies, activities in outside organizations, and exercise routines helped her cope with the difficult demands at school.

A change in principals caused Kathy to become extremely frustrated. She hated to go to school because she felt she could do nothing right and the principal would not even say good morning. She sought alternative careers in textbook sales but could not find a full-time position. Alternative role options and differentiated staffing, a leave of absence, alternative career exploration opportunities, and changes in schools were all incentives that were appropriate for Kathy.

Eventually Kathy received a transfer to another school where the principal was supportive of team teaching and participated with the teachers in summer institutes. She has moved from the frustration stage back into the enthusiastic and growing stage. She is excited about teaching and her colleagues and sharing her expertise with others. She recently asked to have a student teacher placed with her.

The stability stage of the career cycle (see Figure 11-6) can take place at any time for a variety of reasons. It may be a time of pulling back when family demands are greatest or a time when organizational demands become overwhelming. This stage, like the previous one, might never happen to a teacher during his or her career.

In Chapter 8, Jerry represented a teacher who had pulled back from total involvement in teaching. He teaches mathematics in a junior high and also is a part-time real estate broker. His attitude is reflected by this statement:

FIGURE 11-5 • *Summary of Career Frustration Stage*

Stage - Career Frustration

Definition/Description

   * This phase finds disillusionment and frustration with teaching and
     job satisfaction waning
   * Teachers question why they are in this profession

Major Characteristics

   * Teachers feel locked into an unfulfilling job
   * Stress increases and teachers dread going to work
   * The term "burnout" often used to characterize these teachers

Influences from the Personal Environment

   * Security needs and special family demands often reported
   * The crises associated with children, spouses, aging parents are
     frequently sources of stress

Influences from the Organizational Environment

   * Increased rules and regulations add to frustration
   * Lack of support from supervisor
   * Lack of support from community
   * Lack of opportunity for creativity or autonomy

Growth Needs

   * Updating of skills
   * Released time to explore new career paths
   * New opportunities for leadership

Incentives

   * Positive feedback from supervisors and students
   * Improved working conditions
   * Shared decision-making roles

Support Systems

   * Supervisor support
   * Counseling help as needed

I was excited when I first started teaching and I still enjoy seeing kids learn but it seems that fewer and fewer kids these days come to school ready to learn and they don't care about the work that math requires for learning. Because of all the problems which I'm not equipped to handle, teaching isn't as much fun as it used to be.

Jerry says that he uses his business experience to make the subject matter more relevant to his students. For example, they might have to figure interest percentages or taxes on assessed values.

FIGURE 11-6 • *Summary of Career Stability Stage*

<u>Stage</u> - Career Stability

<u>Definition/Description</u>

* Teachers at the stable stage have plateaued in their careers
* They may be doing a competent job but are not committed to further growth
* It could be a "holding stage" until personal or organizational influences stimulate continued growth

<u>Major Characteristics</u>

* May be characterized as putting "a fair day's work for a fair day's pay"
* Do what is expected but little more
* Close the door and teach but will not volunteer for any extra activity

<u>Influences from the Personal Environment</u>

* Demands of a growing family might require teacher to devote less time to the job
* Midlife examination of how time is to be spent might have teachers cut back on job demands
* Family crises could require less job involvement

<u>Influences from the Organizational Environment</u>

* Social criticism of teachers can cause teachers to say "just let me teach!"
* Parental apathy and mistrust may be present
* Frequent supervisor and peer negativism

<u>Growth Needs</u>

* Encourage experimentation and improve working conditions
* Consultive management style
* Ask teachers their opinions
* Provide released time for interacting with other teachers
* Sabbatical leaves

<u>Incentives</u>
* Parent and student praise
* Telephones, office space, secretarial service
* Increased reinforcement and opportunities for leadership

<u>Support Systems</u>
* Peer support with peer coaching and experimentation with new teaching strategies
* Team teaching with teacher being the "expert" on team

Incentives and support for Jerry need to come from a variety of sources. Recognition of his expertise in the business world could be used to upgrade the curriculum to make it more relevant to situations encountered in life. Praise and encouragement from his principal and department head could bring him the recognition he needs. Perhaps a leave to pursue his outside work full-time would allow him the career exploration time he needs to decide where his energies should be spent.

The career wind-down stage (see Figure 11-7) can come at any point in one's career. It frequently comes after a number of years in teaching but can take place voluntarily or involuntarily at any time. The reduction-in-force mandates of the 1970s saw a number of teachers enter the career wind-down stage each April, many of whom repeated this pattern for a number of years. Statistics indicated that approximately 50 percent of those entering the profession leave

---

FIGURE 11-7 • *Summary of Career Wind-Down Stage*

<u>Stage</u> - Career Wind Down

<u>Definition/Description</u>

* The period when a teacher is preparing to leave the profession
* It may be a positive experience after a rewarding career or a negative period following an unfulfilling teaching experience

<u>Major Characteristics</u>

* Uncertainty about the future and changes in life structure
* May be positive or negative, depending on experiences and specific environmental influences.

<u>Influences from the Personal Environment</u>

* Family and friends are significant figures
* Health issues and financial concerns may influence this stage
* Hobbies and outside activities become more important

<u>Influences from the Organizational Environment</u>

* For teachers quitting the profession, restrictive rules, regulations and management style of supervisor can influence decision
* Retiring teachers can provide support and leadership in professional organizations and community groups

<u>Growth Needs</u>
* Opportunities for experienced teachers to share their expertise
* Peer coaches, mentors, curriculum production, supervisors of student teachers

<u>Incentives</u>
* Pleasant work environment
* Recognition for career achievements
* Good retirement benefits and insurance options
* Student praise
* Influence in school decision-making and teacher hiring
* Released time for professional activities

<u>Support Systems</u>
* District workshops on financial planning, job transitions
* Leadership opportunities to share expertise
* Professional organization work and work with local universities in teacher preparation programs

within the first five years, resulting in a very different type of wind-down period than the type associated with the current "bulge" of early and regular retirements.

In Chapter 9 we met Brenda, a 62-year-old who will retire in a year. She is staying an extra year to put a new reading program in place in her first-grade class. Brenda has taught for 27 years and feels very positive about teaching, students, parents, and colleagues.

Brenda's personal environment has been extremely important to her throughout her career. As a minority she experienced discrimination in her first job search and in the community. Her mother's support and her own determination allowed her to complete certification requirements and secure a permanent teaching position. Her positive outlook helped her through a number of personal crises.

Brenda now feels support from parents and the community, which looks to her as a spokesperson for district policies. She sees herself in a role of helping to change public attitudes and garner community support.

Brenda enjoyed the role of assistant principal because it afforded her opportunities to work with other teachers in her own school and from other districts. Brenda values her work as a cooperating teacher for the student teachers from a local college. She also found support in this stage from district-sponsored seminars on health issues and retirement planning.

Brenda is moving into retirement with a feeling of having made a difference with her students, her family, and her community. She reflects on a career of fulfillment and is an excellent example of Erickson's (1959) model of generativity.

The career-exit stage (see Figure 11-8) is not related to age or length of service, although it is one stage that every teacher will experience. When school districts experience reductions-in-force, the newest teachers are often put in the exit stage. Currently, early retirement plans have changed the career-exit profile to teachers who have 25 to 30 years in the profession and who are choosing to take advantage of attractive retirement benefits. The characteristics of these two groups of teachers are markedly different.

In Chapter 10, three teachers were introduced who exited the profession for very different reasons and at different point in their lives. Their common enthusiasm for teaching marks them as people who continue to have positive feelings and support for schools and teachers. Peter felt he was in a rut in teaching and needed the variety and flexible use of time that his current career in business affords him. Donna's dissatisfaction with inequities in the system led her into union work, where she felt she could make life better for teachers. Her dedication to the profession is obvious, although she exited teaching to take on another role related to education. Gladys exited teaching after a long and successful career. She retired fourteen years ago and is still using her expertise by working with senior citizens at a bank, keeping in touch with former colleagues and students.

FIGURE 11-8 • *Summary of Career—Exit Stage*

<u>Stage</u> - Career Exit

<u>Definition/Description</u>
  * Period of time after the teacher leaves the job for
    retirement or other reasons
  * Possibly a period of unemployment after involuntary job
    termination or a temporary career exit for child rearing
  * Possible time for alternative career exploration or moving
    to a new role in education, such as administration

<u>Major Characteristics</u>
  * If exit is involuntary, it may be a bitter, resentful time
  * May be characterized be enthusiasm of looking forward to
    a change in career
  * May be a time of reflection and satisfaction with a long
    and rewarding career

<u>Influences from the Personal Environment</u>
  * Life stage can cause examination of how one wants to spend
    the rest of a career
  * Need for personal challenge may influence change in career
    choice
  * Family crises may cause early retirements
  * Financial needs may cause early exit to higher paying job

<u>Influences from the Organizational Environment</u>
  * Legislation promoting early retirements may move up retirement
    date
  * Reduction-in-force policies may force some to leave the
    profession against their will
  * Lack of support for leaves of absence or sabbatical leaves
    force teachers to leave the field

<u>Growth Needs</u>
  * Leaves of absence to explore other career options
  * Shared leadership at school and district levels
  * Continued sharing of expertise once retired

<u>Incentives</u>
  * Secure benefits for retirement
  * Flexible schedules to meet demands of family in crisis
  * Leadership opportunities in the community and in education

<u>Support Systems</u>

  * For reduction-in-force teachers, employment assistance
  * Seminars on retirement, wellness, insurance, etc.
  * Reunions and support groups
  * Professional organizations involving their retired members
    in useful ways

All of these teachers appreciated the importance of colleagiality in the schools and stressed the importance of working together. They all wanted diversity in their jobs and leadership opportunities. Autonomy, flexibility, and feedback were important to them as motivators to do their best work. They all talked about intrinsic motivation and stated that money was important but not what drew them away from teaching.

As we attempt to retain the best teachers in the classroom, it is imperative that they are provided with roles that will allow them to use their expertise and feel that they have some control over their lives. Differentiated staffing, shared decision making, and flexible use of time are all possible designs to promote change in a rigid, confining job structure. Challenges and support must be available to allow teachers to feel worthwhile and creative. Recognition is essential to those of retirement age, and support for their changing needs can make their retirement years happy and productive.

This section has summarized each stage of the career cycle and has illustrated the interactive nature of the model by revisiting the case studies that were presented in the preceding chapters. In the following section, the use of the model as a proactive staff development tool will be described.

The Career Cycle Model as a Professional Development Tool

The Career Cycle Model can be used as a tool for sensitizing teachers to their own growth needs and for building individual and school improvement programs. The following are suggested components of a comprehensive use of the model.

As a first step, the constructs of the model should be presented to the staff in the form of readings, seminars, presentations, and discussion sessions. Chapter 2 of this book could be used as a primer for the model, with subsequent chapters serving as more detailed illustrations of specific stages and case studies. Emphasis should be placed on understanding the dynamic nature of the model and the need to explore how the various stages relate to personal and organizational environmental influences.

As part of their orientation to the model, teachers should be engaged in introspection and reflection. They should be encouraged to assess where they see themselves in the career cycle. A useful tool here would be for them to complete the Teacher Career Cycle Inventory (TCCI), which can be found in Figure 11-9. Most teachers identify with the various stages in the model in terms of where they see themselves today, as well as stages they have experienced previously.

An assessment of support systems currently available in a school can yield valuable information to assist in planning needed changes. An activity that can assist in that process would be to use the worksheet found in Figure 11-10. Teachers can be asked to survey the support systems currently available to assist teachers at various career stages and to indicate the additional support systems that are needed. This exercise can be done individually or in groups and can be valuable in building a plan for the best use of current resources and for adding necessary components to a comprehensive faculty support system.

The use of peer coaching and mentoring strategies has proven to be an

FIGURE 11-9 • *Teacher Career Cycle Inventory*

Self-Assessment of Career Stages

A number of stages in the career cycle of teachers have been identified and are summarized below. Please read the following descriptions and check (on the line provided at the left) which stage best describes where you presently are in your career.

_____ 1.   This stage is the period of preparation for a specific professional role. Typically, this would be the period of initial preparation in a college or university. It might also include retraining for a new role or assignment, either by attending a higher education institution or as part of staff development within the work setting.

_____ 2.   This stage is generally defined as the first few years of employment, when the teacher is socialized into the system. It is a period when a new teacher strives for acceptance by students, peers, and supervisors and attempts to achieve a comfort and security level in dealing with everyday problems and issues. Teachers may also experience this stage when shifting to another grade level, another building, or when changing districts completely.

_____ 3.   During this stage, the teacher is striving to improve teaching skills and abilities. The teacher seeks out new materials, methods, and strategies. Teachers at this stage are receptive to new ideas, attend workshops and conferences willingly, and enroll in graduate programs through their own intiative. Their job is seen as challenging and they are eager to improve their repertoire of skills.

_____ 4.   At this stage, teachers have reached a high level of competence in their job but continue to progress as professionals. Teachers in this stage love their jobs, look forward to going to school and to the interaction with their students, and are constantly seeking new ways to enrich their teaching. Key ingredients here are enthusiasm and high levels of job satisfaction. These teachers are often supportive and helpful in identifying appropriate inservice education activities for their schools.

_____ 5.   This period is characterized by frustration and disillusionment with teaching. Job satisfaction is waning, and teachers begin to question why they are doing this work. Much of what is described as teacher burnout in the literature occurs in this stage.

_____ 6.   At this stage, teachers have resigned themselves to putting in "a fair day's work for a fair day's pay." They are doing what is expected of them, but little more. These teachers are often fulfilling the terms of their contracts, but see little value in professional development programs. They are seldom motivated to participate in anything more than at surface level and are passive consumers of inservice efforts at best.

_____ 7.   This is the stage when a teacher is preparing to leave the profession. For some, it may be a pleasant period in which they reflect on the many positive

FIGURE 11-9 • *(Continued)*

experiences they have had and look forward to a career change or retirement. For others, it may be a bitter period, one in which a teacher resents the forced job termination or, perhaps, can't wait to get out of an unrewarding job. A person may spend several years in this stage, or it may occur only during a matter of weeks or months.

_____ 8.   This stage of a teacher's career represents the period of time after the teacher leaves the job, but includes other circumstances than simply retirement after many years of service. It could be a period of unemployment after involuntary or elective job termination or a temporary career exit for child rearing. It could also be a time of alternative career exploration or of moving to a nonteaching position in education such as administration.

Burke, P. J., Christensen, J. C., Fessler, R., McDonnell, J. H., & Price, J. R. (1987, April). *The teacher career cycle: Model development and research report.* Paper presented at the annual meeting of the American Educational Research Association, Washington, DC. (ERIC Document Reproduction No. ED 289 846.)

effective means of building skills and competencies in a supportive environment. Various models and variations of these approaches have been used successfully to assist teachers in identifying their strengths, weaknesses, and growth strategies. The general format for a peer coaching plan is for teachers to be paired for mutual support. Generally, they take turns coaching each other through a new lesson or growth plan. Components of this process generally include a pre-conference (often several sessions) used to identify growth needs and an action plan, observations of teaching or continued conferences to assess development of the plan, open feedback throughout the process, and an assessment of outcomes. A key feature of this process is that it occurs in a trusting, supportive environment unencumbered by the tensions of performance evaluation that are often present when the supervisor or principal does the "coaching."

The Teacher Career Cycle Model can be used as a framework for pairing and matching mentors and peer coaches. Cross-referencing the various stages can yield a variety of potential matches and mixes. One strategy would be to match individuals at the same stages (e.g., preservice with preservice, induction with induction). An advantage to this approach would be the mutual support that could emerge from the identification of common needs. Two induction-level teachers, for example, could explore a common set of needs emerging from their early career experiences. Their pairing could result in mutual support in a nonthreatening environment. A potential disadvantage of stage-alike pairings is that the perspective or expertise of a different stage is not present. For example, an enthusiastic and growing teacher paired with an induction novice could add

FIGURE 11-10 • *Assessment of Career Cycle Support Systems*

What Support Systems Exist in Your School?	Phase of Career Cycle	What Additional Support Systems Ought to Exist in Your School
	Pre-Service	
	Induction	
	Competency Building	
	Enthusiastic & Growing	
	Career Frustration	
	Stability	
	Career Wind-down	
	Career Exit	

content, knowledge, and wisdom of experience beyond that of another novice. Care must also be taken to avoid partnerships that would feed on mutually negative feelings. For example, two very negative stable/stagnant teachers might use a peer coaching situation to reinforce each other's frustrations. The key here is to examine the specific dynamics and goals for the support system and make pairings that support the desired ends.

An alternative to pairing stage-alike individuals would be to intentionally mix people at different stages for specific purposes. For example, a preservice teacher could be mixed with an enthusiastic and growing veteran. Indeed, this type of pairing may be ideal for pre–student teaching and student teaching arrangements. The prospective teacher gains from the enthusiasm and experience of the mentor, who in turn benefits from the recognition and esteem that come from serving in this leadership role. Some experienced, enthusiastic teachers also indicate that the novice brings renewed energy and ideas to their teaching.

Numerous other pairings can be used to address school and individual teacher needs. For example, one strategy that may have an impact on a frustrated teacher would be pairing with a competency-building individual. Asking an experienced teacher who may be questioning current commitment to teaching to assume a mentoring role with an individual who is attempting to build a collection of skills may help to rekindle that lost spark. Similarly, a person who has settled into a "fair day's work for a fair day's pay" (stable/stagnant), may respond positively to the status and recognition that come from a mentoring experience. Once again, this approach should be used in a thoughtful manner to mix and match individuals who can both benefit from the relationship.

Implications for Supervisors and Administrators

If the notion of individual career stages is to go beyond the "interesting to know" level, there is a need to identify personalized support systems for teachers at various stages of their careers. We have summarized many such strategies in this chapter. In Chapter 1, considerable attention was given to laying the foundation for the Career Cycle Model by reviewing the organizational environment of schools, motivational factors affecting teachers, and approaches to personalized staff development. In addition, one might want to refer to other recent attempts to personalize approaches to supervision and staff development. Particular attention might be given the works of Glickman (1990), Glatthorn (1984), Burke (1987), Krey and Burke (1989), Fessler and Burke (1988), Christensen, McDonnell, and Price (1988), and Levine (1989). Each of these authors presents models and approaches to individualizing professional development that are very supportive of the constructs presented in this book.

Schools and school systems may want to examine their current practices and policies in lieu of the concepts set forth in this book. There is much here to reinforce the traditional use of inservice or staff development activities that emphasize improving teacher skills, especially during the skill-building periods associated with the induction and competency-building stages and, to some extent, during the enthusiastic and growing stage. The ideas presented here also suggest a broadening of the notion of staff development and professional growth to include concern for personal needs and problems of teachers. This might include support systems to assist teachers in dealing with family problems, chemical abuse, financial planning, and crisis resolution. Larger school district systems may want to consider internal employee assistance programs for this purpose, while smaller districts could explore linkages with existing social service agencies.

In addition, organizational policies should be examined to find new and creative ways of supporting teachers at various stages of their careers. Examples could include more liberal sabbatical and leave-of-absence policies, modifications of job assignments, job sharing, internal transfers, and other procedures that would give teachers the opportunity to explore career alternatives or pursue solutions to personal problems.

Finally, school systems must attempt to understand the linkages between teacher career stages and the organizational environment. The leadership and management style of the principal may be the single most important factor in that environment. The recent movement toward school-based management and shared decision making may have a major impact on providing outlets for teacher growth needs. Other organizational environmental factors that must be examined in the context of the concepts set forth in this book include the teacher's time consumed by rules, regulations, and "administrivia," and the atmosphere of trust and professional respect for teachers present in the school system and community. All of these factors relate to the tone and climate set by the administration and have a major impact upon teacher's progression through the career stages.

Implications for Research

As indicated in Chapter 2, the Career Cycle Model was developed through a process of model building that emphasizes the need to continually feed new data back into the process to confirm, refine, and, when needed, dramatically alter model components. For the researcher, the working model offers a framework for further analysis. Model constructs suggest interrelationships among complex phenomena and hypotheses about additional relationships. Some examples of areas needing further study are:

- What is the relationship between career stages and specific teacher and supervisor personality characteristics?

- Can the Career Cycle Model by applied to other role incumbents, such as principals, counselors, or curriculum specialists?
- Is there a relationship between teacher career stages and student achievement?
- Can the concept of teacher career stages be applied to an entire staff to develop a school profile? If it can, what are the implications for school reform and restructuring?

These are but a few of the interesting questions and challenges that lie ahead. The authors welcome the research community to join in efforts to continue to refine and modify model component through additional studies.

Summary

The model presented in this book represents an attempt to describe and analyze the dynamic and interactive nature of the teacher career cycle. The model should be of value to both researchers and practitioners concerned with teacher growth and professional improvement. For researchers, a scheme to view the teacher career cycle process is presented that is rich in questions and conceptualizations that merit further analysis. For the practitioner, the model presents a framework for viewing teacher growth needs and development that holds numerous implications for efforts in school improvements, supervision, inservice, and staff development. It is the authors' hope that this model will stimulate dialogue and activity among both groups.

References

Adams, R. D., and Martray, C. R. 1980. *Correlates of teacher perceived problems.* Paper presented at the 9th annual conference of the Mid-South Educational Research Association, New Orleans (ERIC Document Reproduction Service No. ED 195 567).

Adams, R. D., and Martray, C. R. 1981, April. *Teacher development: A study of factors related to teacher concerns for pre, beginning, and experienced teachers.* Paper presented at the annual meeting of the American Educational Research Association, Los Angeles.

Adams, R. D.; Martray, C. R.; and Alexander, L. 1982. *Relationships among burnout factors and occupational stressors in the teaching profession.* Paper presented at the annual meeting of the Mid-South Educational Research Association, New Orleans (ERIC Document Reproduction No. ED 260 053).

American Association of Colleges for Teacher Education. 1987. *Teaching teachers: Facts and figures.* Washington, DC: AACTE.

Andrews, I. H. 1986, April. *An investigation of the academic paradigms underlying induction programmes in five countries.* Paper presented at the annual meeting of the American Educational Research Association. San Francisco (ERIC Document Reproduction Service No. ED 269 400).

Arends, R. I. 1983. Beginning teachers as learners. *The Journal of Educational Research, 76*(4), 235–242.

Ashburn, E. A. 1987. Current developments in teacher induction programs. *Action in Teacher Education, 8*(4), 41–44.

Ashton, P. T., and Webb, R. B. 1986. *Making a difference: Teachers' sense of efficacy and student achievement.* New York: Longman.

Bandura, A. 1977. *Social Learning Theory.* Englewood Cliffs, NJ: Prentice Hall.

Bandura, A. 1982. Self-efficacy mechanism in human agency. *American Psychologist, 37,* 122–147.

Bartell, C. A. 1987. *Proceedings of a seminar on incentives that enhance the teaching profession: A discussion of the policy issues.* Elmhurst, IL: North Central Regional Educational Laboratory.

Belenky, M. F.; Clinchy, B. M.; Goldberger, N. R.; and Tarule, J. M. 1986. *Women's ways of knowing.* New York: Basic Books.

Bellon, J. 1988. *Career ladder report.* Paper submitted to the Tennessee Commissioner of Education. Knoxville, TN: University of Tennessee.

Borko, H.; Lalik, R.; Livingston, C.; Pecic, K.; and Perry, D. 1986. *Learning to teach in the induction year: Two case studies.* Paper presented at the annual meeting of the American Educational Research Association, San Francisco.

Boyer, E. L. 1988. *Teacher involvement in decision making: A state-by-state profile.* The Carnegie Foundation for the Advancement of Teaching.

Burden, P. R. 1982a, February. *Developmental supervision: Reducing teacher stress at different career stages*. Paper presented at the annual conference of the Association of Teacher Educators, Phoenix, AZ.

Burden, P. 1982b, August. *Implications of teacher career development: New roles for teachers, administrators, and professors*. Paper presented at the annual workshop of the Association of Teacher Educators, Slippery Rock, PA.

Burke, P. J. 1987. *Teacher development, induction, renewal, and redirection*. Cherry Hill, PA: Falmer Press.

Burke, P.; Christensen, J.; and Fessler, R. 1983, April. *Teacher life-span development: An instrument to identify stages of teacher growth*. Paper presented at the annual meeting of the American Educational Research Association, Montreal, Canada.

Burke, P.; Fessler, R.; and Christensen, J. 1984. *Teacher career stages: Implications for staff development*. Bloomington, IN: Phi Delta Kappa.

Burke, P. J.; Christensen, J. C.; Fessler, R.; McDonnell, J. H.; and Price, J. R. 1987, April. *The teacher career cycle: Model development and research report*. Paper presented at the annual meeting of the American Educational Research Association, Washington, DC (ERIC Document Reproduction Service No. ED 289 846).

Carter, K., and Koehler, V. R. 1987. The process and content of initial year of teaching programs. In G. Griffin and S. Millies (Eds.). *The first years of teaching: Background papers and a proposal* (pp. 91–104). Chicago: University of Illinois at Chicago.

Chapman, D. W., and Lowther, M. A. 1982. Teachers' satisfaction with teaching. *The Journal of Educational Research, 75*(4).

Chickering, A. W., and Havighurst, R. J. 1981. The life cycle. In A. W. Chickering and Associates. *The modern American college: Responding to the new realities of diverse students and a changing society*. San Francisco: Jossey-Bass.

Christensen, J. C. (Project Director). 1985. *The role of teacher career stages and professional development practices in determining rewards and incentives in teaching* (Contract No. G008410003). Washington, DC: U.S. Department of Education.

Christensen, J.; Burke, P.; and Fessler, R. 1983, April. *Teacher life-span development: A summary and synthesis of the literature*. Paper presented at the annual meeting of the American Educational Research Association, Montreal, Canada.

Christensen, J.; Burke, P.; Fessler, R.; and Hagstrom, D. 1983. *Teachers' career development*. Washington, DC: ERIC Clearinghouse.

Christensen, J. C.; McDonnell, J. H.; and Price, J. R. 1988. *Personalizing staff development: The career lattice model*. Bloomington, IN: Phi Delta Kappa Educational Foundation.

Collegial Research Consortium. 1985, March. *Master teachers: Do educators agree?* A research symposium presented at the annual meetings of the Association of Teacher Educators, February, and the American Association of Colleges for Teacher Education.

Collegial Research Consortium. 1987. Incentives and teachers' career stages: Influences and policy decisions. In C. A. Bartell (Ed.), *Proceedings of a seminar on incentives that enhance the teaching profession: A discussion of the policy issues*. Elmhurst, IL: North Central Regional Educational Laboratory.

Cornett, L. 1988. *Is "paying for performance" changing schools?* Atlanta, GA: Southern Regional Education Board.

Cresap, McCormick, and Paget. 1984. *Teacher incentives*. Reston, VA: National Association of Secondary School Principals.

Cross, P. 1981. *Adults as learners*. San Francisco: Jossey-Bass.

Cruickshank, D. R., and Callahan, R. 1983. The other side of the desk: Stages and problems of teacher development. *The Elementary School Journal, 83*, 250–258.

Dorman, A., and Bartell, C. A. 1988. *Incentives for teaching: LEA programs and practices in seven states*. Elmhurst, IL: North Central Regional Educational Laboratory.

Dorman, A., and Fulford, N. 1989. *Incentives closeup: Profiles of twenty-one teacher incentive programs*. Elmhurst, IL: North Central Regional Educational Laboratory.

Duke, D. L. 1990. Setting goals for professional development. *Educational Leadership*, *47*(8), 71–75.

Dworkin, A. G. 1987. *Teacher burnout in the public schools*. Albany, NY: State University of New York Press.

Easterly, J.; Williston, A.; and Allen, N. 1982 spring/summer. The implications of development stage theory on the expertise of teachers. *MATE Viewpoints*, 9–12.

Eddy, E. M. 1969. *Becoming a teacher: The passage to professional status*. New York: Teachers College Press.

Erikson, E. 1959. Identity and the life cycle. *Psychological Issues*, *1*(1). New York: International Universities Press.

Featherstone, H. 1988, spring. A time to learn: The first year of teaching. *Colloquy*, *1*(2). East Lansing, MI: Michigan State University National Center for Research on Teacher Education.

Feiman, S., and Floden, R. 1980, February. *What's all this talk about teacher development?* Research Series No. 70, East Lansing, Michigan: Institute for Research on Teaching, Michigan State University. (ERIC Document Reproduction Service No. ED 189 088).

Feistritzer, C. E., and O'Rourke, L. M. (Eds.). 1983. *The American teacher*. Washington, DC: Feistritzer Publications.

Fessler, R. 1985. A model for teacher professional growth and development. In P. J. Burke and R. G. Heideman (Eds.) *Career-long teacher education*. (pp. 181–193). Springfield, IL: Charles C. Thomas.

Fessler, R., and Burke, P. J. 1988. Teacher assessment and staff development: Links in the same chain. *Journal of Staff Development*, *9*(1), 14–18.

Fessler, R.; Burke, P.; and Christensen, J. 1983, April. *Teacher career cycle model: A framework for viewing teacher growth needs*. Paper presented at the annual meeting of the American Educational Research Association, Montreal, Canada.

Freudenberger, H. J. 1974. Staff burn-out. *Journal of Social Issues*, *30*, 159–165.

Freudenberger, H. J. 1982. Counseling and dynamics: Treating the end-stage person. In W. J. Paine (Ed.), *Job stress and burnout: Research, theory, and intervention perspectives*. Beverly Hills, CA: SAGE Publications.

Friedan, B. 1963. *The feminine mystique*. New York: Dell.

Fuller, F. 1969. Concerns of teachers: A developmental conceptualization. *American Educational Research Journal*, *6*(2), 207–226.

Fuller, F., and Bown, O. 1975. Becoming a teacher. In K. Ryan (Ed.), *Teacher Education, Seventy-Fourth Yearbook of the National Society for the Study of Education, Part 2*. Chicago: University of Chicago Press.

Furtwengler, C. B. 1989. *Evaluating career ladder incentive programs*. Atlanta, GA: Southern Regional Education Board.

Galvez-Hjornevik, C., and Smith, J. J. 1986. Support teachers in beginning teacher programs. *The Journal of Staff Development*, *7*,(1), 110–123.

Gehrke, N. J. 1987. On helping the beginning teacher. In G. Griffin and S. Millies (Eds.), *The first years of teaching: Background papers and a proposal* (pp. 105–114). Chicago: University of Illinois at Chicago.

Getzels, J., Lipham, J., and Campbell, R. 1968. *Educational administration as a social process: theory, research and practice*. New York: Harper and Row.

Gilligan, C. 1982. *In a different voice*. Cambridge, MA: Harvard University Press.

Glassberg, S. 1979. A developmental model for the beginning teacher. In K. R. Howey and R. H. Bents (Eds.), *Toward meeting the needs of the beginning teachers*. Lansing, MI: Midwest Teacher Corps Network (ERIC Document Reproduction Service No. ED 206 581).

Glassberg, S. 1980, April. *A view of the beginning teacher from a developmental perspective*. Paper presented at the annual meeting of the American Educational Research Association, Boston.

Glassberg, S., and Oja, S. N. 1981. A developmental model for enhancing teachers' personal and professional growth. *Journal of Research and Development in Education, 14*(2), 59–70.

Glatthorn, A. A. 1984. *Differentiated supervision*. Alexandria, VA: Association for Supervision and Curriculum Development.

Glickman, C. D. 1990. *Supervision of instruction: A developmental approach* (2nd ed.). Newton, MA: Allyn & Bacon.

Goodlad, J. 1984. *A Place Called School*. New York: McGraw-Hill.

Gould, R. 1972, November. The phases of adult life: A study in developmental psychology. *American Journal of Psychiatry, 129*(5), 521–531.

Gould, R. L. 1978. *Transformations: Growth and change in adult life*. New York: Simon and Schuster.

Grant, C. A., and Zeichner, J. M. 1981. In-service support for first year teachers: The state of the scene. *Journal of Research and Development in Education, 14,* 99–111.

Grant, W. V., and Eiden, L. J. 1982. *Digest of education statistics*. Washington, DC: U.S. Government Printing Office.

Gregorc, A. F. 1973. Developing plans for professional growth. *NASSP Bulletin*, Dec., 1–8.

Griffin, G. A. 1984, October. *Crossing the bridge: The first years of teaching*. Paper presented at a hearing of the National Commission on Excellence in Teacher Education, Austin, TX.

Griffin, P. E. 1983. The developing confidence of new teachers: Effects of experience during the transition period from student to teacher. *Journal of Education for Teaching, 9,* 113–122.

Guskey, T. R. 1987. Context variables that affect measures of teacher efficacy. *Journal of Educational Research, 81,* 41–47.

Guskey, T. R. 1989. Attitude and perceptual change in teachers. *International Journal of Educational Research, 13*(4), 439–453.

Hackman, R. J., and Oldham, G. R. 1980. *Work redesign*. Reading, MA: Addison-Wesley.

Hall, G., Wallace, R., and Dossett, W. 1973. *A developmental conceptualization of the adoption process within educational institutions*. Austin, TX: Research and Development Center for Teacher Education, The University of Texas.

Hall, G. E., and Loucks, S. 1978. Teacher concerns as a basis for facilitating and personalizing staff development. *Teachers College Record, 80*(1), 36–53 (ERIC Document Reproduction Service No. EJ 195-495).

Halpin, G.; Harris, K.; and Halpin, G. 1985. Teacher stress as related to locus of control, sex, and age. *Journal of Experimental Education,* 136–140.

Hange, J. 1982, March. *Teachers in their fifth year: An analysis of teaching concerns from the perspectives of adult and career development*. Paper presented at the annual meeting of the American Educational Research Association, New York.

Harvey, O. J.; Hunt, D. E.; and Schroder, H. M. 1961. *Conceptual systems and personality organization*. New York: Wiley.

Herzberg, F.; Mausner, B.; and Snyderman, B. 1959. *The motivation to work*. New York: Wiley.

Hoffman, J.; Griffin, G.; Edwards, S.; Paulissen, M.; O'Neal, S.; Barnes, S.; and Verstegen, D. 1985. *Teacher induction study: Final report of a descriptive study.* (Rep. No. 9063). Austin, TX: The University of Texas at Austin, Research and Development Center for Teacher Education.

Hoover-Dempsey, K. V., and Kendall, C. D. 1982. *Stress and coping among teachers: Experience in search of theory and science.* (Report to the National Institute of Education pursuant to Grant NILE-G-81-0109J). Nashville, TN: George Peabody College.

Hoy, W., and Miskel, C. 1991. *Educational administration: Theory, research and practice.* New York: McGraw-Hill.

Huberman, M. 1985. Educational change and career pursuits. *Interchange, 16*(3), 54–73.

Huberman, M. 1989. The professional life cycle of teachers. *Teachers College Record, 91*(1), 31–57.

Huling-Austin, L. 1988, June. *Overview of the induction scene: Teacher induction as part of the larger picture.* Paper presented at the National Academy for Leadership in Teacher Education (sponsored by the Association of Teacher Educators), Providence, RI.

Huling-Austin, L., and Odell, S. 1987. Teacher induction. In D. M. Brooks (Ed.), *Teacher induction: A new beginning* (pp. 69–80). Reston, VA: Association of Teacher Educators.

Huling-Austin, L.; Putnam, S.; and Galvez-Hjornevik, C. 1985. *Model teacher induction project study findings* (Final report). Austin, TX: University of Texas, Research and Development Center for Teacher Education (ERIC Document Reproduction Service No. ED 270 442).

Hunt, D. E., and Sullivan, E. V. 1974. *Between psychology and education.* Hinsdale, IL: Dryden Press.

Hunt, D. 1975. Person-environment interaction. *Review of Educational Research, 45*(2), 209–230.

Hunt, D. E., and Joyce, B. R. 1981. Teacher trainee personality and initial teaching style. In B. R. Joyce, C. C. Brown, and L. Peck (Eds.), *Flexibility in teaching.* New York: Longman.

Invarson, L., and Greenway, P. 1981. *Portrayals of teacher development.* Washington, DC: ERIC Document Reproduction Service No. ED 200 600.

Jandura, R. M. and Burke, P. 1989. *Differentiated career opportunities for teachers.* Bloomington, IN: Phi Delta Kappa.

Johnson, J. M. 1985. Teacher induction: Problems, roles and guidelines. In P. Burke and R. G. Heideman (Eds.), *Career-long teacher education,* (pp. 194–222). Springfield, IL: Thomas.

Johnson, J. M., and Ryan, K. 1983. Research on the beginning teacher: Implications for teacher education. In K. R. Howey and W. E. Gardner (Eds.), *The education of teachers: A look ahead,* (pp. 136–162). New York: Longman.

Joyce, B. R., and Showers, B. 1983. *Power in staff development through research on training.* Alexandria, VA: Association of Supervision and Curriculum Development.

Kanter, R. M. 1977. *Men and women of the corporation.* New York: Basic Books.

Katz, L. G. 1972. Development stages of preschool teachers. *Elementary School Journal, 73*(1), 50–54 (ERIC Document Reproduction No. EJ 064 759).

Kohlberg, L. 1968. Stage and sequence: The cognitive-developmental approach to socialization. In D. A. Garlin (Ed.), *Handbook of socialization on theory and research,* Chicago: Rand McNally.

Kohlberg, L. 1981. *Essays in moral development. Volume I: The philosophy of moral development.* San Francisco: Harper & Row.

Kohlberg, L. 1984. *Essays in moral development. Volume II: The philosophy of moral development.* San Francisco: Harper & Row.

Kramer, J. 1974. *Reality shock: Why nurses leave nursing.* St. Louis, MO: Mosby.

Kremer, L., and Lifman, M. 1982. Locus of control and its reflection in teachers' professional attributions. *College Student Journal, 16*(3), 209–215.

Kremer, L. 1982. Locus of control, attitudes toward education, and teaching behaviors. *Scandinavian Journal of Educational Research, 26*(1), 1–11.

Krey, R., and Burke, P. 1989. *A design for instructional supervision.* Springfield, IL: Thomas.

Krupp, J. A. 1981. *Adult development: Implications for staff development.* Manchester, CT: Adult Development and Learning.

Krupp, J. A. 1982. *The adult learner: A unique entity.* Manchester, CT: Adult Development and Learning.

Lanier, J., and Little, J. W. 1986. Research on teacher education. In M. C. Wittrock (Ed.), *Handbook of research on teaching* (3rd ed.) (pp. 527–569). New York: Macmillan.

Lebman, T., and Lester, V. 1978. *Adult learning in the context of adult development.* Empire State College Research Series. Saratoga Springs, NY: Empire State College.

Levine, S. L. 1989. *Promoting adult growth in schools.* Boston: Allyn & Bacon.

Levinson, D. J., et al. 1974. The psychosocial development of men in early adulthood and the mid-life transition. In D. F. Ricks, A. Thomas, & M. Roff (Eds.), *Life history research in psychopathology.* Vol. 3. Minneapolis: University of Minnesota Press.

Levinson, D. J.; Darrow, C. N.; Klein, E. B.; Levinson, M. H.; and McKee, B. 1978. *The seasons of a man's life.* New York: Knopf.

Lewis, A. C. 1987. Confusius say, learn from international neighbors. *Phi Delta Kappan, 68*(7), 492–493.

Lickona, T. (Ed.). 1976. *Moral developmental behavior.* New York: Holt, Rinehart & Winston, p. 34–35.

Lightfoot, S. L. 1983. *The good high school: Portraits of character and culture.* New York: Basic Books.

Lind, K. 1990. *Beginning teacher assistance: A program handbook,* (Bulletin No. 9282). Madison, WI: Wisconsin Department of Public Instruction.

Little, J. W. 1982. Norms of collegiality and experimentation: Workplace conditions of school success. *American Educational Research Journal, 19,* 342–360.

Loevinger, J. 1976. *Ego development.* San Francisco: Jossey-Bass.

Lortie, D. 1966. Teacher socialization: The Robinson Crusoe model. In *The real world of the beginning teacher.* Washington, DC: National Commission on Teacher Education and Professional Standards (ERIC Document Reproduction Service No. ED 030 616).

Lortie, D. 1975. *School teacher: A sociological analysis.* Chicago: University of Chicago Press.

Lowenthal, M. F.; Thurner, M.; and Chiriboga, D. 1975. *Four stages of life: A comparative study of women and men facing transitions.* San Francisco: Jossey-Bass.

Lowther, M. A.; Gill, S. J.; and Coppard, L. C. 1981. Worklife issues of teachers and other professionals. In R. Hill, E. Miller, and M. Lowther (Eds.), *Adult career transitions: Current research perspectives.* Ann Arbor, MI: Business Papers No. 66: Graduate School of Business Administration, University of Michigan.

Lowther, M. A.; Gill, S. J.; and Coppard, L. C. 1985. Age and the determinants of teacher job satisfaction. *The Gerontologist, 25*(2).

Maeroff, G. I. 1988. *The empowerment of teachers.* New York: Teachers College Press.

Maslach, C. 1982. Understanding burnout: Definitional issues in analyzing a complex phenomenon. In W. S. Paine (Ed.), *Job stress and burnout: research, theory, and intervention perspectives*. Beverly Hills, CA: SAGE Publications.

Maslach, C., and Jackson, S. E. 1981. The measurement of experienced burnout. *Journal of Occupational Behavior, 2,* 99–113.

Maslow, A. H. 1960. *Motivation and personality*. New York: McGraw-Hill.

McCoy, V. R., Ryan, C., and Lictenberg, J. W. 1978. The adult life cycle: Training manual and reader. Lawrence: University of Kansas.

McDonald, F. J., and Elias, P. 1983. *The transition into teaching: The problems of beginning teachers and programs to solve them* (Summary report). Berkeley, CA: Educational Testing Service.

McDonnell, J. H.; Christensen, J. C.; and Price, J. R. 1987. Incentives and teachers' career stages. In C. Bartell (Ed.), *Incentives that enhance the teaching profession: A discussion of policy issues*. Elmhurst, IL: North Central Regional Educational Laboratory.

McDonnell, J. H.; Christensen, J. C.; and Price, J. R. 1989, April. *Teachers' career stages and availability and appropriateness of incentives in teaching*. Paper presented at the annual meeting of the American Educational Research Association, San Francisco (ERIC Document Reproduction Service No. ED 318 704).

Metropolitan Life. 1985. *Survey of former teachers in America*. New York: Metropolitan Life Insurance Company.

Metropolitan Life. 1986. *Survey of the American teacher*. New York: Metropolitan Life and Affiliated Companies.

Metropolitan Life. 1988. *Survey of the American teacher 1988*. New York: Metropolitan Life Insurance Company.

Miller, S. 1983. *Assessing stages of teacher growth: a professional development tool*. Unpublished master's thesis. National College of Education, Evanston, IL.

Milstein, M. 1989. *Plateauing on an occupational phenomenon among teachers and administrators*. Paper presented at the annual meeting of the American Educational Research Association, San Francisco.

Murphy, M. J.; Hart, A. W.; and Walters, L. C. 1989, April. *Satisfaction and intent to leave responses of new teachers in target populations under redesigned teacher work*. Paper presented at the meeting of the American Educational Research Association, San Francisco.

Myers, B.; Kennedy, J. J.; and Cruickshank, D. R. 1979. Relationship of teacher personality variable to teacher perceived problems. *Journal of Teacher Education, 30*(6), 33–40.

Near, J. 1984. Reactions to the career plateau. *Business Horizons,* (July–August), 75–79.

Neugarten, B. L. 1968. *Middle age and aging: A reader in social psychology*. Chicago: University of Chicago Press.

Newberry, J. M. 1977, April. *The first year of experience: Influences on beginning teachers*. Paper presented at the annual meeting of the American Educational Research Association, New York (ERIC Document Reproduction Service No. ED 137 299).

Newman, K. K.; Burden, P. R.; and Applegate, J. H. 1980, February. *Helping teachers examine their long-range development*. Paper presented at the annual meeting of the Association of Teacher Educators, Washington, DC (ERIC Document Reproduction Service No. ED 204 321).

Newman, K. K.; Burden, P. R.; and Applegate, J. H. 1980b, October. Adult development is implicit in staff development. *Journal of Staff Development, 1*(2), 7–56.

Odell, S. J. 1987. Teacher induction: Rationale and issues. In D. M. Brooks (Ed.),

Teacher induction: A new beginning, (pp. 69–80). Reston, VA: Association of Teacher Educators.

Odell, S. J.; and Loughlin, C. L. 1986, February. *Innovative inservice in a collaborative internship/induction program.* Paper presented at the sixty-sixth annual meeting of the Association of Teacher Educators, Atlanta, GA.

Oja, S. N., and Smulyan, L. 1989. *Collaborative action research: A developmental approach.* New York: Falmer Press.

Orpen, C. 1983. The career patterns and work attitudes of plateaued and non-plateaued managers. *International Journal of Manpower, 4,* 32–36.

Peterson, A. 1979, April. *Teachers' changing perceptions of self and others throughout the teaching career: Some perspectives from an interview study of fifty retired secondary school teachers.* Paper presented to the Southwest Educational Research Association, San Francisco.

Price, J. R. 1986, April. *The teacher career cycle: Development and validation of research instruments.* Paper presented at the annual meeting of the American Educational Research Association, San Francisco.

Rhodes, M. 1989, April. *Work alienation, teacher efficacy, and career ladder reform.* Paper presented at the meeting of the American Educational Research Association, San Francisco.

Rosenholtz, S. J. 1985. Effective schools: Interpreting the evidence. *American Journal of Education, 93,* 382–388.

Rosenholtz, S. J. 1987a. Education reform strategies: Will they increase teacher commitment? *American Journal of Education, 95,* 534–562.

Rosenholtz, S. J. 1987b. Workplace conditions of teacher quality and commitment: Implications for the design of teacher induction programs. In G. Griffin and S. Millies (Eds.), *The first years of teaching: Background papers and a proposal,* (pp. 15–34). Chicago: University of Illinois at Chicago.

Rosenholtz, S. J. 1989. *Teachers' workplace: The social organization of schools.* New York and London: Longman.

Ryan, K. (Ed.). 1970. *Don't smile until Christmas: Accounts of the first year of teaching.* Chicago: University of Chicago Press.

Ryan, K. (Ed.). 1980. *Biting the apple: Accounts of first year teachers.* New York: Longman.

Ryan, K.; Flora, R.; Newman, K.; Peterson, A.; Burden, P.; and Mager, J. 1979. *The stages in teaching: New perspectives on staff development for teachers' needs.* (ASCD audio-tape). Presentation to the Association for Supervision and Curriculum Development, Anaheim, CA.

Sacks, S. R., and Harrington, G. N. 1982, March. *Student to teacher: The process of role transition.* Paper presented at the annual meeting of the American Educational Research Association, New York.

Schwab, R. L., and Iwanicki, E. F. 1982. Perceived role conflict, role ambiguity, and teacher burnout. *Educational Administration Quarterly, 18*(1), 60–74.

Sergiovanni, T. (Ed.) 1975. Human resources supervision. In Sergiovanni, T. (Ed.) 1975 *Professional Supervision for Professional Teachers.* Washington, D.C., Association for Supervision and Curriculum Development. (Categories and descriptions from Sergiovanni, p. 18.)

Sergiovanni, T., and Carver, F. 1980. The new school executive. New York: Harper & Row.

Sergiovanni, T., and Starratt, R. 1983. *Supervision: Human perspectives.* New York: McGraw-Hill.

Sheehy, G. 1976. *Passages: Predictable crises of adult life.* New York: Dutton.

Snyder, T. D. (Project Director). 1989. *Digest of educational statistics*. Washington, DC: U.S. Department of Education National Center for Educational Statistics.

Spencer, D. A. 1986. *Contemporary women teachers: Balancing school and home*. New York: Longman.

Sprinthall, N. A., and Thies-Sprinthall, L. 1983. The teacher as an adult learner: A cognitive-developmental view. In G. A. Griffin (Ed.), *Staff development* (Eighty-second Yearbook of the National Society for the Study of Education). Chicago: University of Chicago Press.

Tabachnick, B. R.; Zeichner, K.; Densmore, K.; Adler, S.; and Egar, K. 1982, April. *The impact of the student teaching experience on the development of teacher perspectives*. Paper presented at the annual meeting of the American Educational Research Association, New York.

Unruh, A., and Turner, H.E. 1970. *Supervision for change and innovation*. Boston: Houghton Mifflin.

Veenman, S. 1984. Perceived problems of beginning teachers. *Review of Educational Research, 54*(2), 143–178.

Veiga, J. 1981. Plateaued versus non-plateaued managers: Career pattern, attitudes, and path potential. *Academy of Management Journal, 24,* 566–578.

Vonk, J. H. C. 1984. The professional socialization of teachers. In F. Busch and K. Spelling (Eds.), *School life today*. Proceedings of the ATEE-Conference in Aalborg. Oldenburg/Copenhagen.

Vonk, J. H. C. 1989. *Becoming a teacher, brace yourself*. Unpublished paper. Vrije University, Amsterdam.

Weathersby, R. 1978. Life stages and learning interests. In *The adult learner: Current issues in higher education*. Washington, DC: American Association for Higher Education.

Yinger, R. J. 1987. In G. Griffin and S. Millies (Eds.), *The first years of teaching: Background papers and a proposal,* (pp. 65–90). Chicago: University of Illinois at Chicago.

Zeichner, K. M., and Gore, J. M. 1990. Teacher socialization. In W. R. Houston (Ed.), *Handbook of research on teacher education* (pp. 329–348). New York: Macmillan.

Zeichner, K. M., and Tabachnick, B. R. 1985. The development of teacher perspectives: Social strategies and institutional control in the socialization of beginning teachers. *Journal of Education for Teaching, 11*(1), 1–25 (ERIC Document Reproduction Service No. EJ 316 079).

Name Index

Subject Index

Impact stage, 172
Importance of teaching, recognition of, 57
Incentives
  career exit stage and, 238–243, 240, 241
  career frustration stage and, 167
  career wind-down stage and, 211–215, 212–213
  competency building stage and, 107–112
  enthusiastic and growing stage and, 123, 138–146
  motivation and hygiene factors, 12, 14
  organizational, competency building and, 108–109
  preservice stage and, 55–57
  stability stage and, 184, 186–187
Individual disposition
  career exit stage and, 226
  career wind-down stage and, 197
  enthusiastic and growing stage and, 126
  importance of, 37
  induction stage and, 67–68
  preservice stage and, 50–51
Induction stage
  alternatives, 83–84
  career exit and, 220
  characteristics of, 41, 59
  as crucial transition stage, 85–86
  incentives, 78–82
  organizational environment influences, 71–76
  personal environmental influences, 65–70
  phases of survival, 61
  potential for failure and, 60
  professional growth needs, 76–78
  stages of concern, 61–62
  summary of, 252
  support systems, 80–85
  teacher profiles, 62–65, 253
  views of, 60–62
Initial teaching period, in teacher career cycle, 22–23
Innovative instruction techniques, 99
Insurance, 211
Isolation, burnout and, 168

Job change. See also Career exit stage
  career frustration and, 168
Job-enlargement ladders, 16

K–12 institution
  influences on preservice education, 51–53
  support systems, 56
Knowledge production
  in Career Lattice Model, 19
  career wind-down stage and, 208
  competency building stage and, 105
  enthusiastic and growing stage and, 134–135

Leadership
  career exit stage and, 238
  in Career Lattice Model, 19
  career wind-down stage and, 209, 216
  enthusiastic and growing stage and, 122, 134
Learning
  competency building and, 104–105
  preservice education and, 57
Leaves, career exit stage and, 238
Life-cycle phases, 4
Life stages
  career exit stage and, 225
  description of, 38
Life-stage theories, 3, 5
Loans and loan forgiveness, 55–56

Management style
  career exit stage and, 230
  career frustration stage and, 163
  career wind-down stage and, 206–207
  competency building stage and, 99
  enthusiastic and growing stage and, 129, 132
  importance of, 39
  induction stage and, 71–72
  stability stage and, 180
Master teacher, enthustiastic and growing stage and, 140
Mastery learning, 166
Materials production, 135
Maturing period, in teacher career cycle, 22–23
Maturity stage, 23–24, 27, 172. See also Stability stage